The Inquisition Revealed In Its Origin, Policy, Cruelties, And History, With Memoirs Of Its Victims

Thomas Timpson

THE

Inquisition Revealed;

IN

ITS ORIGIN,
POLICY, CRUELTIES, AND HISTORY,

WITH

Memoirs of its Victims

IN FRANCE, SPAIN, PORTUGAL, ITALY, ENGLAND,
INDIA, AND OTHER COUNTRIES.

DEDICATED TO CARDINAL WISEMAN.

BY

REV. THOMAS TIMPSON,
AUTHOR OF THE "COMPANION TO THE BIBLE," &c. &c.

"Drunken with the blood of the Saints, and with the blood of the Martyrs of Jesus."—REV. xvii. 6.

"THEY SHED INNOCENT BLOOD. This single circumstance shall, God willing, ever separate me from the Papacy. For this crime of cruelty I would fly from her communion as from a den of thieves and murderers!"—LUTHER.

LONDON:
AYLOTT AND JONES, PATERNOSTER ROW.
MDCCCLI.

LONDON
J. UNWIN, GRESHAM STEAM PRESS.
BUCKLERSBURY.

TORTURES OF THE PULLEY AND THE FIRE.

TORTURES OF THE HORSE AND SUFFOCATION.

CONTENTS.

DEDICATION.

TO

HIS EMINENCE, CARDINAL WISEMAN.

My Lord Cardinal,

Roman Catholics and Protestants are alike interested in this volume: designed, as it is, to advance pure Christianity. They have an equal right to profess their own peculiar faith, and to propagate their religious opinions. But, in the free exercise of that right, they are equally bound, by every principle of justice and charity, to cherish towards each other mutual esteem and benevolence.

Romanists, however, do not admit the Holy Scriptures as the sole authority in religion; and their principles will not allow them, therefore, to grant toleration to those who dissent from them. Their intolerance arises from the policy of the Hierarchy and the reception of unscriptural traditions. Hence their illiberality in Italy, Sardinia,

Spain, Portugal, the Brazils, and other countries, where the priesthood is dominant. Hence the inveterate hostility of the Romish priests against the popular reading of the Bible. Their people are kept thus in ignorance, deluded by false doctrines; and theirs being not exclusively the principles of the Holy Scriptures, cannot be the religion of our Lord Jesus Christ.

My Lord Cardinal—Every Briton should understand the character and claims of the Papacy. For, as predicted in "the oracles of God," Protestants hold that Popery is the "man of sin,"—the "mystery of iniquity,"—the "MOTHER OF HARLOTS AND ABOMINATIONS OF THE EARTH,"—"drunken with the blood of the saints, and with the blood of the martyrs of Jesus."—2 Thess. ii. 3—7; Rev. xvii. 5, 6.

Every British Christian is deeply interested in studying the doctrines of Popery; its *Priestly power — Absolution — Transubstantiation — Tradition —* and *Purgatory;* and in considering its evil doings in *Auricular confession—Penance—Mariolatry—Priestly celibacy—Spiritual domination*—and the INQUISITION. The history of these is the condemnation of Popery.

This volume contains the substance of the valuable

works of Limborch, Llorente, Dellon, Gavin, Buchanan, Bower, Newton, Gibbon, Watson, Ranke, Sismondi, Jones, Puigblanch, Edgar, Elliott, Mendham, Giesler, Dowling, D'Aubigné, De Castro, Achilli, and many others, regarding the Inquisition.

This volume is designed as an Antidote to Popery; especially *as a present to young persons*; and it is believed, by judicious friends, to be most seasonable, to instruct inquirers, and to advance the truth of the Gospel of Jesus Christ.

Having these objects in view, this work is dedicated, with due respect, to

YOUR EMINENCE,

BY THE AUTHOR.

THE INQUISITION REVEALED.

CHAPTER I.

POPERY AS PREDICTED IN SCRIPTURE.

The Court of Inquisition cruel and execrable—Christianity
benevolent—The Inquisition predicted, 2 Thess. ii. 3, 4;
1 Tim. iv. 1-3; Rev. xvii. 1-18—Comments by Elliott,
Bp. Newton, and Scott.

RELIGION, as taught by the Romish priesthood,
has been enforced and guarded by pains and penalties during many ages. For the last *six* centuries,
this has been done chiefly by a court, denominated,
in all countries where it has been established,
"THE HOLY INQUISITION." But this court has
been execrated, in every country in which it has
existed, as the most dreadful, cruel, and sanguinary
of all tribunals, even by professors of the faith of
Rome. Still it is supported by the papal hierarchy, as the agents of the Pope may be able to
obtain permission of the governments who observe
the Romish religion.

Christianity has thus been dishonoured in the
assumption of its sacred name by Roman Ca-

tholics, while they have practised these cruelties, so contrary to the letter and to the spirit of the religion of Jesus Christ; for all His principles and precepts manifest Divine benevolence, as chanted at the birth of the Redeemer, by a multitude of the heavenly host, praising God, and saying, "Glory to God in the highest, and on earth peace, good-will towards men."

Christianity is the religion of love, and like its ever blessed Author, the Son of God. "God is love; and he that dwelleth in love, dwelleth in God, and God in him." It enjoins upon all its professors the practice of benevolence. It requires them to possess and exemplify that spirit. Its moral code is comprehended in that summary of the Divine law, as given by our Saviour, "Thou shalt love the Lord thy God with all thy heart, and with all thy soul, and with all thy mind. And thou shalt love thy neighbour as thyself." Its chief practical maxim is, "Whatsoever ye would that men should do to you, do ye even so to them: for this is the law and the prophets." These precepts were followed by the early believers of the Gospel, constraining the heathen to admire their benevolence, exclaiming, "See how these Christians love one another!"

False teachers, however, having corrupted the doctrines and ordinances of Christ, were influenced by another spirit; and, in the course of a few ages, the professed ministers [of the loving Redeemer exhibited intolerance, malevolence, and cruelty, exceeding what had ever been witnessed under any form of religion. These enormities have been seen chiefly in the operations of the Roman Catholics, and especially by their execrable "Court of INQUISITION," as this has been established in Spain, France, Portugal, India, and Rome. This court, though denominated "Holy," has been the most arbitrary, inhuman, and sanguinary that ever existed among men; and because of its enormities, by its various machinery, and by its savage armies, it is symbolised in the Holy Scriptures under the emblem of a harlot, deluding the nations with her intoxicating draughts, and herself "drunken with the blood of the saints, and with the blood of the martyrs of Jesus."—(Rev. xvii. 6.)

Before we enter upon the direct history of the Inquisition, therefore, it will be necessary to notice the inspired prophecies relating to this apostate and cruel hierarchy of popery; and to take a brief review of the rise and progress of that terrible and hated system of Antichrist.

"Known unto God are all his works from the beginning of the world." And equally foreseen were all the forms of falsehood, cruelty, and evil upon the earth. Hence the inspired predictions concerning the hateful enemy of Christ.

Our blessed Lord repeatedly admonished his disciples concerning false teachers, who would be distinguished by their inhumanity; and the apostle Paul, in correcting the mistakes of some, regarding the day of judgment as being near, says, "Let no man deceive you by any means: for that day shall not come, except there come a falling away first, and that man of sin be revealed, the son of perdition; who opposeth and exalteth himself above all that is called God, or that is worshipped; so that he, as God, sitteth in the temple of God, showing himself that he is God."—(2 Thess. ii. 3, 4.) Again, he represents the character of Romish teachers, and says, "Now the Spirit speaketh expressly, that in the latter times some shall depart from the faith, giving heed to seducing spirits, and doctrines of devils; speaking lies in hypocrisy; having their conscience seared with a hot iron; forbidding to marry, and commanding to abstain from meats, which God hath created to be received with thanksgiving of them who believe and know the truth."—(1 Tim. iv. 1—3.)

Still more remarkable is the prediction described by the apostle John : "And there came one of the seven angels which had the seven vials, and talked with me, saying unto me, Come hither; I will show unto thee the judgment of the great whore that sitteth upon many waters: with whom the kings of the earth have committed fornication, and the inhabitants of the earth have been made drunk with the wine of her fornication. So he carried me away in the spirit into the wilderness: and I saw a woman sit upon a scarlet-coloured beast, full of names of blasphemy, having seven heads and ten horns. And the woman was arrayed in purple and scarlet colour, and decked with gold and precious stones and pearls, having a golden cup in her hand full of abominations and filthiness of her fornication: and upon her forehead was a name written,

MYSTERY, BABYLON THE GREAT, THE MOTHER
OF HARLOTS AND ABOMINATIONS OF THE EARTH.
And I saw the woman drunken with the blood of
the saints, and with the blood of the martyrs of
Jesus; and when I saw her, I wondered with great
admiration. And the angel said unto me, Wherefore dost thou marvel? I will tell thee the mystery
of the woman, and of the beast that carrieth her,
which hath the seven heads and ten horns. The
beast that thou sawest was, and is not; and shall
ascend out of the bottomless pit, and go into perdition. The seven heads are seven mountains, on
which the woman sitteth. And there are seven
kings. And the ten horns which thou sawest are
ten kings, who have received no kingdom as yet;
but receive power as kings one hour with the beast.
These shall make war with the Lamb, and the Lamb
shall overcome them: for he is Lord of lords, and
King of kings: and they that are with him are
called, and chosen, and faithful. And he saith unto
me, The waters which thou sawest, where the
whore sitteth, are peoples, and multitudes, and
nations, and tongues. And the woman whom thou
sawest is that great city, which reigneth over the
kings of the earth."—(Rev. xvii. 1—18.)

All these several predictions have been fulfilled
with the most striking completeness; and we may
have to refer to them in the course of this work;
but the descriptions in those from the Revelation
require our very special notice, as they lead us
more particularly to the Romish hierarchy, and to
the terrible court of inquisition. The Rev. Mr.

Elliott, in his "Commentary" on this chapter, says :—

"This vision represented pictorially a gaudily dressed drunken harlot, seated on a beast of monstrous form, with *seven* heads, and on the seventh *ten horns*. The beast, in respect of its body, depicted the papal empire of the ten western European kingdoms ; and in respect of the seventh, or rather, eighth head, the succession of Roman popes, constituting, from after the sixth century, that empire's spiritual rulers. So the *woman* represented *Rome* in its character of the papal see, and mother-church of Western Christendom ; including, doubtless, as part and parcel of herself, the ecclesiastical state, or Peter's patrimony, in Italy, and vast dominions, convents, churches, and other property appertaining to the papal church elsewhere, both in Europe and over the world.

"1. As the beast's body both upheld and was subject to the woman, the rider, so the empire, as a whole, with the power of its secular kingdoms and many peoples, upheld, and was also at the same time ruled by papal Rome, the mother-church of Christendom.

"2. As the woman was here depicted before St. John under a double character, viz., as a harlot to the ten kings, and a vintner or tavern-hostess vending wines to the common people, just according to the custom of earlier times, in which the harlot and the hostess of a tavern were characters frequently united ; so the church of Rome answered to the symbol in either point of view ; interchanging mutual favours, such as might suit their respective characters, with the kings of Anti-Christendom; and to the common people dealing out for sale the wine of the poison of her fornication, her indulgences, relics, transubstantiation-cup, as if the cup of salvation, &c. (see the Pope's own medal, holding out the cup of her apostacy, struck at Rome on occasion of the Jubilee in 1825), therewith drugging and making them besotted and drunk.

"3. With regard to the portraiture of the woman, robed in purple and scarlet, and adorned with gold, and precious stones and pearls, it is, as applied to the Romish church, a picture, characteristic and from life; the dress specified being distinctively that of the Romish ecclesiastical dignitaries, and the ornaments those with which it has been bedecked beyond any church called Christian; nay, beyond any religion, probably, that has ever existed in the world; not to add that even the very name on the harlot's forehead, *Mystery*, (a name allusive, evidently, to St. Paul's predicted *mystery of iniquity,*) was one, if we may repose credit on no vulgar authority, once written on the Pope's tiara; and the apocalyptic title, 'Mother of harlots and of the abominations of the earth,' the very parody, if I may so say, of the title Rome arrogates to herself, 'Rome, mother and mistress.'

"4. As to the harlot's being depicted 'drunken with the blood of the saints,' its applicability to the Romish church, throughout the latter half, at least, portion of the beast's 1260 predicted years of prospering, is written in deep-dyed characters on the page of history."

Nothing can be more evident than that "Babylon the Great" designs the mystical city of the papal commonwealth, a regnant system of spiritual wickedness — an idolatrous church. This was the judgment of all the chief reformers in Germany, Switzerland, France, England, and Scotland. Some even of the Roman Catholics had the same conviction; and Petrarch, the celebrated Italian poet, calls the papal court "The Babylonian harlot, mother of all idolatries."

Bishop Newton, having reviewed the prophecy, says, "Moreover, the woman, like other harlots who give philters and love-potions to inflame their lovers, hath 'a golden cup in her hand, full of abominations, and filthiness of her fornication,' to signify the specious and alluring arts wherewith she bewitcheth and inciteth men to idolatry, which is 'abomination and spiritual fornication.' It is an image copied from Jeremiah li. 7, 'Babylon hath been a golden cup in the LORD's hand, that made all the earth drunken.' And is not this a much more proper emblem of *pontifical* than of *imperial* Rome?

"Yet farther to distinguish the woman, she has her *name* inscribed *upon her forehead* (verse 5), in allusion to the practice of some notorious prostitutes, who had their names written in a label upon their foreheads. The inscription is so very particular, that we cannot easily mistake the person; '*Mystery, Babylon the great, the mother of harlots*, or rather, of fornications and abominations of the earth.' Her name, *Mystery*, can imply no less than that she dealeth in *mysteries;* her religion is a mystery, a mystery of iniquity; and she herself is mystically and spiritually 'Babylon the great.'   But the title of *mystery* is in no respect proper to ancient Rome, more than any other city; and neither is there any mystery in substituting one heathen, idolatrous, and persecuting city for another; but it is indeed a mystery, that a Christian city, professing and boasting herself to be the city of God, should prove another Babylon in idolatry and cruelty to the people of God.   She glories in the name of *Roman Catholic*, and well, therefore, may she be called 'Babylon the great.'

"Infamous as the woman is for her idolatry, she is no less detestable for her cruelty, which are the two principal characteristics of the antichristian empire. 'She is drunken with the blood of the saints, and with the blood of the martyrs of Jesus,' (ver. 6) which may indeed be applied both to pagan and to Christian Rome, for both have in their turns cruelly persecuted 'the saints and the martyrs of Jesus;' but the latter is more deserving of the character, as she hath far exceeded the former, both in the degree and duration of her persecutions.   It is very true, that if Rome pagan hath slain her thousands of innocent Christians, Rome Christian hath slain her ten thousands; for, not to mention other outrageous slaughters and barbarities, the crusades against the Waldenses and Albigenses; the murders committed by the Duke of Alva in the Netherlands; the massacres in France and Ireland, will probably amount to above ten times the number of all the Christians slain in all the ten persecutions of the Roman emperors put together. St. John's *admiration* also plainly evinces that Christian Rome was intended, for it could be no matter of surprise to him that a heathen city should persecute the Christians; but that a city professedly Christian should wanton and riot in the blood of Christians, was a subject of astonishment indeed; and well might he, as it is emphatically expressed, 'wonder with great wonder.'"

Mr. Scott, in his commentary on 2 Thessalonians ii. 3, 4, remarks, "No apostacy of equal magnitude and duration, no delusions equally pernicious and abominable, have taken place since the apostle's days, as those of Rome. The imposture of Mohammed alone can be compared with it, and this could not be intended; for that impostor and his successors were not placed in the temple of God, the visible church (Rev. xi. 1, 2), but *without* it, and in direct opposition to the very name of Christianity; they propagated their delusions mainly by the sword, and not lying miracles; and, indeed, the impieties of Mohammed never equalled the blasphemies here predicted. This 'man of sin' would be the 'son of perdition' (John xvii. 12); a genuine descendant of Judas, the apostle and traitor, who sold his Lord for money, and destroyed him with a kiss; a peculiar factor and agent of Satan, in destroying the souls of men, and finally sinking into perdition as his inheritance. It is manifest, that no succession of men have yet appeared on earth to whom this description fully accords, except that of

the Roman pontiffs. This deceiver would oppose
and exalt himself above all that is called God, or is
'worshipped,' either by Christians or pagans;
thus the Roman pontiffs have opposed the truths,
commandments, and disciples of Christ, in every
age; the prophetical office of Christ, by teaching
human inventions—his priestly office, by the doctrine of human merits and created intercessors—
and his kingly office, by changing and dispensing
with his laws. They have exalted themselves 'above
all that is called God,' and is 'worshipped,' by
claiming authority to forgive sins; by granting
indulgences to men to break the commandments of
God; by dispensing with his laws, and presuming
to give meaning and authority to the Scriptures
themselves. Moreover, this 'man of sin' 'sits as
God' in the temple of God; and we must, therefore,
look for him within the visible church; there he
blasphemously usurps the throne of God, 'showing himself to be God.' Many Roman emperors
affected divine honours, and demanded adoration;
but there was no antecedent apostacy from Christianity or the worship of JEHOVAH; and they might
rather be said to sit in the temple of Jupiter or
Mars, than in that of God, whose temple must be
considered to be among his professed worshippers,
and not among avowed heathen. But the Roman
pontiff—claiming to be the universal head of the
whole church of God, called by his flatterers 'Vice-
God,' a 'God upon earth,' arrogating the title of
'His Holiness,' boasting of 'infallibility,' claiming a
right to depose kings and bestow kingdoms on

whom he pleases—answers exactly to the description here given. While the Roman pontiff opposes the worship of God, by enjoining the worship of images, of saints, and angels, and the authority of his laws, to enforce subjection to his own edicts, he himself may be called the great idol, as well as the great tyrant, of the Romish church!"

Human sagacity could by no means have conjectured such a character rising up among the people of God, and such deeds perpetrated in the name and form of religion. This required the prescience of the Infinite Mind. But we shall see them all in their dreadful enormity, as we pursue the history of the Romish Inquisition.

CHAPTER II.

PROGRESS OF ANTICHRIST.

Spirit of Antichrist—Priests, Clergy, and Laity—Ceremonies —Mosheim—" Pious Frauds "—Splendour of Prelates— Constantine — the Hierarchy — Titles — Creeds — Arianism — Persecution — Rome and Constantinople — Pope John — Pope Gregory — Mohammed — Claims of the Pope—Henry IV.—Corrupt principles.

DIVINE Wisdom having foreseen, and thus foretold, all the dreadful corruptions of the Christian church, we are interested in marking the steps by which the progress was made. The spirit of popery we behold in the conduct of the judaising teachers of the early Christians, as censured by Paul, and as seen in the proceedings of Diotrephes, who is believed to have been a pastor. John complained of his refusing to "receive the brethren," the messengers of the apostle, and of his "malicious words," persecuting some, and casting others out of the church.—(2 John 9, 10.)

This ambitious spirit led the pastors in some of the larger churches, early in the second century, to assume the character and title of *priests*, as peculiar to their order. They claimed the privilege of being the Lord's "heritage," or clergy, which belonged to the faithful, as distinct from their ministers.— (1 Pet. v. 31.) But they persuaded the people that they had succeeded to the rights of the Jewish priesthood, as God's clergy; and hence the distinction of *clergy* and *laity*, which has no foundation in Christianity. This distinction being established, gave immense force to the spirit of popery, which advanced rapidly among the ignorant people. Dr. Mosheim states, "The Christian doctors had the good fortune to persuade the people, that the ministers of the Christian church succeeded to the character, rights, and privileges of the Jewish priesthood; and this persuasion was a new source of honour and profit to the sacerdotal order. This notion was propagated with industry, some time after the second destruction of Jerusalem [A.D. 135] had extinguished all hopes of seeing their government restored to its former lustre, and their country arising from its ruins. And, accordingly, the *bishops* considered themselves invested with a rank and character similar to those of the *high priests* among the Jews, while the *presbyters* represented the *priests*, and the *deacons* the *Levites*."

Christianity having no splendid ceremonial to recommend the preaching of the Gospel, priests devised various forms to be added to the Lord's supper, which was administered every Sabbath, and ceremonies were invented, partly derived from the Jews and 'some from the idolators, to attract the minds of the people, and with a view to gratify the converts from heathenism. The performance of these, especially in the Lord's supper, served also as the means of employing the priests in their newly created offices; and they were called *mysteries*, as having a hidden meaning and a peculiar virtue, after the manner of the rites of the Pagan priests. Hence originated the term *sacraments*, the Latin word for *mysteries*, applied to various rites, especially baptism and the Lord's supper.

Dr. Mosheim, therefore, remarks, "The bishops, by an innocent allusion to the Jewish manner of speaking, had been called 'chief priests;' the elders or presbyters had received the title of 'priests,' and the deacons that of 'Levites.' But in a little time these titles were abused by an aspiring clergy, who thought proper to claim the same rank and station, the same rights and privileges, that were conferred with those titles upon the ministers of religion under the Mosaic dispensation. Hence the rise of tithes, first-fruits, splendid garments, and many other circumstances of external grandeur, by which ecclesiastics were eminently distinguished."

Priestly power was greatly augmented at this time by the meetings of the bishops, as delegates from the churches, to consult respecting their mutual defence and security against their persecuting enemies. In these synods or councils, as they were called, various decisions were formed unfriendly to the interests of the people; for the bishops soon asserted authority to prescribe laws, and to impose creeds, which led to the most grievous persecution in the following ages. Superiority was claimed in these assemblies by the bishops of the chief cities, especially by the bishop of Rome, as the imperial metropolis. Dr. Mosheim, therefore, states, "Toward the conclusion of this century, Victor, bishop of Rome, took it into his head to force the Asiatic Christians, by the pretended authority of his laws and decrees, to observe the Roman custom of keeping Easter." They refused compliance; and, as Milner says, "Victor, with much arrogance, as if he had felt the very soul of the future papacy formed in himself, inveighed against the Asiatic churches, and pronounced their excommunication."

In the second century, popery was further advanced by the peculiar practices of the Egyptian monks being cherished among the Christians. They magnified the virtues of fasting, celibacy, and a solitary life, as the perfection of excellence; and hence the origin of the Romish monks, nuns, and celibacy of the clergy.

Christianity, in the third century, was still more corrupted by the priesthood; for "pious frauds," or false miracles, were commonly practised. Several of the teachers were guilty of these in the second century; but, to the dishonour of religion, they were now publicly defended, even by some good men, provided they were employed with a design to convert men and advance the cause of Christianity!

Popery continued to advance in this century by rapid strides; for the clergy maintained their various dignities with determined zeal. The simple ordinances of Christ in the ministry of the Gospel were laid aside for the performance of priestly rites. Ecclesiastical government degenerated towards the form of a religious monarchy; while the people were, in most cases, excluded from all share in the management of their own affairs in the churches. Dr. Mosheim, therefore, testifies — "The bishops assumed, in many places, a princely authority, particularly those who presided over the most opulent assemblies. They appropriated to their evangelical function the splendid ensigns of temporal majesty. A throne, surrounded with ministers, exalted above his equals the servant of the meek and humble Jesus, and sumptuous garments dazzled the eye and the mind of the multitude into an ignorant veneration for their arrogated authority. The example of the bishops was ambitiously imitated by the presbyters, who, neglecting the sacred duties of their station, abandoned themselves to the indolence and delicacy of an effeminate and

luxurious life. When the honours and privileges
of the bishops and presbyters were augmented, the
deacons also began to extend their ambitious views,
and to despise those lower functions and employments which they had hitherto exercised with
such humility and zeal; and the effects of a corrupt
ambition were spread through every rank of the
sacred order."

Ecclesiastical ambition was not satisfied with the
creation of a hierarchy of bishops, priests, and
deacons; but various lesser orders of ministers
were now instituted, on account of the increasing
ceremonies which had been adopted in imitation of
the heathen mysteries. Various forms of prayer
and consecration were prepared for these ceremonies; the table of the Lord was converted into
an altar; wax tapers were burnt upon it; the bread
and wine were regarded as possessing a kind of
saving virtue; and much solemn pomp was observed
in celebrating the Lord's supper. Baptism was
preceded by a terrifying process—exorcism, to expel
the evil spirit, and the newly baptised persons were
required to taste milk and honey, as indicating
spiritual food, and the converts from heathenism
were sent home from the ceremony adorned with
crowns and white garments.

Popery received a vast accession of power, in the
beginning of the fourth century, by the conversion
of the Emperor Constantine. He became a most
munificent patron of Christianity, as by its profession he succeeded to the throne of the Cæsars.
The extravagant claims of the ambitious prelates

were now confirmed, and the spiritual institution of
Jesus Christ was transformed into a worldly
system, framed to resemble the civil government of
the empire. The bishops of Rome, Antioch, and
Alexandria were already regarded as superior to
the other prelates—as archbishops, with the title of
patriarch; and to these was added a fourth, for
the new imperial city of .Constantinople. Under
this first Christian emperor, as Dr. Haweis remarks,
"the prelatical government became modelled, after
the imperial, into great prefectures, of which Rome,
Alexandria, Antioch, and Constantinople, claimed
superiority; whilst a sort of feudality was established, descending from patriarchs to metropolitans, archbishops, bishops, some with greater, and
others with less extensive spheres of dominion.
Instead of the people choosing their own bishops
and presbyters, they were no more consulted. The
presbyters wholly depended on the bishops and
patrons; the bishops were the creatures of patriarchs and metropolitans; or, if the see was
important, appointed by the emperor. So 'church
and state' formed the first inauspicious alliance;
and the corruption, which had been plentifully sown
before, now ripened by court intrigues for political
bishops of imperial appointment, or at the suggestion of the prime minister."

"This pernicious example," says Dr. Mosheim,
"was soon followed by the several ecclesiastical
orders. The presbyters, in many places, assumed
an equality with the bishops, in point of rank and
authority. Those more particularly of the presby-

ters and deacons, who filled the first stations of these orders, carried their pretensions to an extravagant length, and were offended at the notion of being placed upon an equal footing with their colleagues. For this reason, they assumed the titles of *archpresbyters* and *archdeacons*."

These newly created dignities required a corresponding style of address, which was soon contrived. It may be remarked, that all these things are contrary to the New Testament; for though all Christians are there described as *saints*, or holy persons; they are never addressed with pompous titles. Even the apostles are never called *Saint* John and *Saint* Peter; these titles are the inventions of popery. Lord Chancellor King remarks, therefore, " It is very seldom, if ever, that the ancients give the title of *saints* to those holy persons, but singly style them Peter, Paul, John, &c.; not *Saint* Peter, *Saint* Paul, *Saint* John." Priestly dignities originated the addresses of " reverend," " very reverend," " right reverend," " most reverend," " your grace," " your holiness."

Constantine having arranged the offices of his government in church and state, soon found it necessary to attempt to produce *uniformity of faith*, especially as Arius, a presbyter of Alexandria, had declared his belief that the Son of God is inferior to the Father, of another nature, and only the first of all created beings. Finding this heresy prevail, he called the bishops of all the provinces to an assembly, A.D. 325, at Nice, in Bithynia. This assembly, famous, as the *first general council*, con-

sisted of about *two thousand and fifty* persons, of
whom *three hundred and eighteen* were bishops.
These prelates delivered to the emperor letters of
grievous accusation against each other, but the
prudent sovereign threw the whole into the fire,
and referred them to the day of judgment for a
settlement. After two months' deliberation, they
agreed on that form denominated "*The Nicene
Creed*," which required to be believed by all Christians. But, by this celebrated act, the foundation
was laid for the pernicious influence of a political
priesthood, and for the authority of councils in
ecclesiastical matters, above even the Holy Scriptures; and this authority, claimed and acted upon,
produced all the superstition, intolerance, and
cruelty, which characterise the terrible *Inquisition*.

Constantine having established the "creed,"
required its universal reception. But the Arians
refused; and the bishops prevailed on him to issue
edicts against them, as enemies of truth, forbidding
their public meetings, and giving their places of
worship to the orthodox. He banished Arius, and
decreed that his books should be burnt; and that
whosoever should dare to keep any of them, as soon
as this was proved, should suffer death! In two or
three years after, the emperor recalled Arius, and
repealed his severe laws against his heresy, which
prevailed under his son and successor, Constantius.
Athanasius, patriarch of Alexandria, became the
champion of orthodoxy; and thus two parties arose
among the clergy.

Decrees and state power authorised *inquisition*

and *persecution;* and "Hence," says Dr. Mosheim, "arose endless animosities and seditions, treacherous plots, and open acts of injustice and violence, between the two contending parties. Council was assembled against council, and their jarring and contradictory decrees spread perplexity and confusion throughout the Christian world." One fact will illustrate the spirit of party in this age: *eighty* orthodox bishops having waited on the Emperor Valerius, to complain of his appointing an Arian bishop of Constantinople, they were murdered by his order, on shipboard, at sea, A.D. 370.

Popery prevailed amid all the contentions; and, A.D. 410, four bishops, deputed from Carthage, obtained an edict from the Emperor Honorius, which doomed to death every one who differed from the Catholic faith. From this edict serious persecutions arose. But, A.D. 451, the council of Chalcedon resolved, "that the same rights and honours conferred on the bishop of Rome, were due to the bishop of Constantinople," confirming his jurisdiction, which he had before claimed, over all the provinces of Asia.

Imperial dominion, however, was now declining, under a succession of feeble princes. At the opening of the *fifth* century, Constantinople was the eastern capital, in which Arcadius presided as emperor, while Rome continued the western metropolis; though Honorius kept his court at Ravenna. Swarms of savage hordes, from the northern regions of Europe, under the names of Goths, Visigoths, Vandals, Franks, Burgundians, overran the richest provinces, sacking cities, and committing every species of barbarity and cruelty. Some of these barbarians had embraced the name of Christ from Arian teachers; and many of those bishops who held the true divinity of Christ were tortured, banished, or massacred with their people.

Religion became still more corrupted; and public worship consisted chiefly in the performance of ceremonies, differing but little from those of the pagan Greeks and Romans. Both of them had a splendid ritual, gorgeous robes, tiaras, mitres, wax tapers, crosiers, processions, lustrations, images, and many such circumstances of pageantry, were to be seen equally in the heathen temples and in Christian churches. To engage the admiration of the ignorant population, pictures and statues of Christ, of the Virgin Mary with the infant Jesus in her arms, and of numerous saints, were set up in the churches, to be admired and worshipped. An invincible efficacy, in expelling evil spirits and healing diseases, was attributed to the presence of the bones of martyrs. The riches and magnificence of the churches exceeded all bounds; and the altars and the chests for the relics of saints were made of the richest materials, some of solid silver.

Everything in the forms of the Catholic religion appeared to produce false ideas, or to excite the worst passions of the human heart. Hence superstition and intolerance, and dreadful persecution among the different parties. Mr. Gibbon states, of the party called Donatists, that *three hundred* bishops, with many thousands of the inferior clergy,

were torn from their churches, stripped of their
ecclesiastical possessions, banished to the islands,
and proscribed by the laws, if they presumed to
conceal themselves in the provinces of Africa."

"Religion in the sixth century became still
more corrupt; it lay expiring," as Dr. Mosheim
remarks, "under an enormous heap of superstitious
inventions. The worship of Christians was now
paid to the remains of the true cross, to the images
of the saints, and to bones, whose real owners were
extremely dubious. The progress of vice among
the clergy was truly shocking. In those very
places which were consecrated to the advancement
of piety, and the service of God, there was little
else to be seen but ghostly ambition, insatiable
avarice, pious frauds, intolerable pride, and a superstitious contempt of the natural rights of the people,
with many other evils still more enormous."

Episcopal claims continued to be the subjects of
constant disputes, especially between the patriarchs
of Rome and Constantinople. John of Rome visited
the eastern capital, A.D. 525, to serve his own
purpose, but charged by Theodore, the Gothic king
of Italy, to engage the emperor Justin to cease from
persecuting the Arians. With a crowd of the
nobility and clergy, the emperor met him, and bowed
down to the very ground before the vicar of the
blessed Peter, and coveting the honour of being
crowned by him, received at his hands the imperial
diadem! The patriarch invited the Pope to perform Divine service in the great church together
with him; but he would neither accept the invita-

tion, nor even see the patriarch, till he agreed not only to yield him the first place, but to seat him on a kind of throne above himself, alleging no other reason than *because he was the Roman High Priest!* The patriarch indulged him in everything he required, and they celebrated Easter together, with extraordinary pomp and solemnity. The Pope officiated in the Latin tongue, according to the rites of the Latin church.

Pre-eminence being thus acknowledged by the patriarch of Constantinople to the pontiff of Rome, it cannot be matter of wonder that Justinian, the nephew and successor of the emperor Justin, in his epistle to the new Pope, John II., writes, A.D. 533, "We hasten to SUBJECT *and to unite to your holiness all the priests of the whole East.* Nor do we suffer anything which belongs to the state of the church, however manifest and undoubted, that is agitated, to pass without the knowledge of your holiness, the *head of all* the holy churches!"

This pre-eminence was given more fully, two years after, in a memorial to the pontiff, by "the bishops and clergy of Constantinople." It was addressed— "To our most holy lord, and most blessed father of fathers, Agapetus, archbishop of the Romans and patriarch, the bishops of the oriental diocese, and those who dwell in the holy places of Christ our Lord, with the residents and other classes assembled in this royal city." Plain Christians may wonder at all this sacerdotal blasphemy, so utterly at variance with all that they read in the New Testament, except of the predicted Antichrist!

But the dignity of "universal patriarch" being assumed by the bishop of Constantinople, "Gregory the Great" denounced it as a "*profane*," "proud," "antichristian" title; as "impious," "execrable," "blasphemous," "infernal," "diabolical." On this occasion, Gregory assumed the title of affected humility, ever since retained by the Popes, "SERVANT OF THE SERVANTS OF GOD!" Still that lofty title, which he condemned in his ambitious brother John, he sought for himself, as is evident from his adulatory letter to those monsters of wickedness, Phocas and his wife Leontia.

Phocas had opened a passage to the imperial throne, by the murder of Mauricius and his six sons; and afterwards, most barbarously, of the empress Constantia, and her three daughters, dragging them from their refuge in one of the churches of Constantinople. Mauricius is commended as a prince of many virtues, and of but few vices; and Gregory, in his letters to him, hypocritically declares, that "his tongue could not express the good he had received of the Almighty, and his lord the emperor; and that he thought himself bound, in gratitude, to pray incessantly for the life of his most pious and most Christian lord; and that, in return for the goodness of his most religious lord to him, he could do no less than love the very ground on which he trod."

Mauricius, however, favouring the title assumed by the patriarch John, Gregory was offended; and, like many a courtier, congratulated the murderer, Phocas, on his being proclaimed emperor; saying,

with the most consummate hypocrisy, "Let the
heavens rejoice! let the earth leap for joy! let the
whole people return thanks for so happy a change!"
In the same strain he wrote, in reply to the first
letter of Phocas, and to the Empress Leontia he
says, "What tongue can utter, what mind can
conceive, the thanks we owe to God, who has placed
you on the throne, to ease us of the yoke with
which we have hitherto been so cruelly galled?
Let the angels give glory to God in heaven! let
men return thanks to God upon earth! for the
republic is relieved, and our sorrows are banished!"

Mr. Bower, in his "Life of Gregory," asks,
"Who would have expected such letters from a
Christian bishop to a usurper! a tyrant! a murderer! a regicide? Who would not have thought
Gregory, of all men, the least capable of becoming
his panegyrist, of applauding him in his usurpation,
murder, and tyranny? Gregory, I say, whose
manners and whole conduct have hitherto appeared
irreproachable! But what virtue can be proof in a
Pope against the jealousy of a rival?"

"Gregory the Great" died A.D. 604, without attain-
ing his object; but he has been highly extolled by
the Romish church, by whom he has been canonised
as a *saint*. He was a man of profound talents, and
of equal priestcraft, as the venerable martyrologist,
John Fox, says of this Pope, "Of the number of all
the first bishops before him in the primitive time,
he was the *basest*; of all them that came after him
he was the *best*."

Sabinian succeeded to the popedom, A.D. 605;

and Boniface, A.D. 607. This latter priest, formerly *nuncio* of Gregory, by flattering the emperor, as his master had done, prevailed on Phocas to "revoke the decree of Constantinople in 588, entailing the title of *universal bishop* on the bishop of Constantinople, and to transfer it to Boniface and his successors, declaring the bishop of Rome *the head of the universal church !*"

Pope Boniface, therefore, on receiving this imperial edict, assembled a council in the church of St. Peter at Rome, consisting of *seventy-two* bishops, and *thirty-four* presbyters, and all the deacons and inferior clergy of the city, and issued a decree as absolute monarch of the church ! His successors pursued his policy; "nor did their boundless ambition allow them or the world," as Mr. Bower states, "to enjoy any rest, till they got themselves acknowleged for UNIVERSAL MONARCHS, as well as UNIVERSAL BISHOPS !"

Throughout the seventh century, popery advanced, while the name of Christianity was dreaded, and by many abhorred, on account of the wicked lives of its professed ministers. It was dishonoured by various heresies and idolatries. Some of their leaders filled the eastern empire with carnage and assassinations, of which, indeed, the Catholics were scarcely less guilty; so that the vengeance of the Christians was regarded with the deepest horror. This shocking exhibition was observed with astonishment by reflecting Jews and pagans; when Mohammed, an Arab travelling merchant, a young man of singular talents, ambition, and enthusiasm,

having witnessed these abominations, formed a
design of a new system of religion, which should
destroy the popular idolatries. Aided, and perhaps
prompted by a learned Jew, and an apostate from
Christianity, he succeeded. His system rejected
the idolatry of the Arabs, and the worship of saints
and relics by professed Christians, while it included the chief facts of patriarchal history in
the Scriptures, mingled with many Arabian and
Jewish fables. This he pretended was the pure
religion taught by Moses, by the prophets, and
by Jesus Christ. By this artful device, and as
a military chief, he engaged multitudes of followers; and thus, by rapine and war, he soon
obtained the sovereignty of Arabia and several
adjoining countries. In this century, therefore,
" the mystery of iniquity" prevailed, fulfilling the
Divine prophecies regarding Antichrist in the west,
as monarch in the church at Rome, but in the
language of Scripture, a " BEAST;" and, in the east,
by the imposture of Mohammed, as the predicted
" FALSE PROPHET." (Rev. xvi. 13—xvii.)

Mohammedanism reigned, in all its savage bigotry,
in the *eighth*, *ninth*, and *tenth* centuries, under
the Saracen and Turkish military leaders, over the
finest parts of Asia and Africa, and in several kingdoms of Europe; and as image-worship prevailed
among professing Christians, with endless priestly
abuses and pious frauds, the Scriptures being almost
unknown to the people, many families, nominally
Christian, relinquished the name of Christ, assuming that of the false prophet, Mohammed.

Popery still advanced in the west; and the barbarous nations proselyted from paganism, being kept in ignorance of the Holy Scriptures, were unable to detect the gross impositions of the priests, who pretended to possess the power of forgiving the sins of men. Hence, many of the princes and nobles, having acquired wealth by rapine and murder, gave large donations to their religious instructors, to save them from the torments in the future world due to their crimes. These gifts were commonly called "The price of transgression for the redemption of souls!" Pepin, king of France, transferred to Pope Stephen III., A.D. 756, the Italian provinces, which he had conquered from the Lombards; and this was enlarged by the addition of Rome itself, by Charlemagne, a few years after. From that time to the present, that territory has been regarded as "the temporal patrimony of St. Peter."

Immense riches were by this means soon possessed by the priesthood. Emperors, kings, and princes invested bishops with the possession of whole provinces, cities, castles, and fortresses, with the rights of sovereignty! But, among all these, the Pope maintained his pre-eminence; and this was willingly conceded, as essential to the usurped dominations of the inferior prelates. The western barbarians who received the name of Christ, looked upon the bishop of Rome as they had regarded their arch-druid; and the ignorant people yielded to the bishops a boundless authority, which they had given to their priests in paganism. The con-

sequences of this superstition were most pernicious;
for it gave to the Roman pontiff a despotic power
in civil affairs; and hence arose the horrible notion,
*that all those who were excommunicated by the Pope
forfeited thereby all their rights as citizens, and the
common claims of humanity.*

Twenty-eight popes, amid five dreadful schisms,
are enumerated in the *tenth* century; several were
sons of the infamous prostitutes Theodora and her
daughters, Theodora and Merozia influencing the
chief ecclesiastics. Their premature deaths or deposition were the fruits of their flagitious lives, details
of which cannot stain these pages. Dr. Mosheim
truly states, "the history of the Roman pontiffs that
lived in this century, is a history of so many monsters, and not of men, and exhibits a horrible series
of the most flagitious, tremendous, and complicated
crimes." Cardinal Baronius describes them as
"monstrous and infamous in their lives, dissolute in
their manners, and villanous in all things."

Popery attained its highest elevation in the
eleventh century; and this will be seen in its genuine
form, as the "man of sin," "exalting himself
above all that is called God, or that is worshipped,"
in the extravagant titles now assumed by the popes.
They were called "universal fathers," and "masters
of the world." Notwithstanding vigorous opposition
from several sovereigns, they carried their insolent
pretensions so far as to proclaim themselves, "lords
of the universe," "arbiters of the fate of nations,"
and "supreme rulers of the kings and princes of the
earth!" One instance of this abominable assump-

tion will best illustrate the hateful spirit of popery, while the reading of it will not fail to shock the feelings of every Christian.

Henry IV., emperor of Germany, opposed the arrogant claims of Gregory VII. The haughty pontiff at once excommunicated him, and excited the princes of the empire to make war upon him. Being ignorant of the Holy Scriptures, and bowed down by superstition, he was terrified by the anathemas of the Pope, as if he had command over the destinies of men, as the pretended vicar of Christ; he was, therefore, persuaded to throw himself into the hands of the pontiff, to yield to his clemency, and to await his dread decision. Filled with apprehension of eternal consequences if he refused, Henry consented; and submitted to the degrading penance which had been prescribed; so as to stand, with his empress and family, at the gates of the fortress of Canusium, during three days, in the open air, in a severe February, A.D. 1077, having his feet bare, his head uncovered, and with no other raiment than a piece of coarse woollen cloth thrown over his body, to cover his nakedness. On the fourth day he was with difficulty admitted to the presence of that lordly priest, who, with the utmost hypocrisy, as a minister of religion, and with much ceremony, granted him absolution! But he forbade him ever after to assume the title or the ensigns of sovereignty! Such a daring outrage upon humanity, as well as royalty, excited universal abhorrence; but not one of the greatest princes in Europe had the courage to utter a word of reproof to the terrible

ANTICHRIST!! Such was the spirit and the power that originated and carried on the execrable COURT OF HOLY INQUISITION!!

With these advances of the papal power there was a corresponding corruption in the doctrines and ceremonies of religion. While Romanists pretend that theirs is the only pure form of Christianity, we know that all their peculiarities are novelties, the contrivances of priests, to serve their own purposes. Their doctrines were never formed into a system or settled until the council of Trent, at the close of which, A.D. 1564, they were first published in the creed of Pope Pius IV. And one of the greatest points, — relating to the Virgin Mary, whether she were *conceived in sin*,—fiercely contested between monkish sects in the Romish Church,—was determined in the affirmative, first by Pope Pius IX., in 1849.

Many of the practices had previously been inculcated by individuals, before their establishment as follows:—

	A.D.
The celibacy of the clergy first ordained	305
The invocation of Saints and Angels	350
The Virgin called Mother of God	431
The Virgin invoked in litanies	620
The worship of images	787
Transubstantiation originated	831
Transubstantiation established	1215
Auricular confession, and priestly pardon	1215
Purgatory affirmed, A.D. 1140: Decreed	1563

CHAPTER III.

ORIGIN OF THE ROMISH INQUISITION.

Persecution of the Paulicians—Albigenses—Their sufferings in Languedoc—In England, Spain, France—Counts Raymond and Roger—Massacre of their People—Dominic, founder of the Inquisition.

INTOLERANCE seems essential to the office of a priest; as no sooner was this character assumed by Christian pastors, than they commenced persecution against those who disputed their claims. Hence originated the Inquisition. Its operations have ever been directed against all who differed from the ruling prelates, even when making their appeal to the Holy Scriptures. And such there were from the time of the apostles. Among the earliest of those who were put to death by professing Christians were the Paulicians.

These people are thought to have been so called from Paul, a preacher, of the Armenian church, in the seventh century; but some consider Constantine of Samosata their founder, about A.D. 660. He received from a pious deacon, who had escaped from captivity among the Mohammedans, a copy of the New Testament. This he esteemed as a precious gift; and, finding the instruction of the Scriptures different from the prevailing super-

D

stitions, he formed a system of theology for himself from the sacred oracles. Constantine devoted himself to the work of the ministry, assuming the name of Sylvanus, a companion of the apostle Paul. His colleagues in preaching were called Timothy, Titus, and Tychicus; and six of their churches were named after those to whom Paul had addressed his Epistles. They rejected human traditions in religion, the worship of the Virgin Mary, of images, and of the cross. They abolished the lofty titles of the priesthood, and instituted pastors, with perfect equality, and without robes to distinguish them from the people. In Asia Minor they increased greatly, and the Greek emperors persecuted them grievously. An officer named Simeon was sent, as an inquisitor, to seek Sylvanus, and he was apprehended, with some of his followers, at Colonia. As the price of liberty, they were required *to stone their pastor!* One only among them, Justus, was found sufficiently base; and he murdered thus his faithful teacher, who fell a martyr for Christ, after having laboured for twenty-seven years, diffusing the doctrine of the Gospel. Justus aggravated his guilt by betraying his brethren; while Simeon, observing the grace of God in the joyful sufferers, embraced the Gospel, forsook the world, preached the faith, and died also a martyr for Jesus.

From the Paulicians arose, as it is believed, a branch of the celebrated Christian confessors, the Valdenses, or Waldenses. Dr. Haweis, therefore, says of them, "At the close of the seventh century we see the first traces of a small but precious body, afterwards named Valdenses, which some suppose a branch of the Paulicians. Retiring from the insolence and oppressions of the Romish clergy, and disgusted with their vices, they sought a hiding-place in the secluded valleys of the Pais de Vaud, embosomed by the Alps, and removed from the observation of their persecutors, where they might enjoy purer worship and communion with God."

These Paulicians increased, and scriptural knowledge was eagerly sought by several persons, who became eminent preachers in the southern parts of France, in Savoy, in Piedmont, and in the contiguous districts of Germany. Their followers were called after their teachers, or by various contemptuous appellations, taken from their peculiar customs or principles. Some were *Petrobrusians*, from Peter de Bruys, who, after twenty years' labour, became a martyr for Christ; *Henricians*, from Henry, a disciple and colleague of Peter; *Albigenses*, from the city of Albi, where they were condemned in a council; *Cathari*, or Puritans, from their seeking the purity of Christian doctrine; and *Waldenses*, from Peter Waldo, a merchant of Lyons, in France. This great man procured translations of several parts of the Scriptures, and commenced his ministry, having relinquished his trade, about A.D. 1180, especially in France and Lombardy. The converts of these zealous men became very numerous; and they soon attracted the notice of the papal court in this century.

Egbert, a German abbot, says of them, "They

are increased to great multitudes throughout all countries. In Germany, we call them *Cathari;* in Flanders, they call them *Pipples;* in France, *Tisserands* (weavers), because many of them are of that occupation."

Among these people many churches were formed, with intelligent and devout pastors of their own choosing. The *Cathari*, especially in Piedmont, formed separate societies, which were screened, in a great measure, from the popish prelates, by the retired seclusion of their habitations in the valleys, from which they were called *Valdenses.*

These people were regarded with jealousy by the prelates, and their enemies commonly accused them of grievous errors ; but it is well known that they were slandered, and that, while they rejected the claims and idolatries of the Romish priesthood, they generally held the essentials of the Gospel, as they derived their principles from the Scriptures. Egbert, the abbot, says of them, "They are armed with all those passages of Holy Scripture, which, in any degree, seem to favour their views: with these they know how to defend themselves, and to oppose the Catholic truth, though they mistake entirely the true sense of Scripture, which cannot be discovered without great judgment."

Evervinus, an abbot in Cologne, in a letter to Bernard, the most famous priest of the church of Rome of his time, called *St. Bernard*, says, A.D. 1140, "There have been lately some heretics discovered among us, near Cologne, though some of them have, with satisfaction, returned again to the church. One of their bishops and his companions openly opposed us in the assembly of the clergy and laity, in the presence of the archbishop of Cologne and of many of the nobility, defending their heresy by the words of Christ and his apostles. Finding that they made no impression, they desired that a day might be appointed for them, on which they might bring their teachers to a conference, promising to return to the church, provided they found their masters unable to answer the arguments of their opponents, but that otherwise they would rather die than depart from their judgment. Upon this declaration, having been admonished to repent for three days, they were seized by the people in the excess of zeal, *and burnt to death;* and what is very amazing, they came to the stake, and bore the pain, not only with patience, but even with joy! Were I with you, father, I should be glad to ask you, how these members of Satan could persist in their heresy with such courage and constancy as is scarcely to be found in the most religious believers in Christianity."

St. Bernard himself was a violent persecutor, yet he says of them, "If you ask them of their faith, nothing can be more Christian; if you observe their conversation, nothing can be more blameless; and what they speak they prove by deeds." Claudius, archbishop of Turin, writes, "Their heresy excepted, they generally live a purer life than other Christians." Cassini, a Franciscan friar, says, "That ALL THE ERRORS of these Waldenses consisted in this, that they denied the church of Rome

to be the HOLY MOTHER-CHURCH, AND WOULD NOT
OBEY HER TRADITIONS!" Thuanus, a Catholic
historian, says they are charged with holding,
"That the church of Rome, because it renounced
the true faith of Christ, WAS THE WHORE OF
BABYLON, and the barren tree which Christ himself cursed and commanded to be plucked up; that,
consequently, NO OBEDIENCE WAS TO BE PAID TO
THE POPE, or to the bishops who maintain her
errors; that a monastic life was the sink and
dungeon of the church; that the orders of the
priesthood were marks of the great beast mentioned in the Revelation; that the fire of purgatory, the solemn mass, the consecration days of
churches, the worship of saints, and propitiation
for the dead, were devices of Satan."

Exemplary as were their morals, and scriptural
as were their principles, thus testified by their
enemies, cruel persecution was carried on against
these dissenters; and the inquisitors, sent by the
Pope to search for and to destroy them, brought
multitudes to suffer as martyrs for Christ. Some,
we have seen, fell victims at Cologne, while others
escaped from the power of their enemies. They
found, however, the intolerance of popery where-
ever they went. This will be illustrated by one
fact in English history of that period. Thirty of
these persecuted Germans sought an asylum in
England, and settled as a church near Oxford, A.D.
1159, but they were apprehended by order of the
clergy. Their pastor, Gerard, was a man of learning; and he professed that they believed the

doctrines of the apostles, though they disbelieved in purgatory, prayers for the dead, and the invocation of saints. But they were condemned in an ecclesiastical council, and delivered to the magistrates to be punished. The king, Henry II., at the instigation of the ruling clergy, ordered them to be branded on the forehead with a red-hot iron; to be whipped through the streets of Oxford; and, having their clothes cut short at their girdles, to be turned into the open country. None being allowed to afford them shelter, they perished with cold and hunger!

Dr. Milner, in his valuable "Church History," in recording this fact concerning these earliest dissenters from popery, who were put to death in England, makes this natural reflection:—"What darkness must at that time have filled this island! A wise and sagacious king, a renowned university, the whole body of the clergy and laity, all united in expelling Christ from their coasts! Driven, most probably, from home by the rage of persecution, they had brought the light and power of the Gospel with them into England. Brief as is the account of them, it is evident they were the martyrs of Christ."

Papal vengeance was threatened against all whom the prelates regarded as heretics; and, A.D. 1163, in the synod of Tours, it was commanded to all bishops and priests in Languedoc, whose capital was Thoulouse, "to take care, and to forbid, under pain of excommunication, every person from presuming to give reception, or the least assistance to the followers of this heresy, *which first began in the country of Thoulouse*, whenever they shall be discovered. As many of them as can be found, let them be imprisoned by the Catholic princes, and punished with the forfeiture of all their substance."

In like manner, Pope Alexander III., A.D. 1179, issued an edict, which expresses his mind thus:— "Because in Gascony, Albi, in the parts of Thoulouse, and other regions, *the accursed perverseness of the heretics*, Cathari, or Patrenas, or Publicans, or distinguished by sundry names, has so prevailed: We therefore SUBJECT TO A CURSE, both themselves and their defenders and harbourers; and, *under a curse, we prohibit all persons from admitting them into their houses, or receiving them upon their lands, or cherishing them, or exercising any trade with them.* But if any die in their sin, *let them not receive Christian burial*, under pretence of any privilege granted by us, or any other pretext whatever!"

Some of the Waldenses having escaped to Arragon, in Spain, King Ildefonsus, A.D. 1194, issued an edict, by which he banished them from his kingdom, and all his dominions, as enemies of the cross of Christ, profaners of the Christian religion, and public enemies, adding, "If any, from this day, shall presume to receive into their houses the aforesaid Waldenses, or other heretics, or to hear their abominable preachings, or to give them food, let him know that he shall incur the indignation of Almighty God and ours, and without appeal be punished as though guilty of high treason. However, we give these wicked wretches liberty till the day after All Saints (though it may seem contrary to justice and reason), by which they must be gone from our dominions; but afterwards they shall be plundered, whipped, and beaten, and treated with all manner of disgrace and severity."

Pope Innocent III., about A.D. 1198, having just ascended the pontifical throne, deputed two monks of Citeaux, Guido and Regnier, to proceed to Narbonne, as inquisitors, to search after and punish heretics; and in the following year, Peter of Castelnau was added to that mission, with in-creased authority. They promised indulgences to all who afforded them aid against the heretics; and they succeeded in this office, but rendered them-selves hated for their bigotry and cruelty, wherever they carried on their antichristian work. They were assisted greatly by the services of a body of preaching friars, under their leader, Dominic. Francis, another zealous monk, with a numerous company of disciples, was deputed by the Pope to contend against the heretics in Italy; and these two leaders became the founders, about A.D. 1200, of the famous, but opposed orders of friars, called, after them, *Dominicans* and *Franciscans*.

Castelnau projected the extension of his mission into the territories of Thoulouse, A.D. 1207; but the prince refused his sanction to this invasion, for such a purpose, and the haughty priest excommu-nicated Raymond. This audacious act received the express sanction of the Pope, but it led to contests; and one of the friends of Raymond, provoked by the insulting denunciations of the agent of the pontiff, struck him with his poniard, and killed him.

Innocent, incensed to fury by the murder of Castelnau, seized the occasion to prosecute the designs of his cruel bigotry, and summoned the counts, barons, and knights of the four provinces of the southern parts of France, to invade the territories of Count Raymond, authorising them to seize the property of the heretics. As the same indulgences were promised to those engaging in this war, as had been assured to the crusaders against the Saracens in the Holy Land, au army of *fifty thousand* cross-bearers was soon assembled, and placed for service, during the period of forty days, under the direction of Arnald Almeric, abbot of Citeaux. The Pope gave directions regarding this crusade :—" We counsel you, with the apostle Paul, to employ guile with regard to the count; for in this case it ought to be called prudence. We must attack separately, those who are separated from unity. Leave, for a time, the count of Thoulouse, employing towards him a wise dissimulation, that the other heretics may the more easily be defeated, and that afterwards we may crush him, when he shall be left alone."

Raymond and his nephew, Roger, count of Beziers, waited upon Arnald, to avert the impending storm; but to no purpose. Raymond submitted to the terrible power, and joined the army that was marching against his own subjects and those of his nephew ; but he first performed the dreadful penance appointed for him on account of the murder of Castelnau. He was made to swear upon the host, as the body of Christ, and upon the relics of the saints, that he would *obey the Pope*, and the holy Roman church, and pursue the Albigenses, *with fire and sword*, till they were extirpated. Having taken this oath, he was ordered *to strip himself naked, from head to foot*, with only a linen cloth around his waist; the legate threw a priest's stole round his neck, and leading him by it into the church, nine times round the pretended martyr's grave, he inflicted the discipline of the church upon the naked shoulders of the humbled prince. He then granted him absolution, on his taking another oath, inviolably to maintain all the rights, privileges, immunities, and liberties of the church and the clergy!

Count Roger offered terms of reconciliation; but the legate rejected his proposals, and intimated that no mercy would be shown to him. The city of Beziers was taken; and the inhabitants, who had crowded into the churches, were barbarously massacred; so that *seven thousand* corpses were said to have been found in the church of St. Magdalen. Some were desirous of sparing the Catholics who might be among the heretics, and they applied to the legate for that purpose; but, in a rage, he replied, *"Kill them all; the Lord knoweth them that are His!"*

Beziers contained a population of about *fifteen thousand;* and Arnald, in his report to the Pope, acknowledged that so many were massacred! But as multitudes, especially women and children, from the surrounding country, had sought a refuge there, in hope of security against the invading army, and none were spared, historians of fidelity reckon that *sixty thousand* were then murdered by the agents of the Pope, and the city was then burnt to ashes !

Count Roger had escaped to Carcassonne, which was next besieged, as he had shut himself up with the inhabitants in that city ; but he offered to capitulate. Dissimulation was practised, as enjoined by the Pope ; so that the prince, with three hundred knights, were admitted to confer with Arnald, who, with the leaders of the army, had given a solemn oath for their safety ; but having them now in his power, he perfidiously arrested them, delivering them over to the general of the army, Simon de Montfort. The citizens, however, made their escape, during the night, and fled to other provinces ; but a few of them being captured, *four hundred* of the captives were burned alive, and *fifty* more were hanged, by Simon de Montfort, under the direction of Arnald, as legate of the Pope. The noble Count Roger was thrown into prison, and soon died by violence, as acknowledged by the Pope.

It would be impossible to detail the sufferings of the poor Albigenses, under Simon de Montfort. With an army of cross-bearers, A.D. 1210, he took several strong castles, and hanged the inhabitants and refugees on gibbets. He selected more than a hundred of the people of Brom, *tore out their eyes, and cut off their noses*, and sent them, under the guidance of a one-eyed man, to Cabaret, to terrify the inhabitants by their example. In the following year, he stormed La Vaur, and destroyed the inhabitants by fire and sword. He hanged Almeric, the governor, lord of Montreal, and then massacred *eighty* of the chief citizens. His sister, Girarda, the lady of the castle, by order of the count, was thrown into a pit, and covered with stones. He afterwards collected all the heretics in the castle, and burned them, with rejoicing. He took possession of the castle of Cassero, which surrendered; but "the pilgrims, seizing nearly *sixty heretics, burned them with infinite joy,*" as testified by the Catholic historian, Petrus Pallensis. At Castris de Termis they put Raymond, the governor, into prison, where he died shortly; and, in one large fire, they burned his wife, his sister, and his daughter, with some other noble ladies, whom they could not prevail upon to return to the profession of the church of Rome. Thus they were sacrificed to papal bigotry, as faithful martyrs for Christ! What adds to the revolting character of these murders was, as usual, the bishops and priests present in the army, in their pontifical habits, who expressed their satisfaction in witnessing the carnage, by singing *Veni Creator!*

Historians scarcely know how to speak of these enormities. Sismondi states, that "hundreds of villages had seen all their inhabitants massacred with a blind fury, and without the crusaders giving themselves the trouble to examine whether they contained a single heretic. We cannot tell what

credit to give to the numbers assigned for the
armies of the cross, nor whether we may believe
that, in the course of a single year, five hundred
thousand men were poured into Languedoc." But
this we certainly know, that armies, much superior
in numbers, and much inferior in discipline, to those
which were employed in other wars, had arrived for
seven or eight successive years; that they entered
this country without pay, and without magazines;
that they provided for all their necessities with the
sword; that they considered it as their right to
live at the expense of the country; and that all the
harvests of the peasants, all the provisions and
merchandise of the citizens, were on every occasion
seized with a rapacious hand, and divided among
the crusaders. No calculation can ascertain, with
any degree of precision, the dissipation of wealth,
or the destruction of human life, which were the
consequences of the crusade against the Albigenses.
"There was scarcely a peasant who did not reckon
in his family some unhappy one cut off by the
sword of Montfort's soldiers. More than three
quarters of the knights and landed proprietors had
been spoiled of their castles and fiefs, to gratify
some of the French soldiers—some of Simon
de Montfort's creatures. Thus spoiled, they were
named *Faidits*, and had the favour granted them of
remaining in the country, provided they were
neither heretics nor excommunicated, nor suspected
of having given an asylum to those who were so;
but they were never to be permitted to enter a
walled city, nor to enjoy the honour of mounting a

war-horse. Every species of injustice, all kinds of affronts, persecutions of every name, had been heaped on the heads of the unhappy Languedocians, under the general name of Albigenses."

So truly horrible was this bloody work, that a native of Thoulouse, a *poet* and a *Catholic*, who witnessed this crusade against the Albigenses, afterwards delivered the following denunciation against Antichrist:—" I know I shall be censured if I write against Rome, that sink of all evil; but I cannot hold my peace. It is no wonder that the world lies in wickedness. It is you, treacherous Rome, who have sown confusion and war. By the baits of thy delusive pardons, thou deliverest up the French nobility to persecution, and dost establish thy throne in the bottomless pit. Heaven will remember thy pilgrimage to Avignon, and the murders thou committest there. In what book hast thou read that it was thy duty to exterminate Christians? Like an enraged beast, thou devourest both great and small. Rome, your head and whole body is arraigned for having committed that horrible murder at Beziers. Under the appearance of a lamb, with an air of modesty and simplicity, you are inwardly a wily serpent and a ravenous wolf. Rome, I comfort myself in the assurance that thy power will decay, and thou wilt soon be no more. If thy dominion is not destroyed, the world will be overthrown!"

Dominic witnessed many of these sad outrages and dreadful slaughters; and he proceeded, as the chief inquisitor, to search out the number and quality of the alleged heretics, to excite the princes and prelates to extirpate them, and so to fulfil his commission from the Pope. His success he fully reported to Rome; and formed a plan of a regular Court of Inquisition. In this he was aided by a nobleman, with whom he had resided at Thoulouse; for having been seduced by that zealous monk to the Catholic faith, he devoted his mansion and his other property to the service of that father. Dominic submitted his scheme to the papal legate, Arnald, by whom it was highly approved; and that abbot appointed him inquisitor-general in Gallia Narbonensis, about A.D. 1208; and he was confirmed in that office, in the fourth Lateran Council, A.D. 1215, at which Dominic was present, and greatly honoured by the Pope on account of his exploits against the Albigenses.

Dominic was a native of Spain, of the noble family of Gusman. His mother dreamed, before his birth, that she was delivered of a whelp carrying a lighted torch in his mouth; that he alarmed the world by his barking, and set it on fire by his torch. These were interpreted of his preaching, by which he terrified the people, and of his dreadful Inquisition. His promotion was the consequence of his fiery zeal and activity; and his priestly domination will appear from a few passages in his imposition of penance on a reclaimed heretic, as follow:—

" Brother Dominic, the least of preachers, to all Christ's faithful people, to whom these presents shall come, greeting in the Lord:—

" By the authority of the Cistertian abbot, who

hath appointed us to this office, we have reconciled the bearer of these presents, P. Rogerius, converted by God's blessing from the heretical sect, charging and requiring him, by the oath which he hath taken, that three Sundays, or three festival days, he be led by a priest, naked from his shoulders down to his drawers, from the coming into the town unto the church doors, being whipped all the way!" Most rigorous rules for the whole of his life, and total separation from his wife, were also imposed on him, on pain of excommunication!

Dominic founded sixty monasteries, in different provinces, forming the centres of so many courts of inquisition; and he died, A.D. 1221, esteemed as an extraordinary character; so that he was canonised, A.D. 1234, by Pope Gregory IX. The Dominicans were called *Jacobins* in France, and *Black Friars* in England.

CHAPTER IV.

THE INQUISITION IN SEVERAL COUNTRIES.

Inquisition in France—Pontifical decrees—Used by Princes—
Arragon, Castile, Navarre and Portugal—Various countries—Sicily, Rome, Venice—Apostolics—Knights Templars—Beghards—Beguins—Lombardy—Milan.

PAPAL policy, by courts of inquisition, continued to prevail in many countries where they had been established. Raymond the younger recovered the

E

dominions of his father, and banished the inquisitors from Thoulouse. But his chief city was
besieged and taken by Amalric, son of Simon de
Montfort. In the presence of two cardinals,
therefore, he was led up before the high altar in
the church, covered with only a linen garment, and
there absolved; but it was on the hard condition
of resigning the greater part of his dominions.
The Inquisition was then restored, and laws still
more severe than before were passed against
heretics.

Louis, the French king, to oblige and gratify
the Pope, made laws against the heretics, constituting every bishop in France a kind of inquisitor, with power to punish those whom he judged
enemies of the Pope. Provincial councils were
held at Thoulouse, A.D. 1229, and, A.D. 1230, at
Rome, where several persons were burnt alive the
following year; and at Narbonne, A.D. 1235, in
which the prelates made severe laws against the
heretics. These laws were collected by order of
Pope Gregory IX.; and, with other decretals of
Pope Boniface VIII., they formed the laws for the
"Court of Holy Inquisition."

Frederick II., emperor of Germany, issued
severe edicts, ordaining that those who should be
adjudged as heretics by the prelates of the church,
should be put to death without mercy; and that
his imperial protection should be enjoyed by the
Predicant friars.

Louis, to ingratiate himself with Pope Alexander, as Innocent IV. had appointed the provincial

of the Predicant friars inquisitor to extirpate
heretics in Thoulouse, requested that pontiff to
constitute the prior of the Predicant order at Paris
inquisitor over the whole kingdom. The proposal
was too pleasing to be refused by him; and he
nominated him, therefore, to that office, with ample
power. Besides, as many, who had excited the
fury of the inquisitors, fled to the churches for the
benefit of ecclesiastical immunity, the Pope abolished that privilege. With this he republished
seven terrible laws, empowering magistrates to aid
the inquisitors in punishing heretics, as ordained
by the Emperor Frederick. These pontifical decrees, authorising inquisitors in their proceedings
generally, exhibit the will of the Pope regarding
those who rejected his religion for the doctrine of
Christ in the Scriptures :—

"We being willing to prevent the danger of so
many souls, entreat, admonish, and beseech your
wisdom, and strictly command you, by these apostolical writings, as you have any regard for the
Divine judgment, that you appoint some of the
brethren committed to your care, men learned in
the law of the Lord, and such as you know to be
fit for this purpose, to be preachers generally to the
clergy and people ; and, in order the more effectually to execute their office, let them take into
their assistance some discreet persons, and carefully inquire out heretics. And if they find out
any, either really culpable, or such who are defamed, let them proceed against them according to
our statutes. And that they may more freely and

effectually execute the office committed to them,
we, confiding in the mercy of God Almighty, and the
authority of the blessed apostles, Peter and Paul,
remit, for three years, the penance enjoined them,
to all who shall attend their preaching for twenty
days. And as for those who shall be happy to die
in the prosecution of this affair, we grant a plenary
pardon of all their sins, for which they are contrite
in their hearts, and which they confess with their
mouths."

This dreadful tribunal was found, by the sovereign princes, to be a convenient engine for
revenging supposed or real injuries received by
them; since it was necessary, for their purpose,
only to bring against their victims the charge of
heresy. By this means, a great number of individuals, known to be devoted Catholics, were prosecuted to death by the Emperor Frederick. Yet
both he and Louis, as it suited their interests,
made vigorous opposition to the proceedings of the
Inquisition; for which, however, they paid dearly,
as they were threatened and humbled by the
haughty Antichrist. Hence arose a series of
ruinous contests between the intolerant pontiff
and the mightiest sovereign princes.

Spain, at this period, comprehended the four
Christian kingdoms of Arragon, under James I.;
Castile, under Ferdinand III.; Navarre, under
Sancho VIII.; and Portugal, under Sancho II.
Arragon was found, A.D. 1232, to contain some of
the Waldenses; and the Pope commanded King
James to proceed in the work of extirpating them

as heretics. A synod was held against them, A.D. 1240, at Tarracon, when the archbishop, with his suffragans, and Peter Cadente, were appointed inquisitors for the province.

Castile and Leon also received this court, A.D. 1290, as it had been established in Arragon. And during the thirteenth century the Inquisition was set up in various other countries, where the Pope possessed influence, especially in Austria, Hungary, Poland, Dalmatia, Ragusia, Bosnia, Croatia, Istria, and several provinces of Germany. It was extended, also, to Syria and Palestine, for the purpose of proceeding against Jews as well as heretics. The policy of the inquisitors, however, differed in different places; but the Austrian Inquisition appears to have been conducted with extreme cruelty; as Catholic historians testify, that many thousands of those deemed heretics were apprehended, and being condemned, were burnt, by the order of the sacred judges, in the city of Crema.

Sicily received the Inquisition about A.D. 1224. It was at first opposed, both in the town of St. Mark, and at Palermo; but the Emperor Frederick is said to have ordained, as a regulation of the profits arising from its proceedings, that "one-third part of the confiscated goods should be appropriated to the common treasury, another third be reserved for the Pope, and the remainder to be shared by the inquisitors; that the spiritual husbandmen should not be defrauded of their reward." This privilege seemed to satisfy the ruling powers; it was renewed, A.D. 1452, by King Alphonsus, and confirmed, A.D. 1477, by Ferdinand and Elizabeth; and various other privileges were accorded to the inquisitors by the Emperor Charles V.

Rome had become the court of appeal for the bishops from an early period. This was a most politic arrangement of the Pope. But, to prevent inconvenience to himself, Urban IV. created Ursarius inquisitor-general, A.D. 1265. This office was continued, with some intermissions, until the Reformation under Luther. The doctrines of that great man were disseminated so extensively in Italy, as well as Germany, that the Romish court became alarmed. Pope Clement VII., therefore, ordered that the utmost rigour should be used against all who professed the doctrines of the reformer; and, as their number appeared to increase, exhibiting the utmost boldness, patience, and zeal, Paul III., A.D. 1543, constituted the "Holy Office" with more extended powers, appointing six cardinals as "inquisitors-general." To these cardinals were added a "commissary-general," always to be a Dominican; an "assessor-general," and the "master of the sacred palace." This court was carried on with magnificence and ceremony suited to the grandees who composed it; and on certain occasions the Pope presided in person. By its dreadful operations the doctrines of the reformers were suppressed, and its professors exterminated from Italy.

Venice received the Inquisition about A.D. 1249, while the contests were being carried on between the Pope and the Emperor. Many persons of different opinions, and, perhaps, under several denominations, fled to Venice, to live in the greater security and quiet of that famous city; but the magistrates, being excited to prevent their city from being polluted by foreign doctrines, chose certain grave persons, zealous for the Catholic faith, to inquire after heretics. Full power was given to the patriarch of Grado, and other Venetian bishops, to judge of those opinions; and it was decreed that whosoever was pronounced an heretic by any bishop should be condemned to the fire. In this process, secular judges made inquisition against heretics, and the duke and senators pronounced the fatal sentence.

Father Paul states, "Notwithstanding the instant requests of Pope Innocent, Alexander, Urban, Clement, and seven other Popes, their successors, the most renowed commonwealth could never be persuaded to receive the office of the *friar inquisitors*, instituted by the Pope. The secular sufficed it, instituted by itself, and brought forth good fruit for God's service."

Nicholas IV., a minor friar, being exalted to the pontifical throne, got the Inquisition to be received by a public decree at Venice, A.D. 1289. Still, this court was established on different principles from those which govern it in other countries; for while the judgment concerning the doctrine for which a person may be pronounced an heretic, is determined by ecclesiastics, the judgment of the fact, or who maintains that doctrine, and the pronouncing of the sentence, are held to belong to the secular judges in Venice. So that they determine what books shall be prohibited, as well as who are heretics, and their court is far milder, and less under the influence of the Pope, than the other inquisitions in Italy.

Among the heretics accused by the inquisitors, there were some forming a sect called *apostolics*, from their professing to imitate the zeal of the apostles of Christ. They attracted the notice of Pope Honorius, A.D. 1290. Sagarelli, their leader, was condemned by the Inquisition and burned. Dulcinus, another of their teachers, withdrew, with about six thousand adherents, to the valleys of the Alps; but Pope Clement V. sent inquisitors to seek them with an army of crusaders, by which many were driven among the mountains, and perished with cold and hunger. Some of them were captured, including Dulcinus and his wife, who were sacrificed at the stake, as victims to the cruelty of their anti-christian persecutors.

Clement V., jealous of the Knights Templars, who possessed large property in France, gladly listened to the accusations against them by the king. Their grand-master, De Molai, and many others, therefore, were arrested, A.D. 1307. The order was abolished in the council held at Vienne, A.D. 1311, and nearly sixty of the prisoners were condemned and burnt. Several others were brought to the stake in Paris, where they protested their innocence; but their property was shared by Pope Clement and Philip, king of France.

Others of the reputed heretics were *Beghards*, so called from their ardour in prayer; *Beguins*, pious females of that society; and Lollards, so named from their singing psalms in social worship. These were hunted in several provinces, and punished in the usual manner by the officers of the Inquisition as enemies of the Pope. Some of the Beguins were patronised by persons of distinction; and a famous controversy arose respecting their opinions regarding the possession of property. Four of their leading men were burnt at Marseilles, A.D. 1318; and they were condemned as heretics and archheretics by the Pope, A.D. 1329.

Lombardy received the Inquisition before A.D. 1233, when Pope Gregory IX. appointed, as chiefinquisitor, Pietro da Verona, a Dominican. He was the first that put heretics to death at Milan. In the course of his ministry he burnt many, but he was assassinated, A.D. 1252; and another fell a sacrifice to his own cruelty, Pagano da Lecco, A.D. 1277.

About A.D. 1320, the Pope excommunicated Matthew Galeacius, viscount of Milan, his sons, and followers. The city was deprived of its charter, and all its municipal privileges; the citizens, who might favour the viscount, were given up to be seized by the faithful as slaves, in full right, and their property was granted to any who might lay hold of it. All who should supply the city with provisions were in like manner denounced; and this state of things continued during three years, in which the viscount set at nought the papal censures. With a view to humble him, the Pope, John XXII., prosecuted the viscount for heresy; and, after several citations, pronounced the definite sentence against him. The Pope also commanded Aycard, the archbishop of Milan, and the inquisitors in Lombardy, to proceed against him and his adherents; and the bishop of Padua and two abbots published these sentences.

Raymond Cardonus was ordered to collect an army to invade his dominions. Several cities were taken, and the viscount routed; when the senate of Milan sent a deputation of twelve of their elders to implore peace and absolution. Matthew resigned his principality to his son Galeacius, and himself repairing to the cathedral, protested, with a solemn oath, against the Pope's legate as having treated him unjustly. He left the city, and made the same oath next day in the church of Monza, where he died of fever, through grief. His sons buried him, but his body was sought for to be burned, by order of the cardinal-legate and the inquisitors.

CHAPTER V.

THE WYCLIFFITES AND HUSSITES.

Wycliffe's ministry—The Lollards—Sawtree—Other Martyrs —Wycliffe's bones burnt—His writings—Martyrdom of Huss and Jerome—Persecution of the Hussites—The Waldenses.

DIVINE prophecy dooms a perpetual overthrow to popery; and it declares also that this is to be

accomplished by the light of the Gospel of Christ.
Instruments and agents, therefore, are needed for
this important work; and these began to increase
in the *fourteenth* century. But the Inquisition was
fearfully employed in various forms to destroy
them.

Among the most distinguished opponents of the
papacy, we must number John Wycliffe, justly
called "The Morning Star of the Reformation!"
He was born A.D. 1324; and being enlightened by
the Holy Scriptures, his ministry, under the Spirit
of God, and his numerous writings, especially his
translation of the Bible, contributed very much to
prepare the way for the Protestant Reformation.
This great man was impelled, not only by love to
the truth of Christ, but by an extensive knowledge
of the enormous evils manifestly arising from the
Romish priestcraft. The papal exactions in England were grievous, estimated at five times the
amount of the royal revenue; and the parliament
determined, therefore, A.D. 1374, to seek redress
by a remonstrance, sent by delegates, who should
present it to the Pope. Wycliffe was one of them;
and during two years, near the seat of "his
holiness," he had an opportunity of observing the
intrigues and iniquities of the court of Rome.

Wycliffe became the more determined in his
opposition to the friars, who, as agents of the Pope
and the Inquisition, were enemies to the welfare of
the country. Their false doctrines, avarice, and
wickedness were exposed by the reformer, with the
light of Divine truth; and he possessed the best

opportunities of doing good service to the cause of Christ, as professor of divinity in the university of Oxford. But his boldness in the Gospel provoked the papal court; and the Pope addressed letters to the heads of the colleges, requiring them, by inquisitors and punishment, to suppress his doctrine, and to deliver him in custody to the archbishop of Canterbury or the bishop of London. He then appealed to those prelates, requiring them to apprehend the daring reformer, and to keep him in irons till they should receive his further orders from Rome. The king also was required by the Pope to aid those prelates in proceeding against Wycliffe. He was cited before the prelates, at the palace of the archbishop of Canterbury; but he was secure under the protection of John of Gaunt, the great duke of Lancaster.

Divine Providence favoured this zealous servant of Christ, so that he escaped the prison, and died in peace, A.D. 1384. Multitudes were enlightened by his controversial and evangelical writings, and by his translation of the Scriptures. Many from the Continent sought his instruction and copies of his works; by which he contributed to produce a revolution in religion, not only in England, but in several other kingdoms in Europe.

Wycliffe's enemies were indefatigable during his life; and after his death they persecuted his disciples. Oxford was regarded as infected with his heresies; and those who followed his scriptural doctrines were distinguished as "Lollards." The heads of the university were, therefore, required, on pain of excommunication, to inquire, every month, whether any scholar held doctrines contrary to the decisions of the church. "Twelve inquisitors of heresy—for this dreadful name," as Dr. Southey remarks, "had been introduced among us—were appointed at Oxford, to search out heresy and heretical books."

King Richard II. being deposed, was succeeded, A.D. 1392, by Henry II., a dupe of the prelates; and under him they procured the sanguinary statute, *ex officio*, which authorised the bishops, as inquisitors, to proceed against all persons suspected of heresy. This was the first law in England for the burning of men on account of religion.

William Sawtree, parish priest of St. Osith's, London, was the first that was condemned to the stake in England, A.D. 1400; and the forms of degradation and execution were carefully observed, that it might be an exact precedent for future occasions. These forms, Dr. Southey states, "were probably derived from the practice of the accursed Inquisition in Languedoc; and they were well devised for prolonging the impression on the spectators." After the ceremonies of degradation, "the cap of a layman was placed upon his head, and Archbishop Arundel then delivered him, as a lay person, to the secular court of the high constable and marshal of England there present; beseeching the court to receive favourably the said William Sawtree, unto them thus recommitted. For with this hypocritical recommendation to mercy the Romish church always delivered over its victims to be burnt alive! Sawtree accordingly suffered martyrdom at the stake in Smithfield, leaving a name slandered by the Romanists, but held in deserved respect for the sake of the Gospel by British Christians."

Wycliffe's disciples continued to be sought after by the inquisitors, and many suffered at the stake for Christ. But volumes are required to detail their sufferings and triumphs.

Archbishop Arundel procured "a law for ever," A.D. 1410, "that whosoever they were that should read the Scriptures in the mother tongue," which was then denounced as "Wycliffe's learning," should "forfeit lands, cattle, body, life, and goods, from their heirs for ever, and so be condemned for heretics to God, enemies to the crown, and most arrant traitors to the land."

Bale says, "Anon after, that Act was proclaimed throughout the realm, and then the bishops, the priests, and the monks, had a world somewhat to their minds. For then were many taken in divers quarters, and suffered most cruel deaths. And many fled out of the land into Germany, Bohemia, France, Spain, Portugal, and into Scotland, Wales, and Ireland, working there many marvels against the false kingdom, too long to write. In the Christmas following was Sir Roger Acton, knight, Master John Browne, and Sir John Beverly, a learned preacher, and divers others, imprisoned for quarrelling with certain priests. In January following, A.D. 1413, was the before-named Sir Roger Acton, Master John Browne, Sir John Beverly, and *thirty-six* more, of whom the more part were gentlemen of birth, convicted of heresy by the bishops, and condemned of treason by the temporality, and, according to the Act, were first hanged and then burned in the Giles-field. In the same year, also, one John Claydon, a skinner, and one Richard Turning, a baker, were both hanged and burned in Smithfield by that Act, besides what was done in all other quarters of England; which was no small number, if it were thoroughly known." Fox calls Sir Roger Acton "this worthy, noble, virtuous knight," in giving an account of the dreadful persecutions of these faithful martyrs of Christ.

Wycliffe's ashes were not allowed to rest in quiet: for, A.D. 1415, by the council of Constance, forty-four conclusions, drawn from his writings, were declared to be heretical, and their author condemned as an obstinate heretic. Inquisitors sought his bones, which were ordered to be dug up and cast upon a dunghill; but the sentence was not executed till A.D. 1428, when Pope Martin V. sent order to Fleming, bishop of Lincoln, once a professed favourer of the reformed doctrine. The inquisitors obeyed the order of the bishop—the bones were burnt, and the ashes were cast into the adjoining rivulet, Swift. From Lutterworth, as Dr. Fuller beautifully remarks, "this brook conveyed his ashes into the Avon; Avon into Severn; Severn into the narrow seas; they into the ocean. And thus the ashes of Wycliffe are emblems of his doctrine, which is now dispersed all over the world!"

Wycliffe's writings were copied and circulated

among studious inquirers after the Gospel in
several nations; and, as the sister of Wenceslaus,
king of Bohemia, had become the queen of Richard
II., learned Bohemians frequented England. One
of these, Jerome of Prague, on his return from
study at Oxford, A.D. 1400, carried with him some
of Wycliffe's books, which became the means of
enlightening John Huss, a famous divine of Prague
university. He laboured to promote a reformation,
opposing the false miracles, and impostures, and
evil lives of the priests. But the archbishop being
incensed against him, accused him before the Inquisition, from which he appealed by proctors to
Cardinal Colonna, who declared him contumacious,
and excommunicated him. He then appealed to
the Pope, who confirmed the sentence, and excommunicated his followers. But he continued his
labours in teaching and writing, until he was summoned before the council of Constance. The
Emperor Sigismund pledged his honour for his
protection, and John, Count of Chlum, interposed
on his behalf; but that holy synod violated the
solemn engagement of the emperor, seizing his
person, and requiring him to plead guilty of heresy
in thirty propositions extracted from his writings.
With this requisition of the inquisitors Huss could
not comply; yet he protested his readiness to yield
to the testimony of Holy Scripture. Being then
presented before the council, in the presence of
the emperor, the princes of the empire, and an
immense assemblage of prelates, he was condemned
to the stake, and his writings to be burned.

Dignified priests endeavoured in vain to induce him to recant. The bishops stripped him of his priestly robes, and put on his head a mitre of paper, on which devils were painted, with the inscription, "Ringleader of Heretics." They then delivered him to the unworthy emperor, and he to the duke of Bavaria. His books were burnt at the church gate, and he was led to the stake at the suburbs of the city. He manifested the true spirit of a martyr for Christ. Multitudes attended his execution, and were astonished at his piety, saying, "What this man has done before, we know not; but we hear him now offer up most excellent prayers to God."

Huss wished to address the people; but the elector palatine prevented him, ordering that he should immediately be burnt. The martyr then cried with a loud voice, "Lord Jesus, I humbly suffer this cruel death for thy sake; I pray thee forgive all my enemies." Thus suffered Dr. John Huss, as a faithful martyr of Jesus, A.D. 1415; leaving a most instructive example to the church of God, and the fame, as Luther testifies, of being "a most rational expounder of Scripture."

Jerome also was sacrificed to papal bigotry. For, having translated the works of Wycliffe into his native language, and professed himself a reformer of Christian doctrine and worship in connexion with Dr. Huss, when he heard of his friend's danger at Constance, he repaired thither in hope of rendering him some assistance. Jerome found that the inquisitors had caused him also to be cited

before the council, and that his own destruction
had been determined. He returned, therefore, to
Bohemia, after writing to the emperor in favour of
his friend; but he was arrested, and imprisoned for
nearly a year. By the tortures and entreaties of
the inquisitors he was induced to sign a recantation.
His conscience, however, would not allow him to
suffer this to stand; and he was brought again
before the inquisitors. He defended the principles
of his martyred friend, and made a solemn appeal
to his persecutors :—"How unjust is it, that ye
will not hear me! Ye confined me three hundred
and forty days in several prisons, where I have
been cramped with irons, almost poisoned with filth
and stench, and pinched with the want of all neces-
saries. During this time, ye always gave to my
enemies a hearing, but refused to hear me so much
as a single hour. I came to Constance to defend
John Huss, because I advised him to go thither,
and had promised to come to his assistance, in case
he should be oppressed. Nor am I ashamed to
make here a public confession of my own cowardice.
I confess, and tremble while I think of it, that,
through fear of punishment by fire, I basely consented against my conscience to the condemnation
of Wycliffe and Huss. I appeal to the Sovereign
Judge of all the earth, in whose presence ye must
shortly answer me!"

Jerome's judges were implacable, and he was
murdered at the stake, singing a hymn in the
flames, while he yielded up his spirit to his Divine
Redeemer, A.D. 1416.

Many of the nobles of Bohemia regarded the murder of these two excellent men as an outrage against their nation, and they meditated revenge. This passion was inflamed by the policy of Pope Martin, who promoted the organisation of the Inquisition in their country, and excited the Catholics in Moravia to unite in the destruction of the Hussites. King Wenceslaus inclined to support the Pope, but through terror of being opposed in the bloody work, he died, A.D. 1419, when the crown of Bohemia falling to the emperor, Sigismund sent an army on a crusade against the heretics. Multitudes fell victims to their cruel bigotry, and perished in the mines of Kuttenburgh, and by drowning, as well as at the stake. It is said there were thrown into one mine 1,701 persons; into another, 1,038; and into a third, 1,334, A.D. 1420.

The chief magistrate of Litomerici, a cruel bigot, to gratify the inquisitors, caused *twenty-four* of the principal citizens to be arrested and accused of heresy. One of these was the husband of his own daughter. They were imprisoned in a lofty tower; and, when perishing with hunger and cold, they were brought out and sentenced to immediate death by drowning in the river Albis. The magistrate himself had to pronounce the sentence upon them, which he performed, regardless of the tears and entreaties of his daughter; and the whole were conveyed in carts, bound hand and foot, to the river, into which they were plunged, while officers were employed, armed with iron forks and poles, to watch that none might escape, and to stab those who should make the attempt. The young lady, being unable to move her cruel father to pity, plunged into the river, in hope of aiding her husband to escape—but she failed; and the next day the bodies of both were found in the water, her arms clasped around the body of her husband! Other instances of murderous cruelty, equally shocking, are recorded of the bloody operations of the Inquisition.

Many of the Hussites now withdrew to a high mountain, which they fortified; and there they held their religious meetings, administering the Lord's supper, not only in bread, but with wine, which had been forbidden by the Catholics. Their fortification they called *Tabor*, and the people were hence called *Taborites*. They chose leaders, and defeated the troops of the emperor in eleven engagements; so that they gained the use of the cup in the Lord's supper, by the consent of the council of Basil, A.D. 1431.

Part of the Hussites sought more than the cup; they insisted on having a reformation according to the Scriptures. They were still persecuted by the Catholics, and obliged to conceal themselves in thickets and caves, kindling fire only at night, when they read the Scriptures and united in the social worship of God. Stephen, their last bishop, having been burnt alive for his profession of Christ, the Bohemian brethren united with the Waldenses, A.D. 1480.

CHAPTER VI.

THE INQUISITION IN SPAIN.

Spain under Ferdinand and Isabella—Holy Office—Torquemada, inquisitor—His victims and policy—Persecution
of Jews—Diego Deza—Cisneros—Charles V.—Philip II.
—Acts of faith—Victims under Philip II.—Murder of
his son, Don Carlos.

SPAIN, above every other country, has been afflicted and degraded by the court of inquisition. We have seen that it was introduced into its provinces at an early period, and several persons were publicly burnt, A.D. 1302, in Arragon, by Father Bernard; and one of the spectacles of burning heretics, A.D. 1325, was sanctioned by the presence of King James and his two sons. About A.D. 1356, Nicholas Eymerick, inquisitor-general of Arragon, wrote a book of rules, as "The Guide of Inquisitors;" and this was the chief directory, though the Inquisition greatly declined, until the union of the crowns of Arragon, Castile and Leon, Asturias and Granada, by the marriage of Ferdinand V. of Arragon, with Isabella, queen of Castile, A.D. 1474.

Spain being thus united under one government, the "Modern Inquisition" was established, in a new form, for the discovery of Moors and heretics, but especially Jews. This people, by diligence in trade, had acquired great wealth; they were celebrated for their learning, and some of them had risen to the highest offices in the state. Yet, even from the first, they were subjected to insult, on account of their religion, by the professors of Christianity. Many of the Jews, however, professed to be converted to the faith of Christ, and intermarried with the Spanish nobility; but no sooner had Ferdinand and Isabella ascended the throne, than the Romish prelates appealed to them, as Catholic princes, to give their sanction to an increased activity and power of the Inquisition.

Isabella was unwilling to become thus guilty of the blood of her subjects; but Ferdinand was led by the priests, and the queen at length yielded to their bigoted counsels. Pope Sixtus IV., therefore, A.D. 1471, at her request, granted a bull, enjoining the arrest and punishment of heretics and apostates. Gentle means were employed for two years, as was desired by Isabella; but it was then reported by the priests, that these were insufficient; and, A.D. 1480, Michael Morillo and John de San Martin, both Dominicans, were constituted inquisitors, with various subordinate officers.

Seville was the seat of their first operations. In their progress, they were furnished by the governors of provinces, according to royal orders, with whatever they required; and the citizens, though opposed to the institution, yielded to the royal commission. They issued their first edict, January 2nd, 1481; and many, dreading the vengeance of the Inquisition, fled from the city. The Spanish nobles were commanded by the inquisitors to seize the emigrants as heretics; their property was confiscated, and such numbers were arrested that they were obliged to provide a larger prison. On a tablet of this building was engraved the following, in barbarous Latin:—

"The Holy Office of the Inquisition, established against the wickedness of heretics, commenced at Seville in the year 1481, under the pontificate of Sixtus IV., who granted, and in the reign of Ferdinand and Isabella, who had asked for it. The first inquisitor-general was friar Thomas de Torquemada, prior of the convent of Santa Cruz, of Segovia, of the order of the Preaching Brotherhood. God grant that, for the propagation and maintenance of the faith, it may last until the end of the ages. 'Arise, O Lord, be judge in thy cause—catch the foxes.'"

Terror might reasonably seize the minds of the people; for, January 6th, only *four* days after the first edict, *six* persons were publicly burnt to death by the inquisitors; and, about a month after, a much larger number. On account of the numerous victims, the prefect of Seville erected a stone scaffold. Upon this were placed four large hollow statues of plaster, called "*the four prophets,*" and within, or chained to these, the condemned wretches were burnt. Innocence was by no means a guarantee against imprisonment, confiscation of property, or even death; for the inquisitors invited accusations, and the accusers were secure, as their depositions were kept secret, and the parties accused knew nothing of their being suspected until they had been arrested and chained in the dungeons of the Inquisition.

These inquisitors travelled, and held their courts in different cities, where their agents had filled the prisons. Though the records of the tribunals were not accurately kept, the numbers convicted and punished were most frightful. Llorente estimates the numbers at Seville, A.D. 1481, at 2,000 burnt; 2,000 burnt in effigy; and 17,000] punished by penances; total, 21,000. In 1482, there were eighty-eight burnt; forty-four burnt in effigy; and 625 subjected to penances; total, 757!

Torquemada prosecuted his duties with such vigour and zeal that, A.D. 1483, Pope Sixtus appointed him inquisitor-general of Castile and Leon, and of Arragon. These powers being confirmed by Pope Innocent VIII., A.D. 1485, distinct tribunals were established at Seville, Cordova, Jaen, Villa-Real, and Toledo. King Ferdinand appointed a royal council of the Inquisition, and Torquemada as its president; and this council published, A.D. 1486, a code of laws for the tribunal. These were revised by the president, with additions, A.D. 1488, and again, A.D. 1498. These laws and rules for the Inquisition were worthy of the spirit of their authors, and the genius of the institution, indicating the cunning and malignity of a fiend, rather than the mind of a Christian. Their enforcement, therefore, threw all classes of society in Spain into the deepest misery, such multitudes being condemned and executed. Upwards of *one hundred thousand* families were reputed to have emigrated from the country. Absolution or redress might, indeed, be obtained at the court of Rome for money, and immense sums were expended, until it was found that it affected the salaries of the Inquisition; when the practice of such appeals was abolished, as being a violation of the agreement of the Pope with Ferdinand and Isabella.

Another expedient was adopted to enrich the Inquisition. The inquisitors charged the Jews with persuading their brethren who had professed Christianity to return to the faith of Israel; with crucifying children on Good Friday, in contempt of our Saviour; and with the fact of the Jewish physicians and surgeons, who were esteemed the most skilful of the medical practitioners, having caused the death of Henry III. In their alarm, they offered Ferdinand and Isabella *thirty thousand* pieces of silver, in aid of the war against Granada; and to refrain from all trades and professions that might be filled with Christians. Those sovereigns being about to accept the proposal, Torquemada rushed into their presence, holding a crucifix, and appealing to the king and queen—" Behold Him, whom Judas sold for thirty pieces of silver; do you sell Him for a greater sum ?" Casting down the crucifix, the haughty priest left the royal apartment; but he gained his object, for the king and queen published a decree, March 31st, 1492, commanding all the Jews to leave the kingdom within three months, under the penalty of death and confiscation of their property. Christians were forbidden to afford them the least assistance. They were allowed to sell their stock, and take their furniture, but not any *gold* or *silver* with them. Some of them emigrated to the states of Barbary, where they were cruelly treated by the Moors; so that they returned to Spain and professed Christianity. Others retired to Portugal, where they were permitted to live for a time, and then they were sold as slaves.

How many Jews were thus expelled from Spain, through the Inquisition, cannot be correctly ascertained; some reckon 160,000, and others as many as 800,000. Mariana states that the number was estimated at 170,000 families, or 800,000 souls! But if we suppose only the smaller number, as the Jews were the most intelligent and wealthy part of the community, the expulsion of them was a serious national loss to Spain.

Torquemada having so far prevailed, exhibited his intolerant haughtiness in such a manner that he was dreaded by all. He was not satisfied with the condemnation of thousands of the rich among the laity, but he laboured to subject the bishops to his hated court. Pope Alexander VI. received continual complaints against him; but he feared to suspend him. However, he constituted four others as joint inquisitors-general, A.D. 1494; and Torquemada died in November, A.D. 1498, execrated by the whole community. Aware of the public hatred, he always kept a horn of a unicorn on his table, as the supposed means of discovering poison in his food; and in public he was guarded by a troop of *fifty* familiars of the Inquisition on horseback, and *two hundred* on foot, for which he obtained the licence of Ferdinand and Isabella.

During the period that Torquemada held the office of inquisitor-general, the total number of his victims was more than 10,000, committed to the flames: nearly 7,000 burnt in effigy; and upwards of 97,000 sentenced to confiscation, perpetual imprisonment, or infamy!

That terrible inquisitor was succeeded by Don Diego Deza, a Dominican, archbishop of Seville. He was confirmed in his office by the Pope's bull, December 1, 1498; and proved himself worthy to follow the sanguinary Torquemada. He laboured to re-establish the Inquisition in Sicily and in Naples; and in Granada against the Moors, many of whom, as well as Jews, were cruelly harassed in Spain. Deza prosecuted some of the prelates and the nobility; and the number of his victims, during eight years, were reckoned at 38,440 persons; 2,592 burnt; 896 burnt in effigy; and 34,952 punished by penances.

Ximenes de Cisneros succeeded Deza. He is reported to have been far milder in his temper and administration than his predecessors; yet he re-organised or established the Inquisition in Seville, Cordova, Jaen, Toledo, Estremadura, Murcia, Valladolid, Calahorra, Barcelona, Saragossa, Pampeluna, Cuenca in Valencia, Majorca, Sardinia, the Canary Islands, Oran in Algiers, and America. Yet, with all his moderation, Llorente reckons his victims, during eleven years, as 3,564 burnt; 1232 burnt in effigy; and 48,059 punished by penances; total, 52,855!

Charles V. succeeded his father, Ferdinand, on the throne of Spain, in January, 1517; and during his reign the Cortes made various attempts to reform the Inquisition, that its dreadful proceedings might be conducted publicly, and according to the rules of the common law; but by means of immense presents to the chancellor, and by the representations of Cardinal Adrian, the inquisitor-general, Charles was induced to support the existing enormities of the terrible court. Adrian was elected Pope, in January, 1522; and during the five years of his office, his victims were 28,220; of whom, 1,344 were burnt; 672 burnt in effigy; and 26,214 were punished by penance.

Charles V. was elected emperor of Germany, A.D. 1520, and he became, during nearly forty years, the greatest sovereign in Europe. He sanctioned the Inquisition in persecuting the Lutherans, and all reformers of religion; and how he regarded that pernicious court will appear from his will, in which he commends it to his son Philip thus:—

"Out of regard to my duty to Almighty God, and from my great affection to the most serene prince, Philip II., my dearest son, and from the strong and earnest desire I have, that he may be safe under the protection of virtue, rather than the greatness of his riches, I charge him, with the greatest affection of soul, that he take special care of all things relating to the honour and glory of God, as becomes the most Catholic king, and a prince zealous for the Divine commands, and that he be always obedient to the commands of the church. And, amongst other things, *this I principally and most ardently recommend to him, highly to honour and constantly support the office of the Holy Inquisition,* as constituted by God against heretical pravity, with its ministers and officials; because by this single remedy the most grievous offences against God can be remedied. Also I command him, that he would be careful to preserve to all churches and ecclesiastical persons their immunities." In a codicil to his will, also, he thus enjoins his son:—"I ardently desire, and with the greatest possible earnestness beseech him, and command him by his regards to me, his most affectionate father, that in this matter, in which the welfare of all Spain is concerned, he be most zealously careful to punish all infected with heresy, with the severity due to their crimes; and that to this intent *he confer the greatest honour on the office of the Holy Inquisition,* by the care of which the Catholic faith w be increased in his kingdoms, and the Christian religion be preserved."

King Philip was obedient to these commands of his father, as the proceedings of the inquisitors in his several provinces proved, as well as his sanction to the horrid course of persecutions and martyrdoms under his queen, in England. See Chapter IX.

On Trinity Sunday, May 21, 1559, there was a most solemn *auto da fé* against the Spanish Lutherans, in the Great Square of Valladolid. The

Princess Donna Juana (governess of the kingdom, in the absence of her brother, Philip II.), the Prince Don Carlos, and many grandees of Spain, as well as prelates and nobles of Castile, and a multitude of ladies and gentlemen, all assisted on that occasion. *Sixteen* persons were brought out in that *auto*, to be reconciled by penance; also, the remains and effigy of a lady, already dead, and *fourteen* living persons, to be consumed by the devouring element! The lady was Donna Eleonora de Vibero, proprietress of a convent in the city. Her daughter, Beatrice, and her two sons, Francis and Dr. Augustin Cazalla, were sacrificed at the stake in this dread *auto*, all being convicted of Lutheranism.

At Seville, the same year, another *auto* was celebrated, in which John Pontius, son of Roderic, earl of Villalon, was publicly burnt as a Lutheran. With him were executed, John Gonsalvus, a preacher, with four ladies of note; Bohorques, scarcely twenty years of age; Maria Viroesia, Cornelia, and Vœnia, in whose house assemblies were held for prayer. Besides these, were *seven* others, and among them, a student, a physician, and a nun. The sacrifice of this company of *thirteen* persons, besides several effigies, was attended with great pomp, yet it excited the indignation of not a few of the citizens. Two others escaped the fire, dying previously in prison; Dr. John Egidius, nominated by the emperor as bishop of Drossen, and Dr. Constantine Pontius, the confessor of Charles V. They were victims of the Inquisition, suspected of holding the doctrines of Luther.

Philip being alienated from his queen, Mary, left England in 1557, and proceeded to his army in Picardy; and after his arrival in Spain he demanded an *auto da fé*, which was celebrated with extraordinary magnificence. De Castro, in his very interesting volume, "Spanish Protestants and their Persecutions by Philip II.," says:—

"Although so many were burnt or oppressed with ignominious penances at the before-mentioned *auto da fé*, the inquisitors reserved the greatest number, and most noted of the prisoners for Protestantism, in order to bring them to condign punishment on the arrival of Philip II.; a festival very appropriate to this monarch, whose reign in England, with the barbarous Mary Tudor, had terminated after broiling in the flames there a multitude of Protestants.

"This *auto* was celebrated on the 8th of October, 1559. In order to greater decorum and solemnity, this *most pious* monarch thought it opportune to assist, with all his court, in those horrors, and recreate himself in the frightful destruction of many of his subjects, illustrious for their birth, their virtue, and their learning.

"Don Diego de Simancas, then secretary of the holy office, says, 'The *auto* of those heretics was most solemnly celebrated in the Great Square, upon a stage *made upon a new plan, so contrived, that from all parts the culprits might be seen*. Upon other stages were assembled the council and prin-

cipal persons; and so great was the concourse of
people, who came from all the country round, that
it was believed the number of persons assembled,
including those of the city, could not be less than
200,000! In this fashion the *most pious* king, the
clergy, the nobility, and the people, with tumul-
tuous haste, had recourse to a method of amusement
worthy of cannibals, or the ancient Mexicans.'"

. In the month of October, 1560, *twenty-eight*
persons, many of them members of the noblest
families in Spain, were tied to the stakes and publicly burnt, as Lutheran heretics, in the presence
of the king at Valladolid.

Philip was not satisfied, however, with the sacrifice of his citizens; he extended the Inquisition to
the navy, appointing an inquisitor to his fleet in the
year 1571; so that, among the seamen of Spain,
many were sacrificed in a public *act of faith*, in
the city of Messina. He established this court at
Lima, in 1571, and in Mexico; and in the year
1574, a public *act of faith* was held in the market-
place of that city. In this, there were *eighty* penitents; two of them, an Englishman and a Frenchman, were released; some others, for judaising
and sorcery, were reconciled; but many of them
were burnt to death, in the presence of the viceroy,
the senate, the priests, and a large concourse of
the Mexicans.

Philip II. died in September, 1598, after having
reigned *forty-two* years. His name was abhorred
in his own dominions on account of his sanguinary
bigotry, and his pernicious policy in government.

Historians represent him as worthy to be classed with those monsters of cruelty, Nero and Domitian, deserving the execration of mankind.

The number of the victims of the Inquisition during the reign of Philip II. was estimated at not less than 40,664; of whom, 6,300 were burnt; 3,124 were burnt in effigy; and 31,240 were subjected to various humiliating penances. This was, therefore, the reign of terror in Spain.

Philip's cruelty may be further illustrated by one act of his domestic administration; for he added his own son, and heir to his throne, to the number of his victims. Don Carlos being shocked at the cruelties exercised by the duke of Alva against the Protestants in the Netherlands, [see Chapter VII.] at the entreaty of several nobles, desired a commission to govern that country, as viceroy, that he might give toleration to those who rejected the domination of the Pope. But his father, attended by several of his privy counsellors and twelve guards, entered his chamber in the middle of the night, seized him, and threw him into prison. The nation was astonished at this outrage against the prince; and the Emperor Maximilian besought Philip to set him at liberty; but in vain. A junta, of whom the inquisitor-general was president, was appointed to try Don Carlos; and he was kept in close confinement. None were allowed to visit him, not even the queen, or the princess, Donna Juana, lest the complaints of the prince should become public; those officials only, with one physician, were permitted to see him, who were

G

appointed by the king. Philip himself dared not see him, fearing the reproaches of the injured prince; and he appears to have been secretly murdered,—the prevailing opinion is, by poison,— July 24, 1568, at the age of twenty-three years!

Philip would never satisfy the public regarding the particulars of the prince's death. De Castro says, " Don Carlos fell a victim to his desires to banish from Flanders the horrors of the Inquisition, and set all men's consciences free in matters of religion. The greatest crime of which Carlos was held by his father, the palace favourites, and the inquisitors, to be guilty, was that of entertaining Protestant doctrines. This was the report in and out of Spain. There is one circumstance which confirms the opinion that Don Carlos was murdered, viz., that the Marquis de Bergnes died in the court under the suspicion of having been poisoned; the Baron de Montigny was secretly beheaded in the palace of Segovia, and the Counts of Egmont and Horn perished on a scaffold, before the populace of Brussels,—all of them for their secret correspondence with Don Carlos ! "

Spain greatly declined under this inhuman policy of Philip II., who was succeeded by his son, Philip III., who reigned twenty-three years, dying March 31st, 1621. The number of his victims in the Inquisition in that period was 15,824 ; of whom 1,840 were burnt; 736 were burnt in effigy; and 13,248 were subjected to penances. Philip IV. succeeded his father, and died in 1665, having reigned *forty-four* years; in which period the victims of the Inquisition were 18,304; of whom, 2,816 were burnt; 1,408 were burnt in effigy; and 14,080 suffered severe penances. Philip IV. was succeeded by his son, Charles II., only four years old; and at his marriage, in 1680, he was *honoured* with the celebration of an *auto da fé*, on a scale of great magnificence, at Madrid! A description of this will be found in Chapter XV.

CHAPTER VII.

THE INQUISITION IN PORTUGAL AND THE NETHERLANDS.

Jews in Portugal—Popular hatred against them—The Inquisition against them—In several cities—Established in Goa —Decree against the Jews—Even after they professed Christianity—Luther's followers in the Netherlands—Inquisitors seek them—Alarm in the cities—Edicts of Charles V.—Philip succeeds him—Duke of Alva's murders—"United Provinces."

PORTUGAL, as we have seen, received some of the Jews, who had been persecuted and driven from Spain under the inquisitor-general Torquemada. Every possible effort, by persecution and cruelty, was employed to convert them to a profession of Christianity. Their children were taken from them,—all under the age of fourteen,—and educated in the Catholic belief. Sismondi states,—" On the occasion of a newly-converted Jew, in 1506, who had appeared to disbelieve in some miracle, the people of Lisbon rose, and having assassinated him, burnt his dead body in the public square. A monk, in the midst of the tumult, addressed the populace, exhorting them not to rest satisfied with so slight a vengeance, in return for such an insult offered to our Lord. Two other monks, raising the crucifix, then placed themselves at the head of the seditious mob, crying aloud only these words, 'Heresy! heresy! Exterminate! exterminate!' And during the three following days, two thousand of the newly converted, men, women, and children, were put to the sword, and their reeking limbs, yet warm and palpitating, burnt in the public places of the city. The same fanaticism extending to the armies, converted Portuguese soldiers into the executioners of infidels and the tyrants of the east. At length, in the year 1540, John III. succeeded in establishing the Inquisition, which the progress of superstition had been long preparing."

King John established the "Holy Office" in Portugal, on the model of that in Spain. "How great his zeal was to maintain the faith in its ancient splendour," says a Catholic historian, "his introducing the sacred tribunal of the inquisitors of heresy into Portugal, is an abundant proof, bravely overcoming those difficulties and obstructions which the devil had cunningly raised in the city, to prevent or retard his majesty's endeavours. For he learned experience from others, and grew wise by the misfortunes of many kingdoms, which, from the most flourishing state, were brought to ruin and destruction, by monstrous and deadly heresies. And it is very worthy of observation, that the year in which the tribunal of the Holy Inquisition against heretical pravity was brought into Portugal, the kingdom laboured under the most dreadful barrenness and famine. But when the tribunal was once erected, the following year was remarkable for an incredible plenty, commonly called '*the year of St. Blaze*,' because before his festival the seed could not be sown in the ground for want of rain, whereas, afterwards, provision was so cheap, that a bushel of corn was sold for two-pence."

Didacus de Silva was the first inquisitor-general in Portugal, and he erected tribunals in several cities, the first at Evora, A.D. 1537, appointing John de Mello the first inquisitor in that city. The tribunal at Lisbon was erected in 1539, by Cardinal Henry, the second inquisitor-general; and another court at Coimbra, in 1541.

Portugal possessed several foreign provinces, among which was Goa, on the Malabar coast of India. Francis Xavier, A.D. 1545, signified to King John III., "that the Jewish wickedness spread every day more and more, in the parts of the East Indies subject to the kingdom of Portugal; and therefore he earnestly besought the king, that to cure so great an evil he would take care to send the office of the Inquisition into those countries." Upon this, Cardinal Henry, then inquisitor-general in the kingdom of Portugal, erected the tribunal of the Holy Inquisition in the city of Goa, the metropolis, and sent into those parts inquisitors, and other necessary officials, who should take diligent care of the affairs of the faith. Alexius Diaz Falcano entered

upon his office, as inquisitor at Goa, A.D. 1541. And
from that period this tribunal has continued, so
that by its intolerance, victims, and cruelties, it has
brought the province to the lowest stage of degradation, and a burden as well as a disgrace to
Portugal.

On several occasions, general indulgences were
granted to the Hebrew converts in Portugal, in
hope of reconciling them fully to the papacy. The
first was by Pope Clement VII., A.D. 1535; and
this was confirmed by Pope Paul III., A.D. 1536.
The *second* was issued by the same pontiff, A.D.
1547; at the same time the inquisitors were required
to proceed with greater vigour against judaisers in
that kingdom. Still he granted a general pardon
to the new converts and their children.

Sebastian, king of Portugal, on the occasion of
his preparation for his unfortunate expedition into
Africa, in which he fell, granted to the descendants
of the Jews, A.D. 1577, for a large sum of money,
that their effects should not be confiscated for ten
years. This pretended liberality, though sanctioned
by Pope Gregory XIII., was contrary to the advice
of Philip II., his uncle, the king of Spain; but upon
the defeat of the king's army by the Saracens, the
same year, Cardinal Henry, the king's great uncle,
succeeding him on the throne, immediately recalled
the said grant, with consent of the Pope, declaring,
as the reason of this revocation, "that after the
most mature consultation of learned men, they all
agreed that he was bound to make such revocation,
because the good of the faith required it."

Cardinal Henry dying in the year 1580, the crown of Portugal fell to Philip, king of Spain; and the new Christians, as the conforming Jews were called, offered him a large sum of money, on condition of his obtaining for them a general indulgence from the Pope; but his divines declared, "that God was greatly offended with such money; and that he could not reasonably expect any prosperous success from it." So Philip disregarded their offers of money, though he was engaged in an expensive war with England and France.

These Jewish Christians in Portugal continued for many years to endeavour, by repeated entreaties, to procure the abolition of the Inquisition, or at least the mitigation of its laws and policy. But they were only deluded by empty words and flattering promises: for they have remained liable to the penalties ordained against heretics, and to the terrors of the Inquisition, on being accused, as being in every way opposed to the principles and doctrines of Rome.

Charles V., the famous emperor of Germany and king of Spain, was the great supporter of the Inquisition in the Netherlands. These provinces, comprehending Belgium, Holland, and several adjacent countries, he inherited from his father. At an early period, many of their divines procured the writings and embraced the doctrines of Luther; and, therefore, the Inquisition was introduced there, A.D. 1521, by Francis Vander Hulst, chancellor of the emperor in Brabant, and Nicolas Van Egmont, a Carmelite friar. These were appointed inquisitors-

general; and their characters and policy we learn
from the celebrated Erasmus. He says, in a letter
to the archbishop of Palermo, A.D. 1524, "Now
the sword is given to two violent haters of good
learning, Hulst and Egmont. If they have a spite
against any man, they throw him into prison; here
the matter is transacted among a few, and the
innocent suffers barbarous usage, that they may
not lose anything of their authority; and when
they find they have done entirely wrong, they cry
out, 'We must take care of the faith.'" In
another letter to a friend, he says, "There reigns
Egmont, a furious person, armed with the sword,
who hates me twice more than he doth Luther.
His colleague is Francis Hulst, a great enemy of
learning. They first throw men into prison, and
then seek out for crimes for which to accuse
them. These things the emperor is ignorant
of, though it would be worth his while to know
them."

Many followers of Christ, therefore, suffered
under these cruel inquisitors by various torments,
and the Emperor Charles endeavoured to establish
the Inquisition in the Netherlands, after the manner
of its operations in Spain. For this purpose he
published an edict against heretics; commanding
all magistrates, when required by the inquisitors,
and at the request of the bishops, to proceed
against any in the affair of heresy, and to afford
their utmost countenance and assistance in the
execution of their office, discovering and apprehending those who might be infected with heretical

pravity. This decree authorised them to proceed
against transgressors by execution, whatever their
dignity or privileges.

Terror filled the minds of the people on learning
the character of this edict, and the most gloomy
apprehensions excited many to prepare to emigrate
from Antwerp. The magistrates, therefore, assembled the chief merchants and traders, to ascertain
from them what losses had been sustained by the
city, and what further damage was expected from
the establishment of the Inquisition. They declared
their minds; and a memorial was prepared and
laid before Queen Mary, sister of Charles V., and
at that time governess of the Netherlands, showing
largely, from the edict of the emperor, from the
instructions of the inquisitors, and from the privileges of Brabant, how many evils appeared to
threaten the city and the whole country. They
besought her to intercede with the emperor, that
so rich and flourish a city might not be ruined by
the operations of the Inquisition. The several
orders of Brabant united with those of Antwerp;
and the queen was prevailed on to undertake their
cause. She at once proceeded to Augsburg, where
she obtained another edict, allowing the ecclesiastical judges to demand some persons from the
imperial courts to join with them in proceeding
against any one accused of heresy. This did by no
means meet the case; it was, therefore, received at
Antwerp under protestation, that this edict should
not derogate anything from the statutes and privileges of the citizens. Still they were ill at ease,

such was the dread of the cruelty which had been known of the inquisitors; especially as they saw that those who were privately commissioned by the pope and the emperor to the office of inquisitors, acted as such by themselves, and by their commissaries. For several were shortly condemned as heretics, in many cities; of whom some were beheaded, others hanged, or burned, and some tied up in sacks and drowned!

King Philip succeeding his father, was appealed to against these enormities, and petitioned to grant religious toleration in the Netherlands. But superstition held the mind of the royal fanatic; and he prostrated himself before a crucifix, solemnly imploring—"I beseech the Divine Majesty, that I may never suffer myself to be, or to be called, the lord of those who deny Thee, the Lord!"

Resolved to annihilate the reformation in the Netherlands, Philip converted the *three* bishoprics into archbishoprics, and established seventeen bishoprics, with a court of inquisition, under the direction of Cardinal Granvile. The Prince of Orange, Count Egmont, and Count Horn remonstrated with the Duchess of Parma, against the Inquisition and Cardinal Granvile. This was in vain. The executions of the Inquisition became more frequent and more rigorous than before; and a general combination was resolved on, to procure a redress of the common grievances. The Duchess of Parma remonstrated with Philip; but the infatuated monarch was deaf to every argument; and the only concession which he made was, that, for the future, heretics, instead of being burnt, should be hanged.

Philip, influenced by superstition, and governed by the priests, supported the policy of the inquisitors in the Netherlands. Their cruelties, therefore, increased, until the people broke out into open revolt. The populace made disturbances, throwing down the images in the churches, and committing other acts of violence. The king threatened vengeance upon the transgressors; and submitted the case to the supreme court of inquisition in Spain, to know its judgment concerning the revolters—information and depositions being given by the inferior inquisitors among the disaffected, that court determined that the inhabitants of the Netherlands were guilty of treason.

Philip now indulged his bigotry to the utmost, regardless of the welfare of his subjects. He sent "the Duke of Alva, of infamous memory," into the Netherlands, with a powerful army to destroy the heretics. That monster, whose bigotry, pride, and stubbornness corresponded with those of his royal master, is said to have "poured out the Protestant blood as water on every side; while *one hundred and twenty thousand* fled from the persecution." Throughout all their cities, old and young, men and women, without any distinction of dignity, age, or sex, might be seen suffering by the sword, the gibbet, the fire, and other torments, until the wretched people, roused with indignation, arose as one man, and totally overthrew the horrid Inquisition. William, prince of Orange, undertook the deliverance of his native country, which he accomplished with troops levied among the refugees and the German Protestants. The mortified King of Spain recalled the Duke of Alva; but that "monster boasted that he had delivered into the hands of the executioners above *eighteen thousand* heretics and rebels, besides those who died in the war!"

Father Paul reckons the Belgic martyrs at 50,000; but Hugo Grotius estimates the numbers who suffered by the hands of the executioner at no less than 100,000. Popery, however, with the accursed Inquisition, was thus driven from the country, and the civil war terminated only with a new form of government, which formed a new Protestant state in Europe, under the title of "THE SEVEN UNITED PROVINCES."

CHAPTER VIII.

THE INQUISITION IN FRANCE.

Martyrs in France—Francis I., a persecutor—His mother, Louisa, establishes the Inquisition—Early victims—Francis pursues her policy—His processions and victims—His horrid death—Increase of Protestants—Charles IX.— Massacre—Edict of Nantes—Its revocation—Barbarities of dragoons.

FRANCE supplied a large number of victims to the cruel bigotry of the Inquisition, at the period of the reformation, especially in the reign of Francis I. This great monarch was nephew to

Louis XII., whom he succeeded on the throne at his death, January 21, 1515. Francis was then twenty-one years of age; and no sooner was he seated on the throne than he resolved on an expedition into Italy, in which he was successful. After the battle of Marignan, in which he was victorious, Francis entered Milan, October 23, 1515; and shortly after concluded a peace with Pope Leo X., by which he was confirmed in many privileges, he and the Pope making various concessions. Leo and Francis met at Bologna, where they drew up a treaty, known as the " *The Concordat*," in virtue of which they agreed to sacrifice what were understood as the rights of the church, mutually sharing the spoils. The king conceded to the Pope his supremacy, independent of all councils of the church, while Leo despoiled the ecclesiastical corporations of France of the power to nominate to the bishoprics, bestowing this patronage upon the monarch. This treaty was ratified by the Pope making a public procession to the cathedral at Bologna, the king bearing the train of His Holiness! Francis felt conscious of the iniquitous character of the *Concordat*; and, turning to Duprat, his chancellor, whispered, "there is enough in it to damn us both!"

Francis and Leo having thus linked their interests together, separated, each to pursue his own course: but the king having afterwards been irritated by some delays of the Pope, complained to the papal legate of the conduct of Leo; adding, that if he were not speedily satisfied, he would countenance the Lutherans in his kingdom. The priestly ambassador replied in a manner that silenced the high-spirited monarch. "Sire," said he, "you would be the first and greatest loser by such a step—a new religion demands a new prince!" By this means Francis was prepared, under the influence of superstition and fear for his crown, to show the most ardent zeal for the cause of the Pope and his Inquisition.

Two ladies, at this period, exercised extraordinary influence in religion in France. Margaret, the duchess of Alençon, sister of Francis, entertained opinions far different from those of the king; and she afforded her powerful protection to the reformers, who increased in several parts of France, especially at Meaux and Lyons. Louisa of Savoy, mother of Francis, professedly a Roman Catholic, but in reality a woman of no religious principle, was made regent of the kingdom, while he carried his arms into Italy, in 1524. He was, at first, successful; but, being eager to take Pavia, he was defeated near that city by the imperial forces, and taken prisoner by Lannoy, vice-king of Naples.

Francis I. became a captive in the power of the Emperor Charles V., and was carried a prisoner into Spain. During his absence the terrors of the Inquisition were felt in France. For, no sooner had Louisa obtained possession of the reins of government, by the captivity of the king, her son, than she wrote to the Pope, as the means of conciliating his favour, asking his advice as to the best mode of dealing with the heretics that infested

France. Clement VII., exasperated by the failure
of every attempt to arrest the progress of the
reformation in Germany and Switzerland, was
delighted with the message which laid the heretics
throughout the "Most Christian kingdom of France"
at the mercy of the sovereign pontiff. He re-
sponded with practical effect; and, by a papal bull,
established the Inquisition in France.

For the purpose of carrying out his policy, the
Pope appointed Chancellor Duprat to be archbishop of Sens, and created him a cardinal. Thus
the Inquisition was, at once, constituted in France,
as all the influential powers, — the regent, the
chancellor, and the parliament, — were leagued
with the Pope and the Sorbonne, to exterminate
heresy with fire and sword. A commission was
appointed, consisting of four priests, to whom was
entrusted absolute power to proceed against all
persons suspected of being tainted with Lutheran
doctrines. The highest dignitaries were held responsible to this dread tribunal; and the first
victim of the inquisitors was Briconnet, count of
Montbrun, bishop of Meaux. He was compelled
to answer, like the humblest priest, before two of
the inquisitors, and every appeal that he attempted
to make to the parliament, or to the regent, was
rejected. He recanted the evangelical doctrines
that he had preached; and Lefevre, an aged professor in the university, "the forerunner of the
reformation," fled to Strasburgh. But neither the
fall of the bishop, nor the flight of the doctor,
could satisfy the inquisitors of Paris. Jean

Pavanne was burned at the stake in the Place de Grève, rejoicing that he was counted worthy to suffer death for Christ. Their next victim was "the good hermit of Livry." As he had evangelised the villagers around his dwelling, about nine miles from Paris, it was resolved to make him a public example. A vast pile was raised in the open area in front of the cathedral of Notre Dame, in which this servant of Christ was sacrificed, in the presence of the whole of the clergy, and a multitude of the people, who had been called together by the great bell of the cathedral. To such humble victims others were added of higher rank, and by other means than the prison and the stake. Michael D'Arande, chaplain to the Princess Margaret, was threatened with death, and Anthony Papillon, chief master of requests to the Dauphin, was carried off by poison. The inquisitors, in a few months, had committed to the flames, or driven from France, nearly every individual who had been the object of their envy or suspicion. At length, after a year's captivity in Spain, Francis obtained his freedom, on most humiliating conditions, to the performance of which he was bound by a solemn oath. From this oath to the emperor the Pope gave him absolution, and thereby bound him more closely to himself by such faithless bonds of perjury and deceit. But this favour rendered it the more difficult for him to change the policy which, under the regency of his mother, had delivered up the heretics of France to the inquisitors of Rome.

Francis returned to Paris in the character of a

doubly perjured vassal of the Pope, bound to assume
the office of the persecutor, and take the lead in
devoting to tortures and to death the most virtuous,
enlightened and faithful of his subjects. The great
change which had taken place in the temper of
Francis on his return from Spain, became remarkably
manifest on his delivering up Louis Berquin, called
"the most learned of the nobility," to the vengeance
of the inquisitors. His books were seized, and, in
order to strike at the root of the heresy, Luther's
writings were publicly burnt before the cathedral
of Notre Dame. Berquin remained faithful; he
refused to purchase life by the sacrifice of his faith;
and Francis ceased to be protector and king. When
the parliament interfered with his early schemes of
policy, his haughty reply had been, "There is a
king in France;" and when the court, responding
to the proud spirit of the sovereign, interfered on
the former arrest of Berquin, the king exclaimed,
"Of what is he accused? Of challenging the
custom of invoking the Virgin in place of the Holy
Ghost! *Is it for such trifles that they imprison a
king's officer?* It is an attack, aimed at literature,
true religion, the nobility, nay, the crown itself."
But Francis had descended from this kingly standing to become the wretched tool of a bigoted
priesthood. Berquin, the "king's officer," was
abandoned to his enemies. He was condemned to
have his tongue pierced and *to be burnt alive;* and
the sentence was executed with the most merciless
severity. Berquin held fast his faith; and his execution was followed by that of fourteen other

reformers, who were burnt at the stake, maintaining, to their latest breath, the true faith of Christ.

Francis not only allowed a free course to the inquisitors, and abandoned the nobles of France to their fury, he was drawn to be their humble agent among the executioners of their cruelties. At the beginning of 1535, Jean Morin, the *surintendant-criminel*, flung into prison immense numbers of men, women, and children, who attended the religious meetings of the evangelicals. They were betrayed by a man named Guainier, who had been employed to keep watch at their secret religious assemblies. These furnished victims for a solemn procession, which the king ordered at Paris, January 21, 1535, in expiation of the offence pretended to have been committed in certain placards, which denied the Romish doctrine of transubstantiation.

Laval, in his " History of the Protestant Reformation in France," describes this procession, thus expressed by a modern writer:—" Between the hours of eight and nine in the morning the procession began to issue from the church of Saint Geneviéve.   There was a long line of priests, dressed in their gorgeous garments; the streets were strewed with flowers, and the windows were crowded with spectators. First were borne the bodies and relics of all the martyrs preserved in the different churches of Paris,—St. Germain, St. Merry, St. Marceau, St. Geneviéve, St. Opportune, St. Landré, St. Honoré; and all those relics of the Holy Chapel which had never been exposed to the public gaze since the grand and mournful day of the funeral of

Saint Louis. Then followed a great number of cardinals in their scarlet robes; of bishops, abbés, and other prelates, and all the members of the University of Paris, marching in regular order. Then came Du Bellay, bishop of Paris, carrying in his hands the holy sacrament. Then the king, with his head bare, and bearing a large waxen taper in his hand; then the queen; the princes of the blood; two hundred gentlemen; the king's guard; the court of parliament; the master of requests, and all the officers of justice. The ambassadors of the emperor, of England, of Venice, &c., were present. The procession, in grave order, proceeded through all the larger streets of Paris; and at *six* principal places there were erected at each a *reposoir*, or temporary altar, adorned with flowers, crucifixes, candlesticks, &c., &c. Little children, dressed as angels, or holding the lamb of peace, are usually to be seen at these reposoirs; but here was now a terrible spectacle prepared. At each altar a scaffold and a pile had been arranged, where were very cruelly burned *six people*, amid the marvellous shouts and rejoicings of the populace, so highly excited, that it was with difficulty they were prevented from snatching the victims out of the hands of the executioners and tearing them in pieces. But if the fury of these was great, the constancy of the martyrs was greater still. The cruelty of the people, in tearing these sufferers to atoms, would have been mercy, compared to the barbarity of the king. He had commanded that these victims should be fastened to a very lofty machine, the beam of

which projecting, was, by means of pulleys, raised
and lowered alternately; and as it rose and fell it
plunged the martyr into a blazing pile below, and
raised him up again in order to prolong his sufferings. This continued till the flames had destroyed
the cords which bound him, and the body sank into
the fire. This horrible machine was not set in
motion till the king, queen, and all present might
enjoy the satisfaction of seeing the heretic tormented
with the flames; during which time the king,
handing his torch to the Cardinal de Loraine,
joined his hands, and prostrating himself humbly,
called down the blessing of heaven upon his people;
and in this attitude remained until the agonies of
the victim had terminated.

"The procession ended where it began, at the
church of St. Geneviéve. The holy sacrament was
replaced in the tabernacle, and the mass was sung
by the archbishop of Paris. After this there was
a splendid dinner, at which the archbishop received
the king, the peers, the ambassadors, the courts of
parliament, &c., &c. At the conclusion of which
entertainment, the king, addressing the numerous
guests, after expressing his grief at the execrable
opinions that were disseminated in his dominions,
said 'that he had determined and commanded that
the most rigorous punishment should be inflicted
upon the delinquents; and he required all his subjects
to denounce every one whom they should know to be
adherents unto, or accomplices in such blasphemies,
without regard to alliance, lineage, or friendship.
As for himself, *if his very arm were thus corrupted,*

*he would tear it from his body; and if his own
children were found guilty of falling into such
enormities, he would at once yield them up as a first
sacrifice to God!'* To give force to his words, the
king ordered the executions of the *sacramentaries*
to continue; and from that time the numbers who
perished by the *balançoire* (or swing) is appalling."

Europe was filled with the reports of these
cruelties on the French reformers, and the Protestant princes remonstrated with the king. But
Francis had become the slave of superstition and
priestly intolerance, and governed by the inquisitors
of Rome. He continued his cruel and impolitic
course, under the counsel of the inquisitors; and
issued a terrible edict, in 1540, against the Vaudois,
requiring " that the villages of Mirandol, Cabrieres,
Les Aignes, and other places shall all be destroyed,
the houses razed to the ground; their caverns
and other subterranean retreats demolished; their
forests cut down; their fruit trees torn up by the
roots; the principal chiefs executed; and the women
and children exiled for perpetuity."

These people were reported as exemplary in their
industry; that "they never say mass for the dead;
they have prayer in the vulgar tongue; they have
no bishops, nor priests, but men whom they elect as
simple ministers." The Papists, therefore, hated
their religion, and envied their prosperity, resulting
from industry; so that they prevailed on the king
to abandon his deserving subjects to the exterminating sword and fire of the inquisitors. Men,
women, and children were massacred with fiendish

cruelty. Towns, villages, and hamlets were devoted to the flames. Death was threatened to all who should offer food or shelter to the fugitives, so that those who escaped the sword of the persecutors, perished in the mountains.

Francis is said to have been stung with remorse on reflecting upon this infamous massacre, especially on his death-bed. He died in 1547, as the persecutor dies,—despairing, dishonoured, and undeplored. His eldest son, the dauphin, died of poison, administered by his cup-bearer; and his own death is believed to have been caused by the same instrument of revenge, administered by the husband of a lady whom he had dishonoured. His character, therefore, was worthy of " the mystery of iniquity," the Romish Antichrist.

France exhibited a long series of the most bloody scenes, after the decease of Francis I., the horrid fruit of the Inquisition, the detail of which would require a volume. Notwithstanding persecution, the Protestants increased greatly; so that, in 1570, it is recorded, there were *two thousand one hundred and fifty* congregations of Protestants in France, some of them containing *two thousand* members! Papal intrigues were long employed, under the direction of the inquisitors, for their extirpation; and the pages of history do not contain such another record of monstrous treachery and malignant barbarity, as that of St. Bartholomew, in 1572. It is to be remembered that the deed was perpetrated in the name of the religion of Jesus Christ, the Prince of Peace!

Charles IX., king of France, guided by his wicked
mother, the infamous Catherine de Medicis, was
induced, by the agents of the Pope, to resolve upon
exterminating, by one decisive effort, all the dissenters from the Romish church. For this purpose,
many of the principal Protestants were invited to
Paris, under a solemn oath of safety, to celebrate
the marriage of the king of Navarre with the French
king's sister. The queen dowager of Navarre, a
zealous Protestant, was destroyed before the
marriage was solemnised, by means of poison, concealed in a pair of gloves. The inhuman butchery
commenced at the tolling of the bell of the Palais
de Justice, at two o'clock in the morning of the
24th of August (the Sabbath), by the murder of the
Admiral Coligny, who had been shot at and wounded
two days previously. The hypocritical king of
France visited him, and declared the admiral's
wound was his own. But the shocking work was
conducted by the Duke of Guise, urged on by the
king himself in person!

Most dreadful was the scene. The shrieks of
women and children rent the air, mingled with the
shouts and blasphemous execrations of their murderers. "Imagine," says a French author, "sixty
thousand assassins, armed with pistols, stakes, cut-
lasses, poniards, knives, and other deadly weapons,
rushing along the streets, blaspheming and abusing
the sacred name of God, and murdering and
mutilating the innocent and defenceless, amid a
horrible tempest of yells and savage cries, and
the piteous shrieks of those whom they dragged

through the mire, or flung headlong into the bloody Seine !" *Five hundred* gentlemen, and *ten thousand* of the common people are believed to have been sacrificed in this horrid massacre, in three days, within the walls of Paris alone. But the bloody work extended to all places where these evangelical dissenters were known; and it is calculated that not less than *a hundred thousand* Protestants were at this time destroyed in France !

On the third day of the massacre, the priests led the king in royal state to the cathedral of Notre Dame, when high mass was performed; and then solemn thanksgivings to God were rendered, as for the victory which he had thus granted over the enemies of the church ! This melancholy tragedy was known to have been contrived by the Romish inquisitors. The announcement of it was received by the clergy, at Rome and in Spain, with expressions of unbounded exultation. The messenger who brought the news to Rome was rewarded with a thousand crowns; and when the letters from the papal legate residing at the French court were read in the assembly of cardinals, it was decreed, that the Pope should march with his cardinals to the church of St. Mark, to offer solemn thanks to God for so signal a blessing conferred upon the see of Rome ! Medals to commemorate this horrid deed were struck in Paris and in Rome, by order of the Governments; and that of Pope Gregory XIII., though proclaiming the everlasting dishonour of the papacy and the Inquisition, may still be obtained at the mint of Rome !

Charles IX. raged in savage cruelty against the

Protestants. Even the king of Navarre and the prince of Condé were devoted to the same destruction; but their lives were spared on their professing to be reconciled to the Romish church; the king of France, with a terrible oath, proposing to them, "mass, death, or the Bastile for life!" This royal bigot, however, fell a victim to guilt and remorse; for he died, May 30th, 1574, in the twenty-fifth year of his age, after suffering dreadful bodily and mental anguish, poisoned, as many believed, by the hand of his own mother!

As to the sacrifices of the Protestants in France, it is collected from authentic records that during *forty* years, in the middle of this century, not less than *a million* were the victims of the unrelenting bigotry of the Romish inquisitors!

Protestantism still survived in France; and many again took up arms in their own defence, until 1598, when Henry IV., of Navarre, succeeded to the throne. He granted the famous "Edict of Nantes," which was called "Irrevocable!" and by which the Protestants were allowed liberty of conscience, the free exercise of their religion, and access to all places of public trust and dignity. But the Papists continued by all kinds of intrigues to annoy them. One shameful invasion of their rights succeeded another, by the enactment of inhuman laws, until the reign of Louis XIV., who was prevailed on, in 1685, by the Popish bishops and the Jesuits, contrary to the most solemn obligations which human or divine laws can frame, to revoke the "Irrevocable Edict of Nantes."

By this means it was intended, in one grand effort, to extirpate the very remembrance of the Protestant profession in France. Reconciliation with Rome was required, or banishment from the kingdom. Fifteen days were allowed to the preachers and professors, and many of them fled. About eight hundred thousand, chiefly artisans, escaped from the dragoons, who were commissioned to destroy those who would not conform. Many of the exiles, being weavers, were well received in England, where they contributed greatly to the wealth and prosperity of the nation, by their woollen factories in Yorkshire and the west, and by their silk works in Spitalfields, London.

Those who could not escape were treated with every species of brutality. "The troopers, soldiers and dragoons," says a French Protestant author, in 1686, "went into the Protestants' houses, where they marred and defaced their household stuff, broke their looking-glasses, and other utensils and ornaments. Those things which they could not destroy in this manner—such as furniture of beds, linens, wearing apparel, plate, &c.,—they carried to the market-place, and sold them to the Jesuits and other Roman Catholics. They turned the dining-rooms of gentlemen into stables for their horses; and treated the owners of the houses where they were quartered with the highest indignity and cruelty, lashing them about from one to another, day and night, without intermission, not suffering them to eat or drink. In several places the soldiers applied ret-hot irons to the hands and feet of men and

breasts of women. At Nantes they hung up
several women and maids by their feet, and others
by their arm-pits, and thus exposed them to public
view, stark naked. They bound to posts mothers
that gave suck, and let their sucking infants lie
languishing in their sight for several days and
nights, crying, mourning, and gasping for life.
Some they bound before a great fire, and, being
half-roasted, let them go—a punishment worse than
death. Amidst a thousand hideous cries and blasphemies, they hung up men and women by the
hair, and some by their feet, on hooks in chimneys,
and smoked them with wisps of wet hay till they
were suffocated. They tied some under the arms
with ropes, and plunged them again and again into
wells; they bound others like criminals, put them
to the tortures, and, with a funnel, filled them with
wine, till the fumes of it took away their reason,
when they made them say they consented to be
Catholics. They stripped them naked, and, after a
thousand indignities, stuck them with pins and
needles from head to foot. They cut and slashed
them with knives; and sometimes with red-hot
pincers took hold of them by the nose and other
parts of the body, and dragged them about the
rooms till they promised to be Catholics. They
beat them with staves, and thus bruised, and with
broken bones, dragged them to the church, where
their forced presence was taken for abjuration. In
some places they tied fathers and husbands to their
bed-posts, and, before their eyes, ravished their
wives and daughters with impunity. With these

scenes of desolation and horror the popish clergy feasted their eyes, and made them only a matter of laughter and sport. Though my heart aches, I beg the reader's patience to lay before him two other instances, which, if he hath a heart like mine, he will not be able to read without watering these sheets with tears. The *first* is of a young woman, who being brought before the council, upon refusing to abjure her religion, was ordered to prison. There they shaved her head, singed off the hair from other parts of her body; and having stripped her stark naked, led her through the streets of the city, where many a blow was given her, and stones flung at her; then they set her up to the neck in a tub of water for awhile; they took her out, and put on her a shift dipped in wine, which, as it dried and stuck to her sore and bruised body, they snatched off again, and then had another ready dipped in wine to clap on her. This they repeated six times, thereby making her body exceeding raw and sore. When all these cruelties could not shake her constancy, they fastened her by the feet in a kind of gibbet, and let her hang in that posture, with her head downward, till she expired!

"The other is of a man in whose house were quartered some of these missionary dragoons. One day, having drunk plentifully of his wine, and broken their glasses at every health, they filled the floor with fragments, and by often walking over them reduced them to very small pieces. This done, in the insolence of their mirth they resolved on a dance, and told their Protestant host that he must be one of their company; but as he would not be of their religion, he must dance quite bare-foot; and thus bare-foot they drove him about the room, treading on the sharp points of the broken glasses. When he was no longer able to stand, they laid him on a bed, and, in a short time, stripped him stark naked, and rolled him from one end of the room to the other, till every part of his body was full of the fragments of glass. After this they dragged him to his bed; and, having sent for a surgeon, obliged him to cut out the pieces of glass with his instruments, thereby putting him to the most exquisite and horrible pains that can be possibly conceived!

"These, fellow Protestants, were the methods used by the 'Most Christian King's' apostolic dragoons to convert his heretical subjects to the Roman Catholic faith! These, and many other of the like nature, were the torments to which Louis XIV. delivered them over to bring them to his own church; and as popery is unchangeably the same, these are the tortures prepared for you, if ever that religion should be permitted to become settled amongst you; the consideration of which made Luther say of it, what every man that knows anything of Christianity must agree with him in:—'If you have no other reason to go out of the Roman church, this alone would suffice, that you see and hear how, contrary to the law of God, THEY SHED INNOCENT BLOOD. This single circumstance shall, God willing, ever separate me from the papacy. And if I was now subject to it, and could blame nothing in any of their doctrines; yet, for this crime of cruelty, I would fly from her communion, as from a den of thieves and murderers!'"

CHAPTER IX.

THE INQUISITION IN ENGLAND.

Spiritual Courts—Henry VIII.—His zeal for Popery—Martyrdom of Anne Askew—Queen Mary marries Philip of Spain—The Inquisition and Martyrs—High Commission —Martyrs under Elizabeth—Archbp. Whitgift's cruelty— Udall—Archbishop Laud—Sufferings of Dr. Leighton— Abolition of Spiritual Courts under William III.

ENGLAND also received the horrid Romish Inquisition. For though the "Holy Office" was never constituted here, on precisely the same plan as it was established in the despotic countries of Spain, Portugal, and Rome, nor completely set up till the gloomy reign of Queen Mary, the victims of papal bigotry were numerous, as sacrificed on its cruel altars. Pontifical decrees and statutes were brought into England, and carried into effect by the prelates, acting under the authority of the popes. Spiritual courts were organised in many dioceses, where holy men of God were sought after and punished as heretics, by the bishops and archbishops, as inquisitors of heresy. Their antichristian spirit may be learned from the cruel proceedings of the ecclesiastics against the thirty Germans at Oxford, under Henry II., and against the Wycliffites, as noticed in Chapter V.

Volumes are required to record the sufferings of the "Lollards," and "Gospellers," in England, as they were called, who read the Scriptures, or the books of Wycliffe. Many of them became faithful martyrs of Christ; and though such severity was used, the cause of God continued and gained strength, especially after Luther arose as the great reformer, in 1517. The translation of the New Testament by William Tindal, in 1526, and his labours in completing the entire Bible, aided by John Frith, William Roye, John Rogers, and Miles Coverdale, greatly provoked the prelates, and all these, except Coverdale, fell sacrifices to papal enmity, as martyrs for Christ.

Popery found a worthy supporter in Henry VIII., who, "through the various stages of his reign, outstripped his predecessors in almost every act of arrogance and barbarity, making himself inquisitor-general and grand judge of heretics. When they were condemned to die, he descended to the office of sitting in judgment upon them." He even published a book against Luther, in "defence of the seven sacraments of the Catholic church;" for which he was rewarded by the Pope with the title of "Defender of the Faith," A.D. 1521.

Henry's vanity being gratified by this favour of the Pope, he entered more zealously into the designs of the Inquisition, and issued a royal proclamation, in which he commands that all persons *defamed* or *suspected* of *preaching* or *writing* contrary to the Catholic church should, by the bishops, be arrested and cast into prison. He then adds, "If any person, by the law of holy church, be convicted before the bishop or his commissary, that the said *bishop may keep in prison the said person so convicted, so long as it shall seem best to his discretion;* and may set a fine to be paid to the king, by the person convicted, *as it shall be thought convenient to the said bishop,* the said fine to be levied for the king's use. And if any person within the realm of England be convicted of the aforesaid errors and heresies, he shall be committed to the secular jurisdiction, and shall suffer execution according to the laws of this realm."

Sanctioned thus by the king, the bishops, who appear to have been the authors of this proclamation, proceeded, by vile inquisitors, to search for victims, whom they imprisoned and grievously fined. Their scandalous exactions enriched them, as their inquisitorial power rendered them superior to any law, or screened them from accountability. The temporal lords, and the commons' house of parliament, therefore, presented a petition to the king for relief, declaring the prelates had "*gotten into their hands more than a third part of all his majesty's realm!*" They add, in their appeal to the king against these dreaded inquisitors,—

"And what do all these greedy, idle, holy thieves do with these yearly exactions which they take of the people? Truly nothing, but exempt themselves from the obedience of your grace. Nothing but translate all rule, power, lordship, authority, obedience, and dignity, from your grace to themselves. Nothing but that all your subjects should fall into disobedience and rebellion against your grace, and be under them, as they did to your noble predecessor, King John; who, because he would have punished certain traitors that conspired with the French king, to have deposed him from his crown and dignity, interdicted his land. For which matter your most noble realm hath wrongfully, alas! stood tributary, not to any temporal prince, but to *a cruel, devilish bloodsucker, drunken ever since with the blood of the saints and martyrs of Christ!*

"What remedy is there? Will you make laws against them? It is doubtful whether you are able. Are they not stronger in your own parliament-house than yourself? What a number of bishops, abbots, and priors, are lords of your parliament! Are not all the learned men in your realm in fee with them, to speak in your parliament for them, against your crown, dignity, and realm; a few of your own learned council only excepted? What law can be made against them that will be available? Who is he, though he be sorely grieved, that, for murder, ravishment, robbery, debt, or any other offence, dare lay it to their charge by way of action? If any one do, he is by-and-by *accused of heresy; yea, they will so handle him, that except he bear a faggot for their pleasure, he must be excommunicated, and then all his actions will be quashed.*"

Henry became alarmed by this bold exposure of

I

the wicked deeds of the prelates, and he appointed
a hearing with all the judges and his temporal
council, which resulted in a bill, that soon passed
into a law, altering the statute of Henry IV.
against heretics. Though this did not remove their
liability to burning, it disabled the prelates from
being the sole judges in the cause of heresy.

Still the bishops, as inquisitors, continued their
proceedings, as they were able to secure the sanction
of the king. But we cannot here trace their
operations in destroying the faithful followers of
Christ; yet we must notice their laying a plan to
accomplish the destruction of Archbishop Cranmer,
and Katherine Parr, the queen of Henry VIII.,
who favoured the reformation. They proceeded
first against Anne Askew, a celebrated lady of the
court, in hope of inducing her, by torture on the
rack, to accuse the queen of heresy. She was
imprisoned and examined by Bonner, bishop of
London, and Gardiner, bishop of Winchester;
and, as she denied transubstantiation, they condemned her to the flames as a heretic.

Dr. Southey relates her martyrdom as follows,
referring to her examination on the rack by the
inquisitors:—"Henry's heart was naturally hard,
and the age and circumstances in which he was
placed had steeled it against all compassion. Some
displeasure, indeed, he manifested shortly afterwards, when the lieutenant of the Tower, Sir
Anthony Knevet, came to solicit pardon for having
disobeyed the chancellor, by refusing to let the
gaoler stretch the lady on the rack a second time,

after she had endured it once without accusing any person of partaking her opinions. It was concerning the ladies of the court that she was put to the torture, in the hope of implicating the queen; and when Knevet would do no more, the Chancellor Wriothesley, and Rich, who was a creature of Bonner, racked her with their own hands, throwing off their gowns that they might perform their devilish office the better. She bore it without uttering cry or groan, though, immediately upon being loosed, she fainted. Henry readily forgave the lieutenant, and appeared ill pleased with his chancellor; but he suffered his wicked ministers to consummate their crime. A scaffold was erected in front of St. Bartholomew's church, where Wriothesley, the duke of Norfolk, and others of the king's council, sat with the lord mayor, to witness the execution. Three others were to suffer for the same imaginary offence; one was a tailor, another a priest, and the third a Nottinghamshire gentleman, of the Lascelles family, and of the king's household. The execution was delayed till darkness closed, that it might appear more dreadful. Anne Askew was brought in a chair, for they had racked her until she was unable to stand, and she was held up against the stake by the chain which fastened her; but her constancy, and cheerful language of encouragement, brought her companions in martyrdom to the same invincible fortitude and triumphant hope. After a sermon had been preached, the king's pardon was offered to her, if she would recant: refusing even to look

upon it, she made answer, that she came not there
to deny her Lord! The others, in like manner,
refused to purchase their lives at such a price.
The reeds were then set on fire—it was in the
month of June—and, at that moment, a few drops
of rain fell, and a thunder-clap was heard, which
those in the crowd, who sympathised with the
martyrs, felt as if it were God's own voice, accept-
ing their sacrifice, and receiving their spirits into
everlasting rest." June, 1546.

Henry VIII. dying January 28, 1547, was succeeded by his son, Edward VI., who laboured to
forward the reformation. Those who formed the
regency, his protectors, were Protestants, and the
persecuting laws were soon repealed, with other
measures for the advancement of the religion of
the Scriptures. But this pious young king died,
July 6, 1553, and was succeeded on the throne by
his sister Mary. She was a consistent Papist,
directed entirely by the Romish prelates. They
revived all the powers of the Inquisition, and soon
imprisoned Cranmer, archbishop of Canterbury,
and the other leaders in the reformation, accusing
them of heresy.

Queen Mary accepted the proposal to marry
Philip, son of the Emperor Charles V., though ten
years her junior, and a widower. As a bigot Papist,
"all who had espoused the cause of the reformation
in England," as Bishop Bonner states, "anticipated
not only a change of religion, but the erection of a
Spanish government and Inquisition. Those who
valued the *civil* liberty of their country, without

any concern for religion, concluded that England would become a province of Spain; and they beheld how the Spaniards ruled in the Netherlands, in Milan, Naples, and Sicily; but, above all, they heard of their unexampled inhumanities in the West Indies."

Philip was a man of great talents; but, as it is said of him, " his religion was of the most corrupt kind; it served only to increase the natural depravity of his disposition, and prompted him to commit the most odious and shocking crimes. Of the triumph of honour and humanity over the dictates of superstition, there occurs not a single instance in the whole reign of Philip; who violated the most sacred obligations as often as religion afforded him a pretence, and exercised, for many years, the most unrelenting cruelty, without reluctance or remorse. Few princes have been more dreaded, more abhorred, or have caused more blood to flow, than Philip II. of Spain."

Mary, on the 23rd of October, before the altar in her private chapel, solemnly plighted her troth to Philip; and Bishop Gardiner was despatched to arrange the marriage settlement with the Emperor Charles V., who borrowed *one million two hundred thousand* crowns,—a prodigious sum at that time,—to enable that prelate to secure an obsequious parliament.

Philip landed at Southampton, July 20, 1554, and, on the 25th, he was married to Mary, by Gardiner, in his cathedral at Winchester. On the 29th of November, the formal reconciliation to

Rome was solemnised, with great pomp, in the hall of the palace at Whitehall. The Queen and the King sat in regal state, with the Pope's legate, Cardinal Pole, a prince of the blood. A large number of both houses of the new parliament being introduced, they presented, on their knees, a humble supplication on behalf of the whole nation, beseeching their majesties to intercede with the lord cardinal for their admission within the sacred pale of the church, and for absolution from their offences of heresy, and schism, on condition of repealing all laws against the Catholic religion, passed in the season of their delusion. Mary and Philip having made the intercession, the legate, after a long speech, declaring the paternal solicitude of his holiness for the welfare of England, in the name of the Pope granted a full absolution, which the members of parliament received on their knees; after which, the king, queen, and legate, together with the whole body of the senators of the nation, chanted *Te Deum* in the chapel of the palace, expressive of their joy! The Pope solemnly ratified the act of his legate, and the news of the whole transaction was quickly published throughout Europe!

Preparatory for this absolution, an act was passed for the *revival* of the statutes of Richard II., Henry II., and Henry V., against heretics. They were to come into force on the 20th of January, 1555; so that the year opened with a portentous gloom. Cardinal Pole, on the 23rd of January, received all the bishops at Lambeth Palace, to give them his blessing, and directions how to govern the church ; and on the 25th, there was a solemn procession through London, consisting of *eight* bishops, and *one hundred and sixty* priests, all in their robes; with Bonner, the bishop, carrying the host, to return thanks to God for their reconciliation. After this solemnity, the first measure of the restored church was for the prelates, as inquisitors, to proceed against the reformers, many of whom were imprisoned, under the direction of Bishop Bonner and Bishop Gardiner, who was lord chancellor.

Bishop Burnet remarks, on this cruel policy of the prelates, " Pope Paul was in the right in one thing, to press the setting up of courts of inquisition everywhere, as the only sure method to extirpate heresy. And it is highly probable that the king, or his Spanish ministers, made the court of England apprehend, that torture and inquisition were the only sure courses to root out heresy."

John Rogers, a prebendary of St. Paul's, London, and a famous preacher, who had aided Tindal in the translation of the Bible, was the first victim. He was burnt to ashes in Smithfield, February 4, 1555, triumphing in Christ.

Laurence Saunders was burnt to death on the 8th of February, where he had been minister, and highly esteemed, at Coventry.

Dr. Hooper, bishop of Gloucester, was carried to suffer at the stake in that city, on the 9th of February.

Dr. Taylor was sent to suffer in like manner, in

his own parish, at Hadleigh, in Suffolk, on the 9th of February.

Dr. Farrar, bishop of St. David's, was carried to seal the truth of the Gospel with his blood, and he triumphed in martyrdom, March 30th, at Carmarthen.

Terrible as were these enormities, they did not satisfy the sanguinary queen nor her bigoted chancellor, Bishop Gardiner. They determined to extirpate heresy, and therefore employed local inquisitors. Bishop Burnet states, therefore, "Instructions were given, in March, 1555, to the justices of peace, to have one or more honest men in every parish, secretly instructed on oath to give information of the behaviour of the inhabitants among them. Here was a great step made towards an Inquisition; this being the settled method of that court, to have sworn spies and informers every where, upon whose secret advertisements persons are taken up; and the first step in their examination is to know of them, for what reason they are brought before them; upon which they are tortured till they tell, as much as the inquisitors desire to know, either against themselves or others. But they are not suffered to know, neither what is informed against them, nor who are the informers. Arbitrary torture, and now secret informers, seem to be two great steps made to prepare the nation for an Inquisition."

John Bradford, a prebendary of St. Paul's, London, a powerful and popular preacher, was burnt in Smithfield, July 15th; Bishops Latimer and Ridley were sacrificed in the flames at Oxford, on the 16th of October; and Archbishop Cranmer was executed at the stake, in the same place, March 24, 1556.

Particulars of the sufferings and triumphs of these and the other martyrs for Christ, during the short reign of Mary, cannot here be detailed. *Four, five, six, seven,* and on one occasion, *thirteen* persons, were seen murdered in one fire! Neither sex nor age, the lame nor blind, being spared, if they refused conformity to the imposition of the Romish prelates. Barbarities so shocking terrified the whole nation. Petitions to the Queen against them were transmitted from the Protestant exiles abroad; so that even King Philip was so ashamed, that he caused a Spanish divine, of high celebrity, to preach against the cruelties, though the same things were transacted under his direct sanction, in his own dominions in the Netherlands and Spain.

Mary had no child, and Philip spent most of his time in the Netherlands, being apparently alienated from his queen. She became dejected, through a sense of his unkindness, and chagrined at the loss of Calais, so that her health declined; while she was the victim of superstition, and a prey to remorse for her dreadful cruelties, and she finished her wretched life, November 7, 1558.

Of the martyrs for Christ in the reign of Mary, victims of the Inquisition, there were reckoned, *one* archbishop, *four* bishops, *twenty-one* clergymen, *eight* gentlemen, *eighty-four* tradesmen, *a hundred* husbandmen, labourers and servants, *fifty-five*

women, and *four* children! Cooper estimates the
number of those who suffered for the Gospel, from
February, 1555, to September, 1558, at about 290!
According to Bishop Burnet, there were 284. The
most accurate account is, probably, that of Lord
Burleigh, who, in his treatise called "The Execution of Justice in England," reckons the number of
those who died in the reign of Mary by imprisonment, torments, famine, and fire, to be nearly 400;
of whom those who were burnt alive amounted to
290!

Queen Elizabeth succeeded to the throne on the
death of her sister Mary. She was a Protestant
in profession, and she restored the reformation in
England; but her prelates were persecutors, and
they were allowed to retain the spirit and power of
the Inquisition, but under another name, "The
Court of High Commission."

This Court of High Commission was created in
the name of the queen, for the express purpose of
searching out and punishing the nonconformists.
These commissioners were principally bishops, and
they assumed the power of administering an *oath*.
ex officio, by which the prisoner was obliged to
answer all questions put to him, and even to accuse
himself or his dearest friend. Many refused to
take the oath, choosing rather to suffer imprisonment, which was determined, not according to any
law, but the will of the commissioners. A detail of
the miseries endured by conscientious clergymen,
under the High Commission Court, would require volumes; their *principles*, and many of their

practices, being precisely those of the *execrable* ROMISH INQUISITION.

Archbishop Parker continued a cruel persecutor of the nonconformists: and others of the prelates employed the most dishonourable methods to hunt out and imprison them, hiring unprincipled characters as inquisitors and informers, and making new articles, contrary to the laws of England, for the more certain conviction of those brought before the ecclesiastical courts.

Persecution and cruelty, in character only in accordance with the popish Inquisition, continued even in London. The year 1575 is distinguished by a transaction, which reflects imperishable dishonour on the prelates and the queen. A congregation of Dutch Baptists being discovered on Easter-day, near Aldgate, their house was entered by the bishop's officers, and *twenty-seven* of the worshippers were seized and committed to prison. *Four* recanted; and, according to the popish custom, *they were required to bear faggots during sermon at Paul's Cross, as a token of their deserving the flames! Ten of the men and one woman were condemned to the stake by the ecclesiastical consistory:* but the *woman* was induced to recant; while *eight* of those who could not be convinced of error were banished, and *two* were sacrificed in the flames as *heretics.*

On this occasion, the Dutch residents in London, who were allowed to hold their meetings for religious worship, interceded with the queen for their mistaken countrymen; but she gave them a

positive refusal to their request. John Fox, who
was in favour with her majesty, on account of his
"Acts and Monuments of the Church," made an
application to her on their behalf, in an elegant
Latin letter; but though his arguments appear sufficient to convince the most perverted judgment,
and his appeals to her compassion, as a woman,
calculated to melt the hardest heart, they availed
nothing with the virgin queen! A clergyman of
our time asks, "What are we to think of those
evangelical prelates, who sat in the High Commission Court, and at the council-table, a part of whose
office it was to advise the queen? Alas! that
none could be found, who, on such an emergency,
would give her correct information respecting the
will of Christ, and assure her, ' He, the Son of Man,
was not come to destroy men's lives, but to save
them!' A death-like silence reigned, and the law
took its course."

Queen Elizabeth's intolerance, in the spirit of
an inquisitor-general, extended even to Dr. Grindal,
archbishop of Canterbury. Having enjoyed that
high dignity two years, he was suspended by the
queen, for refusing to suppress the "prophesyings,"
which were meetings of the evangelical clergy to
promote scriptural knowledge by preaching. He
appeals to the queen, "Alas! madam, is the Scripture more plain in anything, than that the Gospel
of Christ should be plentifully preached? If the
Holy Ghost prescribeth, especially, that preachers
should be placed in every town, how can it well be
that three or four preachers may suffice for a shire?

[This was the declared opinion of the queen.] Public and continual preaching of God's Word is the ordinary means of salvation to mankind.

"Concerning the learned exercises and conferences amongst the ministers of the church—the time appointed for this exercise is once a month; the time of this exercise is two hours—some text of Scripture, before appointed to be spoken, is interpreted in this order—prayer, and a psalm follow. I am enforced with all humility, and yet plainly, to profess that I cannot, with safe conscience, and without the offence of the majesty of God, give mine assent to the suppressing of the said exercises; much less can I send out any instruction for the utter and universal subversion of the same. If it be your majesty's pleasure for this, or any other cause, to remove me out of this place, I will, with all humility, yield thereunto. Remember, that in God's cause, the will of God, and not the will of any earthly creature, is to take place; it is the antichristian voice of the Pope, ' *Thus I will—thus I order—my will is reason sufficient!* ' "

Grindal's mode of arguing was precisely that of the Protestants against the Papists, and of the apostles against the rulers of the Jews. But this appeal to the Scriptures availed nothing with the royal inquisitor; the prelate continued in disgrace with his sovereign, though he was permitted till his death, in 1583, to retain his dignity as archbishop of Canterbury.

Dr. Whitgift succeeded as archbishop of Canter

bury, and he was a severe inquisitor and persecutor.
He published *three* articles for every clergyman to
subscribe, declaring from his heart, his approbation
of the whole Common Prayer; besides which, he
drew up *twenty-four* articles to be used in examining those who were brought before the bishops.
Through these impositions, great numbers of pious
clergymen were deprived; among whom were *sixty-
four* in Norfolk, *sixty* in Suffolk, and *thirty-eight*
in Essex; besides those in other counties.

These inquisitorial proceedings induced Lord
Burleigh, the earls of Leicester, Shrewsbury, and
Warwick, Lord Charles Howard, Sir James Crofts,
Sir Christopher Hatton, and Sir Francis Walsing-
ham, secretary of state, to sign a letter, September
20, 1584, to the archbishop, and the bishop of London, complaining of such intolerant inquisition.
But Whitgift disregarded their appeal, sustained in
his pernicious course by the queen.

Among the numerous cases of oppression by the
prelates, that of Giles Wigginton, the vicar of
Sedburgh, Yorkshire, will serve as an example.
After having suffered many hardships in prison for
his nonconformity, his health being impaired, he
was deprived of his living. But, with liberty, his
improved health enabled him to visit his beloved
flock, to whom he preached, from house to house,
the Gospel of Christ. For this he was again imprisoned in Lancaster Castle; from which he wrote
to his patron, Sir Walter Mildmay, one of the
privy council, to procure his release. He says,
"I was arrested at Burroughbridge by a *pursuivant*,

and brought to this place, a distance of *fifty* miles, in this cold winter. I am here within an iron gate, in a cold room, among felons and condemned prisoners, and, in various ways, worse used than they, or recusant Papists."

Several efforts were made in parliament to impose a check on these oppressions, which were yet illegal; but the bishops prevailed, especially in the House of Lords.

John Udall, in 1591, was tried for publishing a book—" A Demonstration of the Discipline which Christ hath prescribed in his Word"—and condemned. The judge offered him his life, if he would recant; adding, that he was now ready to pronounce sentence of death. " And I am ready to receive it," cried the magnanimous confessor; "for, I protest before God, not knowing that I shall live another hour, that the cause is good, and I am contented to receive sentence, so that I may leave it to posterity how I have suffered for His cause."

Udall was condemned, as he would not sign a recantation of his doctrine; nor could any of the doctors move him in conference from appealing in its proof to the Scriptures. His fame was great; so that several lords of the council, and even James VI., afterwards king of England, interceded for his life. Archbishop Whitgift became afraid of his being put to death in public, and the Turkey merchants offered to employ him as one of their chaplains, and at length Whitgift consented to pardon him on his leaving the country; but while

the hard terms were being arranged with the archbishop, Udall died in prison, from his long confinement and ill treatment. Dr. Fuller remarks of
him, that "his wisest foes were well contented with
his death, lest it should be ‚charged as an act of
cruelty on them who procured it." He calls him
"a person of worth, a learned man, blameless for
his life, powerful in his praying, and no less pro-
fitable than painful in his preaching."

Fifty-nine, in different prisons of London, in
1592, petitioned Lord Treasurer Burleigh to be
brought to trial; complaining that "many had
died in the prisons, that they had been imprisoned
contrary to all law and equity, many of them for
the space of *two years and a half*, upon the bishop's
sole commandment." Among these was Henry
Barrowe, a barrister of Gray's Inn, who was apprehended when visiting his relative, Greenwood,
a nonconforming clergyman, who had been in
prison a long time. They were tried on a charge
of "writing and publishing sundry books, tending
to the slander of the queen and government."
Mr. Neal remarks, "They had written only against
the church; but this was the archbishop's artful
contrivance, to throw off the odium of their death
from himself to the civil magistrate. Being condemned, endeavours were made, but in vain, to
induce them to recant. They were exposed under
the famous gallows, at Tyburn, March the 31st;
but this produced no effect on their pious minds,
and they were executed, April 6, 1592. John
Penry, a clergyman, and several others, were

hanged for dispersing the writings of the nonconformists.

Dr. Reynolds, the queen's professor of divinity
at Oxford, attended some of these martyrs for the
Scriptures; and he reported to her Majesty the
calm piety which they displayed, and how they had
blessed and prayed for her, as their sovereign, and
for their enemies; and Elizabeth's heart melted;
but she was urged forward by the chief-inquisitor,
Whitgift, and she consented to sanction him in his
bigotry, by a severer law against the nonconformists. To this was added a form of recantation;
which, if the offenders refused to subscribe, it was
further enacted, "that within three months they
shall *abjure the realm, and go into perpetual banishment;* and if they do not depart within the time
appointed, or if they ever return without the
queen's licence, *they shall suffer death without
benefit of clergy !!*"

Severities towards the nonconformists increased
as the queen and the archbishop advanced in years.
Dr. Aylmer, the persecuting and profane bishop of
London, died in June, 1594. Dr. Fletcher succeeded him, and was banished by the queen. In
1596, Dr. Bancroft, a haughty, unfeeling persecutor, was made bishop of London. Elizabeth died,
March 24, 1602, and Archbishop Whitgift, in
1604, when they were called to render up their
awful account to God.

Queen Elizabeth was a great monarch, and she
was favoured with statesmen of extraordinary
abilities; but, as Dr. Warner remarks, " the severity

K

with which she treated her Protestant subjects by
her High Commission Court, was against law,
against liberty, and against the rights of human
nature. She understood nothing of the rights of
conscience in matters of religion; and, like the
absurd king, her father, she would have no opinion
in religion, acknowledged at least, but her own.
She differed from her sister; and as she had much
greater abilities for governing, so she applied herself more to promote the strength and glory of her
dominion, than Mary did; but she had as much of
the bigot and tyrant in her as her sister."

Dr. Bancroft was translated from London to
Canterbury, on the death of Whitgift, in 1604;
and his severities were sanctioned by the new
sovereign, James I., who became a cruel bigot.
Under their government the nonconformists suffered grievously. The inquisitors prosecuted their
shocking employment, and two men were executed
at the stake on the charge of heresy. One of these,
Bartholomew Legate, of Essex, was condemned
as a heretic, and publicly burnt in Smithfield,
March 18, 1612; the other was Edward Wightman,
of Burton-upon-Trent; he was condemned by Dr.
Neile, bishop of Lichfield and Coventry, and burnt
as a heretic in Lichfield, April 11, 1612. They
were said to be Arians and Baptists, and charged
with many absurd opinions; but it is admitted that
they were exemplary in their morals. They refused
to recant, even at the stake; and popular sympathy
being called forth in favour of these victims of the
prelates, they were the last that publicly suffered

death for their religious opinions in England. There were others in prison under sentence, but they were continued to linger out a miserable existence in Newgate.

Dr. Abbot succeeded Bancroft, in 1611, as archbishop of Canterbury; but, being unfitted for political intrigue, he was suspended in 1620, and Laud, bishop of London, exercised almost unlimited authority in ecclesiastical affairs. His bigotry would have qualified him for inquisitor-general in Rome or Spain, and his evil counsels involved both England and Scotland in most grievous troubles, until his intolerance became the chief cause of his own execution, and that of his misguided master, Charles I., to the astonishment of all Europe.

Dr. Williams, bishop of Lincoln, to whom Laud was under the greatest obligations as his patron, disapproving of his severities by the High Commission Court, incurred his displeasure, when "the warmest professions of friendship were succeeded by the most deadly hatred." Laud became his persecutor, and succeeded, in the second attempt, in obtaining his conviction, on a charge of tampering with the king's witnesses. Williams was fined £10,000 to the king, £1,000 to Sir J. Mounson, and imprisonment in the Tower during the king's pleasure. All his property being seized, his private papers were presumed to contain some reflections on Laud, and he again persecuted him. He was sentenced to pay £5,000 to the king, and £3,000 to the archbishop. "Laud's thirst of revenge out-

weighed his fear of reproach," as remarked by
Dr. Vaughan.

Laud's spirit may be learned more fully from his
persecution of Dr. Leighton, who had written "An
Appeal to Parliament; or, Zion's Plea against
Prelacy." For this he was condemned in the "Star
Chamber," which was a political Inquisition; and
the archbishop being present, as one of the judges,
while the sentence was being pronounced, removed
his cap from his head, and, with an audible voice,
rendered solemn thanks to God for this decision of
the court. The illegal sentence was executed upon
Dr. Leighton; and the archbishop was found to
have made a record in his diary, thus:—"Nov. 6th.
1. He was whipped before he was put in the
pillory. 2. Being set in the pillory, he had one
of his ears cut off. 3. One side of his nose slit.
4. Branded on the cheek with a red-hot iron, with
the letters S.S. On that day seven-night, his sores
upon his back, ear, nose, and face, being not yet
cured, he was whipped again at the pillory in
Cheapside, and had the remainder of his sentence
executed upon him, by cutting off the other ear,
slitting the other side of the nose, and branding
the other cheek!"

Probably, the diary of no other man, in any age
or nation, ever contained such a record in his
private diary, with his approbation. He must have
been a monster; and no language can sufficiently
reprobate such cruelties, illegally exercised, and
that in the abused name of the Prince of Peace!

Leighton bore his sufferings with the meekness

and courage of an apostle. "But the fortitude of the sufferer marred the policy of his oppressors. It brought upon *them* the execrations of the people, and vested *him* with the honours of martyrdom."

Prelatical tyranny at length wearied out the nation, and the people arose, demanding redress of their grievances. "The Long Parliament" was called in 1640, and they decreed the abolition of the civil and ecclesiastical Inquisitions,—the High Commission Court and the Star Chamber. Dr. Leighton, on petitioning Parliament, was set at liberty: as the reading of his petition, describing a series of his sufferings, during *eleven* years, unparalleled, perhaps, in English history, affected many of the senators to tears; and, when released from prison, the venerable man could hardly walk, or see, or hear! Parliament allowed this injured servant of God a pension till his death, in 1644, aged seventy-six. All who were imprisoned by those courts on account of religion were liberated. Dr. Burton, Dr. Bastwick, and Mr. Prynne, a barrister, were met by an immense multitude, and conducted in triumph to London.

Persecution ceased; religious liberty prevailed, in a great degree, under the Long Parliament, and during the Commonwealth. But, after the restoration of Charles II., the principles of the Inquisition, for some years, enabled the prelates to harass the nonconformists, by the "Act of Uniformity," the "Conventicle Act," and the "Five Mile Act." Tyranny triumphed, by these and other shocking statutes, until they were abolished by the "Act

of Toleration," as a shield against priestly oppression, by the "GLORIOUS REVOLUTION" under
William III.

CHAPTER X.

CRIMES ALLEGED BY THE INQUISITION.

Heretics — Open and secret — Schismatics — Favourers of
    Heretics—Hinderers of the Inquisition—Suspected per-
    sons relapsed — Readers of forbidden books — Priests
    soliciting confessors—Blasphemers—Diviners—Witches—
    Polygamists—Jews.

ROMAN Catholics denominate the tribunal of the
Inquisition *Sanctum Officium*, or *Holy Office;* pretending that it is engaged in the sacred service of God,
for the seeking out and extirpation of evil persons
from the church of Christ. The inquisitors, therefore, proceed against alleged heretics, blasphemers,
apostates, relapsed Jews, Mohammedans, witches,
wizards, and all others charged with having violated
the canons of the holy Roman Catholic church.
These classes of alleged offenders require to be
mentioned, as illustrating the intolerant and sanguinary character of the Romish Inquisition.

1. HERETICS.—These, in general, are persons
who, having been baptised, or professed the Romish
faith, hold doctrines condemned by the Pope;—as
the denial of the sacrifice of the mass, priestly
absolution, the worship of the Virgin Mary, tran-

substantiation, or purgatory. Some are reckoned *manifest*, and others, *concealed* heretics. All who hold the doctrines of Luther, or of the other reformers, and all Protestants rejecting the pretended ecclesiastical traditions, and taking the Holy Scriptures as the only rule of faith and duty, are thus declared *heretics* by the Papists. Such are punished variously, some being burnt alive.

2. OPEN AND SECRET HERETICS.—These are described thus, by the Romanists:—"An *open* heretic is one who publicly avows something contrary to the Catholic faith, or who is condemned for it by the judges of the faith. A *secret* or concealed heretic is one who errs in his mind concerning the faith, and purposes to be obstinate in his will, but hath not shown it by word or deed. Although an heretic be thus concealed, yet, if he infects others, he is immediately to be discovered by his judges." These are also called *affirmative* and *negative* heretics. The latter are those, who, according to the law of the Inquisition, are rightly and justly convicted of some heresy before a judge, but yet profess the Catholic faith. Such were many of those converted from amongst the Jews and Moors in Spain. Obstinate heretics are to be doomed to be burnt alive, delivered over to the fire with their mouths gagged, and their tongues tied, lest, by their speaking, they should induce others to embrace their principles. Some are denominated *arch-heretics*, as the inventors or chief teachers of doctrines contrary to those established by the Pope. Among the most distinguished of these,

the Papists reckon Peter Waldo, John Wycliffe, Luther, Calvin, Zuingle, Cranmer, Knox, and others, the leaders of the Protestant reformation. Multitudes of these have been burnt alive, especially in France, Spain, and England.

3. SCHISMATICS.—These are described by the Papists as those who depart from the unity of the church, and believe that there may be salvation and true sacraments without the Catholic church, and differ little from heretics; but others are without blame, and err through probable or insuperable ignorance. The punishments of schismatics are privation of ecclesiastical power, if priests, excommunication, and, finally, death.

4. RECEIVERS OR FAVOURERS OF HERETICS.—These are such as, knowing them to be heretics, defend them when persecuted by the church, afford them lodging or shelter, or allow them to read or preach in their houses. Others are favourers of heretics, who omit to discover them to the bishops and inquisitors. Their punishment is excommunication, and banishment for ever, with confiscation of goods.

5. HINDERERS OF THE OFFICE OF THE INQUISITION.—In various ways the Inquisition may be hindered, directly or indirectly; and those who do not aid the inquisitors are held guilty as hinderers. Thus, in a bull of Pope Alexander IV., he requires of the prelates, " Since, therefore, there are certain predicant friars appointed by the apostolic see, inquisitors against heretics, that they may carry on the business of the faith with a fervent mind and

constant heart, through many tribulations and persecutions, we admonish and exhort all of you in our Lord Jesus Christ, strictly commanding you by these apostolical writings, in virtue of your obedience, and enjoining you, that you favourably assist these inquisitors in carrying on this affair; and that, laying aside the fear of man, you effectually give them your counsel and help. But, as for those whom we shall know to be contemners, besides the Divine judgment that hangs over them, they shall not escape the ecclesiastical vengeance."

6. SUSPECTED HERETICS.—Suspicion may be *light, vehement,* or *violent,* as the Papists declare, and great numbers are accused and imprisoned by the Inquisition only on the suspicion of holding opinions contrary to the Romish church. Those who are lightly suspected are enjoined ceremonial purgation; those vehemently suspected are required solemnly to abjure every heresy; and he who is violently suspected is commonly condemned.

7. PERSONS DEFAMED FOR HERESY.—Common report, especially if certified before a bishop, renders a person suspected, and liable to a process by the Inquisition; and the punishment is canonical purgation, with some other penalty.

8. RELAPSED PERSONS.—Persons relapsed are those who, after having publicly abjured heresy, are convicted of falling into it again. The punishment of such persons is extreme; they are given over to the secular power to be burnt without mercy.

9. READERS OF PROHIBITED BOOKS.—Nothing can exceed the intolerance of the Papists in relation

to the writings of the reformers; and the books of the Waldenses, of Wycliffe, of Luther, and of the other reformers, were sought for with the utmost zeal. Multitudes suffered death, therefore, for reading their writings, especially their translations and commentaries on the Holy Scriptures.

10. THOSE NOT PRIESTS ADMINISTERING THE LORD'S SUPPER.—Such persons are declared to approach idolatry, because they teach the faithful to adore the bread and wine, as though it were the body and blood of Jesus Christ. In like manner, he who is not a priest, and yet hears confessions and gives absolution, is said to abuse the sacrament. Such persons are to abjure, as vehemently suspected, and then be delivered over to the secular power to be punished with death.

11. PRIESTS SOLICITING IN CONFESSION.—Incontinent priests, in the sacramental confession, are known, as a common practice, to solicit and provoke women to commit dishonourable actions. Cases of this kind are very common; but it is dangerous to accuse a confessor of such a crime, as the proof is so very difficult, while he possesses the means of immediate revenge by the Inquisition. But the crime itself is seldom punished, even where many nuns, and even abbesses, have had children by their father confessors.

12. BLASPHEMERS.—Blasphemers are of various kinds—some saying, "I deny God; I do not believe in God;" or, "I deny the faith on the cross, or chrism, which I received in my forehead; or I deny the virginity of our Lady." Heretical blasphemers

are punished by their tongues being tied and pinched with an iron or wooden gag; and being exposed in public, wearing each an infamous mitre, they were whipped and banished; but if the offender were a person of rank, his punishment is lighter, though he was required to abjure heresy.

13. DIVINERS AND FORTUNE-TELLERS.—Those guilty of divination are supposed to use or to imitate the sacraments, or things sacramental, in the practice of their mysteries; they are, therefore, punished with suspension of dignities, whipping; excommunication, or banishment. And those who practise astrology are punished in the same manner, as offenders against the church.

14. WITCHES AND WIZARDS.—These were regarded as a sect supposed to hold intercourse with the devil, especially on the eve of Friday, when he was said to appear in a human shape. They are said to deny their holy faith and baptism, the Lord God, and the blessed Virgin Mary. For these imaginary crimes, it is computed that 30,000 persons were burnt to death, in about a century and a half, by the cruelty of the Inquisition, chiefly in Spain and Sicily.

15. POLYGAMISTS.—Those who marry two or more wives are suspected of heresy, and of disregarding the sacrament of matrimony. Such are punished with penances, fastings, and slavery in the galleys, for five, seven, or ten years. This crime is but lightly considered in Spain, though it is looked upon as more serious by the inquisitors in Rome.

16. JEWS AND JEWISH PROSELYTES.—Divine prophecy declares that the Jews shall continue a

distinct people, scattered among the Gentiles, until
the conversion of Israel to the Messiah, while they
yet shall endure persecution. The Roman Catholics,
ignorant of the nature of the Gospel, have endeavoured wholly to destroy this people, or to compel
them to profess the Christian faith. Edicts, the
most severe and cruel, have been published against
them, from time to time, by different Popes, in
France and Spain. They have been oppressed,
fined, and banished, unless they would turn Christians. Thousands of them, in Spain and Portugal,
professed the name of Christ to escape punishment,
yet, in heart, remaining Jews, abhorring the idolatry
of the Papists. The inquisitors proceeded against
them, therefore, as heretics and apostates. They
are condemned by the inquisitors to endure various
punishments, according to the nature or degree of
the alleged crimes—as, privation of all intercourse
with Jews, penalties, public whipping, and burning
at the stake.

CHAPTER XI.

MINISTERS OF THE INQUISITION.

Inquisi tion in Spain—Inquisitors—Vicars—Counsellors—Pro-
moters-Fiscal—Notaries—Treasurer—Executor—Familiars—Cross-Bearers—Visitors—Privileges—Jurisdiction
—Prohibition of books—Prison-keepers.

SPAIN, Portugal, and Rome have been most notorious for cruelty, by means of the dreaded court of

inquisition. The "Holy Office," in those countries, has been the most extended, and the most complete in its arrangements; its ministers, therefore, have been most numerous. The number of officers in the Spanish Inquisition has been reckoned at about *three thousand*, and its expense to the country about *one million of pounds* sterling per annum!

District courts were formed in many places, of which it is said, "In every province of Spain there ought to be two or three inquisitors, one judge of the forfeited effects, one executor, three notaries, one keeper of the prison, one messenger, one door-keeper, and one physician. Besides these, assessors, skilful counsellors, familiars and others," were appointed for the service of this court. These require some notice, the better to understand the character of the Inquisition.

1. INQUISITORS APOSTOLIC.—These are the chief officers, delegates from the Pope, for the special service of judging heretics. Their rank is exalted in the papacy, as each has the title of "lord," and every inquisitor is styled "most reverend." One among those in Spain was president of the Inquisition, and was called "inquisitor-major," or "inquisitor-general." The Romish cardinals, also, were inquisitors-general.

2. VICARS.—These are appointed by the inquisitors, to serve as their substitutes in case of absence or sickness, and these exercise all the power of their principals, in receiving accusations, and arresting those who may be accused.

3. COUNSELLORS.—These were skilful lawyers,

appointed to advise and assist the inquisitors, who were generally ignorant of legal forms. They were sworn to secrecy.

4. PROMOTER-FISCAL. — This officer also is a lawyer, whose business is to examine the depositions of witnesses, to give information against criminals, to demand their imprisonment, and to frame their indictment against them. He was a kind of counsellor for the Holy Office.

5. NOTARIES.—These officers were short-hand writers, whose duty was to attend the examinations of the prisoners, to note down everything they said, their behaviour, and even change of countenance, while questioned by the inquisitors. They are required to be skilful in different languages; as the prisoners may be French, German, or Italian, before a Spanish Inquisition.

6. TREASURER.—This officer is called, in Spain, the *receiver-general* of the effects and property of the prisoners: in Rome he is called, *treasurer of the Holy Office.* He takes charge of all the effects of the prisoners, letting or selling their lands and houses; so that immense property falls into his hands.

7. EXECUTOR.—This officer is the head of the police attached to the Inquisition; and he directs the mode of the apprehension of accused persons.

8. OFFICIALS.—These are assistants to the executor, or police officers, who pursue and apprehend the persons accused before the inquisitors.

9. FAMILIARS.—These are armed police officers, or soldiers of the Inquisition. They are called *familiars,* or belonging to the inquisitor's family.

10. CROSS-BEARERS.—These also are soldiers, a kind of militia, trained and armed for the defence of the Inquisition, and for the vigorous pursuit of offenders. They are favoured with many privileges, including a "plenary remission of all their sins," to encourage them in the service of the Inquisition. Soldiers having, however, become less needful, these officers have generally been transformed into an order of monks of St. Dominic, with constitutions confirmed by the Pope.

11. VISITORS.—These were magistrates appointed to inspect all the provinces of the inquisitors, and to report the state of the institutions to the inquisitor-general. They are commonly commissioned as occasions seem to require investigation.

12. PRIVILEGES OF INQUISITORS. — Extraordinary are the privileges granted to inquisitors; so that "no delegate of the apostolic see, or sub-delegate under him, no conservator, or executor, deputed by the Pope, shall be able to publish the sentence of excommunication, suspension, or interdict against them, or their notaries, whilst they are engaged in the prosecution of their duty, without the special command of the holy see." The inquisitors only, and not the bishops, can publish edicts against heretics. In like manner, the inquisitors, and no others, can absolve from excommunication for heresy; and persons under the interdict by the inquisitor, cannot be absolved by the ordinary, or any other person, without the command of the Pope, except in the article of death.

13. JURISDICTION OF THE INQUISITION.—This is

so ample, that few persons are excepted from it ; because the inquisitors being judges delegated by the Pope in the cause of the faith, that all heresy may be extirpated, power is given to them against all sorts of persons, except bishops and legates of the Pope.   They may proceed against priests and clergy generally; and laymen without distinction, infected, suspected, or defamed of heresy, not excepting princes and kings.   Even treaties with, or the power of, sovereigns, the inquisitors have set at nought, if they would yield to the assumed authority.   Of this we have a remarkable instance in the king of Portugal, where Thomas Maynard was English consul.   He was arrested and imprisoned at Lisbon, as having spoken against the Romish religion.   When Oliver Cromwell was advised of the fact, the protector sent an express to the deputy, Mr. Meadows, to go to the king and demand his immediate release; but the sovereign professed that he had no power to grant the favour, as he had no authority over the Inquisition.   But Cromwell sent new instructions, requiring from the king his instant liberation, or he declared war against the Inquisition. The terrified inquisitors offered the consul his liberty, which he accepted only on being brought forth honourably and in public by the Inquisition.   This was at once granted, and Mr. Maynard continued unmolested, during the reigns of Charles II. and James II., well-known at Lisbon.

14. PROHIBITION OF BOOKS.—From time to time lists of books have been published by the Popes, as forbidden to be read, and these have

especially included the Holy Scriptures, as fatal to
the pretensions of the papal hierarchy and the
Inquisition. One of the rules of the "Index" of
prohibited books, regarding the Bible, says, "Since
it is plain by experience, that if the Sacred Writings
are permitted everywhere, and without difference,
to be read in the vulgar tongue, men, through their
harshness, will receive more harm than good. Let
the bishop or inquisitor determine, with the parish
priest or confessor, to whom to permit the reading
of the Bible, translated by Catholic authors in the
vulgar tongue." This rule against the Bible is
observed in all Catholic countries, especially in
Spain, where the inquisitors published their prohibition, with a particular stress upon the Scriptures,
"with all parts of them, either printed or manuscript,
with all summaries and abridgments, although historical, of the said Bible in the vulgar tongue."

15. KEEPERS OF THE PRISONS OF THE INQUISI-
TION.—Some bishops in the Romish church have
prisons for the custody of offenders of their laws.
But such places were usually placed under the care
of inquisitors as their keepers. Every person imprisoned is first accused by some one, generally by
two persons, who has heard him utter or suspects
him of holding opinions that are deemed heretical.
This accusation being received, the promoter-fiscal
demands before the inquisitors that such person
may be imprisoned and brought to trial. A warrant is then issued, subscribed by the inquisitors,
and given to the officer, who proceeds to arrest the
person and lodge him in gaol. This gaol, though a

L

horrid place, is called, in Spain and Portugal, *Santa-casa*, or *Holy-house*.

In Portugal, all the prisoners, men and women, without any regard to birth or rank, are shaved, the first or second day of imprisonment. Every prisoner has two pots of water daily, one to wash and the other to drink, and a besom to cleanse his cell; a mat of rushes to lie on; and a larger vessel for other uses, with a cover to put over it, which is changed every four days.

How intolerant and cruel the inquisitors and keepers were, in the sixteenth century, may be learned from two cases: the first was relating to some English persons who put into the port of Cadiz. The familiars of the Inquisition searched the vessel on account of religion. They seized several on board, as they manifested evangelical piety, and they were thrown into gaol. Among these was a child, about ten or twelve years of age, son of a rich gentleman, owner of the ship and part of the cargo. The pretence was, that he had in his hands the Book of Psalms in English. The ship and cargo were confiscated, and the child was imprisoned at Seville, where he lay six or eight months, and became very ill through cruel treatment. The lords inquisitors being informed of his illness, and hoping to profit by his father's reputed wealth, removed him to the Cardinal Hospital. But he lost the use of his legs. The gaoler often observed him lifting up his eyes to heaven and praying for help; so that he reported him as "already grown a great little heretic!" Through the cruel treatment in the prison, he died in the hospital of the Inquisition!

Another case, about the same period, will illustrate the cruelties of the Inquisition. Peter ab Herera, keeper of the tower of Triada, the prison of the Inquisition, had in charge a good matron, and, with her, two daughters, but kept in different cells. They bemoaned their separation, and entreated the keeper to suffer them to be together for a quarter of an hour, that they might have the satisfaction of embracing each other. Moved with compassion for them he granted their request; and after they had indulged their mutual affection for half an hour, he locked them up again in their solitary cells. A few days after, they were examined by torture, and the keeper, fearing that through the severity of their torments they might discover his lenity to the lords inquisitors, went to the holy tribunal and declared what he had done; but they, instead of commending his humanity, regarded him as guilty of a crime, and immediately ordered him into gaol, and to torture. After a year of suffering he was brought out of prison, with a halter round his neck, and led in a public procession, punished with a *hundred* lashes, and condemned to the galleys as a slave, for six years. He became insane through ill treatment, and attempting the life of the alguazil he was sentenced to four years additional slavery in the galleys! Dreadful as these are, they are far from being the most affecting examples of cruelty in the Inquisition.

16. TERRORS OF THE INQUISITION.—No words

can express the dread of the people regarding the tribunal of the inquisitors. They regard the prisoners as lost. So little hope have they of the release of those arrested, that as soon as they are imprisoned, their friends put on mourning, and speak of them as dead, not daring to petition for their pardon, lest they also should be brought in as accomplices, and become themselves victims of the Inquisition!

CHAPTER XII.

TRIAL IN THE INQUISITION.

Edict of Faith—Process at Tribunal—Arrest—Examination— Bill of accusation—Prisoner's counsel—Escaped persons —Process terminated—Abjuration of a penitent—Penance.

ECCLESIASTICAL processes are entered upon with remarkable solemnity, particularly in the court of the inquisition. The court having been set up under the authority of the sovereign, and with full protection to its officers, a commissary is appointed, for the purpose of receiving information or accusations from any persons against others, under the authority of the chief inquisitor. Public preparations are made, therefore, for the commencement of proceedings against them on account of alleged crimes.

1. THE EDICT OF FAITH.—Some Sunday is ap-

pointed by the chief inquisitor, for a sermon on the solemn publication of the object of the court, and this is called the "Edict of Faith." After the sermon by the inquisitor, on the duty of extirpating heresy, a monitory letter is read, requiring all persons, on pain of excommunication, to discover to the inquisitor, within six or twelve days, any heretics known to them, or persons suspected of heresy. Magistrates are made to promise the same upon oath. This edict of faith is repeated every year in the chief city; and from its obligations no one is freed: so that Joan, the daughter of the Emperor Charles V., was counselled by her father to make the required deposition, even if it were against himself, and she immediately deposed against a certain person before the inquisitor-general, the archbishop of Seville.

2. PROCESS BEFORE THE TRIBUNAL.—There are three ways of proceeding—*first*, by *accusation*; *secondly*, by *denunciation*; *thirdly*, by *inquisition*, or *seeking* out heretics. Witnesses are summoned, and the testimony of a wife, of sons, of daughters, and of domestics, is received against, but not in favour of, persons accused of heresy. The testimony of persons guilty of perjury, and of women known to public infamy, and even of outlaws, is allowed. Their depositions are taken in writing concerning the characters and opinions of prisoners.

3. ARREST OF THE ACCUSED.—Persons accused of heresy, living in cities, are usually arrested in the dead of night, by familiars of the Inquisition.

They proceed to the dwelling of the accused, who is required immediately to rise and follow them to a carriage in waiting. Resistance is useless; and people stand so much in awe of the hated court, that parents deliver up their children, husbands their wives, and masters their servants, to its officers, without daring to murmur in the least degree; the prisoners are kept in solitary confinement, generally for a long time, till they are convicted of any crime of which they may have been guilty.

4. EXAMINATION OF PRISONERS.—After solemn prayer to the Holy Spirit has been read, the prisoner is brought before the inquisitor in the chamber of audience. He beholds at a table on his right hand the judge-inquisitor, at the farther end sits the notary, and the unhappy victim, with his arms and feet naked, and his head shaved and uncovered, is allowed to sit on a form at the lower end of the table. Opposite to him, against the wall, is fixed a large crucifix, reaching nearly to the ceiling. He is then interrogated by the inquisitor, who employs every possible artifice to induce him to make confession of every thing that he may have said or done against the Catholic faith. In Spain and Portugal, the inquisitor sometimes sends a person to visit him, exhorting him, as a friend, to make confession, that he may obtain the favour of his judge, and not be separated for ever from his wife and children. Many are thereby induced to confess fictitious crimes, in the vain hope of obtaining liberty.

5. BILL OF ACCUSATION.—The promoter-fiscal exhibits the bill of accusation against the prisoner, thus,—" I, *N.*, fiscal of the office of the Holy Inquisition, do, before you, the reverend inquisitor, delegated judge in causes of the faith against heretical pravity, criminally accuse *M.*, who being baptised a Christian, and accounted such among all persons, hath departed from the Catholic faith." Their various crimes are specified in grievous terms. The witnesses are examined in private, and only their testimony exhibited against the prisoner. This iniquitous course is uniformly pursued. So that the New Christians, as the conforming Jews in Spain were called, in vain offered Charles V. the sum of 80,000 pieces of gold, if he would order the witnesses against some of them to be made known at the tribunal of the Inquisition. In some cases, prisoners are allowed to appeal from the inquisitor, before the trial has proceeded to the definitive sentence.

6. COURSE FOR THE PRISONER.—If the prisoner deny his guilt, he is allowed to select an advocate from a list provided by the inquisitors, but paid from the effects of the accused. If under twenty-five years, he is allowed a curator or guardian.

7. ACCUSED PERSONS ESCAPED.—If an accused person flee from the court, or escape from prison, he is publicly cited in the cathedral, in the parish church, and in his own house, and the temporal lord is required to arrest him: if this fail, he is excommunicated; and, if taken, he is whipped and proceeded against with increased severity.

8. THE PROCESS TERMINATED.—Sentences are pronounced according to the decisions of the inquisitors. Those declared innocent are absolved; and those suspected are subjected to abjuration, purgation, fines, or banishment. When the prisoner is defamed for heresy, but not found guilty by legal evidence or his own confession, he is required to submit to canonical purgation, in severe penances imposed by the bishop. Those of high reputation among the people—as bishops, priests, and preachers—are mostly enjoined some purgation: and those who are condemned, are declared to have been heretics or apostates, and to have incurred the penalties according to law; his effects are confiscated; his opinions and writings are condemned; and he is deprived of all ecclesiastical or public offices and honours, while he is delivered over to the secular power to be punished. If he persist in his opinions, sentence is immediately pronounced, and he is committed to officers to be burnt. The greatest severity is exercised against the Lutherans, as they are regarded as the most decided enemies of the papacy.

9. ABJURATION OF A PENITENT.—A heretic, against whom an information has been laid, confessing his heresy to the bishop or inquisitor, promising to return to the bosom of the church, abjuring all heresy, is not delivered to the secular power, but punished by the inquisitors. He is compelled to abjure publicly, before all the people in the church; where he is required to place his hands on the book of the Gospels, with his head

uncovered, and, falling on his knees, to read a form
of solemn abjuration, or to repeat it while it is read
by the notary. When this is done, he is absolved
from excommunication, on condition of his returning,
with a true heart and sincere faith, to observe all
the commands of the Catholic church; but if he do
not observe them, he forfeits the benefits of his
absolution. In this manner abjuration is enjoined
upon all who return from heresy, even boys of
fourteen and girls of twelve years of age are not
excused, especially persons of dignity and rank as
priests; and doctors, whom they call *dogmatists*,
dogmatisers, and *arch-heretics*.

10. PENANCES OF THOSE WHO ABJURE.—Though
abjuration reconciles to the church, still penance is
required as a wholesome punishment. In some
cases a penitent is required to make a pilgrimage,
with a black habit, carrying the inquisitor's letters,
which must be brought back with letters testimonial
from the predicant friars, or other official personages, as certifying the truth of such visit. In
other cases, a penitent is required to walk in a
procession, destitute of all clothes, except a shirt
and breeches; and in this condition to receive public
discipline by the bishop or priest, to be expelled
the church, and to stand with a lighted candle in
hand, bare feet, and a halter about his neck, at its
principal gate, during the time of solemn mass, on
some holy day, or as the bell was ringing for Divine
service. Others are punished by public whipping
with rods, and if ecclesiastics by their own frater-
nity, in the presence of the notary of the Holy

Office. But the most common punishment is wearing crosses upon their penitential garments, by which they become exposed to the scoffs and insults of the people. He that throws off this garment is more severely punished, some for the whole of life; from which it is difficult to procure release without money, on the application of friends to the chief inquisitors.

CHAPTER XIII.

TORTURES IN THE INQUISITION.

Torture to force confession—Hall of Torture—Stripping—Binding — Squassation — Fire-pan—Rack—Horse—Dice—Wet cloth—Various devices.

PRISONERS in the Inquisition are of different characters; and many of them naturally deny their guilt. Others would only in part confess their faults and crimes, employing different terms in successive examinations. Others again, being innocent of the criminality with which they were charged, could not confess or acknowledge that they were guilty. While others, holding fast the doctrine of Christ, were willing rather to suffer death than deny the Gospel of their Lord and Saviour.

If the prisoner do not confess according to the deposition of the witnesses against him, or do not satisfy the inquisitors, torture is employed, chiefly to induce the accused to confess regarding friends or associates, who may hold opinions deemed heretical. Determined to humble their victims, they employ extensively a most cruel system of torture, the records of which have justly procured for the Inquisition the character of *sanguinary* and *diabolical*. Surely, none but the evil spirit, "the devil, who was a murderer from the beginning," could have devised such revolting methods of cruelty, and prompted men, with the most ingenious devices, so to outrage all the dictates of humanity, as to act on the system which was the practice of the Romish inquisitors. They yet attempt its justification on the plea that "Paul delivered the Corinthian to Satan for the destruction of the flesh, that the spirit may be saved in the day of the Lord Jesus." (1 Cor. v. 5.) Paul inflicted no bodily tortures, but such is the Romish perversion of the Scriptures.

These tortures of the Inquisition it will be necessary here briefly to describe, that the character of the atrocious system may be the more clearly understood by the reader.

1. THE HALL OF TORTURE.—This, in Spain, is a subterraneous chamber, in the centre of the prison, so that the cries of the sufferer may not be heard by any one outside. It is entered by a passage through several doors; at one end of it a tribunal is erected, on which the inquisitors, the inspector, and the notary are seated. The lamps being lighted in this dark room, the prisoner is brought in and delivered to the executioner, who makes a dreadful

appearance; as he is covered all over with a black linen garment down to his feet, and tied close to his body, while his head and face are all hidden with a hood, having in it only two small holes, through which he may see. All this is intended to strike terror into the miserable wretch, when he sees himself in the power of one who has the appearance of an infernal spirit.

Those who are employed as torturers are required to be such as are born of "ancient Christians,"— undoubted Catholics; and they are sworn to secresy as to what is said and done in this terrible place of punishment.

2. STRIPPING.—All who are tortured are stripped naked, both men and women, without regard to decency or honour; and the prisoner has no clothing except a pair of linen drawers. This process, to some, is an inexpressible torment. While he is being stripped, he is exhorted to confess and declare all the truth, being admonished that if he should die under the torture, the judges would be clear from blame, which would rest alone with himself, as a criminal. The notary present writes down everything that is said or done in the act of torture. If the inquisitors are not satisfied with the confession, the prisoner is threatened with various punishments, the instruments of which he is shown in the hall.

3. BINDING.—This is done by cords, fastening the hands behind the back, the wrists bound together, with weights tied to the feet; so that it is impossible for the prisoner to extricate himself from the power of the executioner.

4. THE PULLEY.—By this instrument, the hook being passed under the rope at the wrists, the victim is drawn up till his head reaches near the pulley, fixed to the roof of the hall. Thus he is suspended; so that by the weight of the body, with what is hung at the feet, all the joints of the emaciated frame are dreadfully stretched, and the bones dislocated.

5. SQUÁSSATION.—This is performed by a jerk of the rope, but without allowing the body being suspended from touching the ground. By this a terrible shake is given to the whole frame, and the arms and legs disjointed, by which the sufferer is put to the most exquisite pain. The shock which is thus received oftentimes occasions death. Romish authors observe on this mode, " When the senate orders, ' Let him be interrogated by torture,' the person is lifted or hoisted up, but not put to the squassation. If the senate orders, ' Let him be tortured,' he must then undergo the squassation at once, being first interrogated as he is hanging upon the rope and engine. If it orders, ' Let him be well tortured,' it is understood that he must suffer two squassations. If it orders, ' Let him be severely tortured,' it is understood of three squassations, at three different times within an hour. If it says, ' Very severely,' it is understood that it must be done with twisting, and weights at the feet. When it says, ' Very severely, even unto death,' then the criminal's life is in immediate danger."

6. THE FIRE-PAN.—This was applied to the prisoner while he was fastened in the stocks, when a

fire-pan, full of burning charcoal, was brought near
to the soles of his feet. These were rendered
increasingly susceptible of pain, by being rubbed
with grease; so that they would literally be fried,
and the suffering be most excruciating. During
the process, the prisoner was exhorted to confess;
and if he promised this, a board was put between
his feet and the fire; but if he did not satisfy
them, the board was removed, and the torture renewed. The Rev. Archibald Bower, once an inquisitor, but afterwards a clergyman in the church of
England, states, that frequently the inquisitors and
other officers, regardless of the groans and tears of
the unhappy sufferer, converse before him on city
news, or add insult to his misery while entreating
by all that is sacred for a moment's relief from the
dreadful torment.

7. THE RACK.—Several instruments were so
called: one was a plank with a windlass attached,
having two pulleys. The prisoner, nearly naked,
placed with his back on the board, was drawn by a
rope tied to the iron ring on each wrist; so that his
arms were drawn until they were dislocated, producing extreme agony to the victim.

8. THE HORSE.—This was a frame of wood—a
sort of trough, across which was a round bar, like
the step of a ladder. On this bar the prisoner was
laid, with his feet elevated higher than his head.
He was then bound to the horse by a cord drawn
thrice round each arm, and the same round each
leg. By means of sticks, after the manner of
screws, the cord being twisted, it was thus tight-

ened, and, cutting into the flesh, much bloodshed
was caused. The rope was then removed to the
sounder parts, and the torture repeated, producing
excruciating agony.

9. THE DICE.—Sometimes iron dice were fastened to the heels of the feet, when screws were
forced through the flesh till they reached the bones,
producing indescribable suffering.

10. THE WET CLOTH.—The prisoner, while bound
to the horse, in some cases, had thrown over his
face a thin cloth, forming a bag to pass into his
mouth, so that he was scarcely able to breathe;
and, at the same time, a very small stream of water
was directed to fall into the mouth, sinking the
bag down his throat. Six or seven English pints
of water have been thus poured into one person,
and the convulsive agonies produced were like a
sense of suffocation. Sometimes the cloth was
removed from the face, to allow the wretched victim
to answer the questions proposed by the inquisitors;
when the pain occasioned by the pulling up of the
bag from the throat was as if the bowels were being
drawn through the mouth, and it was found to be
soaked with blood as well as with water. In his
struggling efforts to breathe, the sufferer would
rupture a blood-vessel, and, in not a few instances,
die under the horrid torture.

Various other modes of cruelty were employed
in some courts, according to the will of the inquisitors. Some used canes put between the fingers,
which were then pressed together, so as to dislocate
the joints, and occasion exquisite pain. Others

tied small cords round the thumbs, so tightly as to force blood from under the nails. Red-hot irons were pressed upon the naked breasts, and iron slippers heated were put on the feet, so as to burn the flesh to the bone. And in perpetrating these enormities, especially on the persons of women, the inquisitors behaved in the most inhuman and revolting manner, indicating the execrable character of the Romish "mystery of iniquity."

CHAPTER XIV.

VICTIMS OF THE INQUISITION.

Victims—1. Juan de Salas—2. Donna Johanna Bohorques—
3. Donna Maria Bohorques—4. Melchior Hernandez—
5. Lewis Pezoa.

"*Justice and Mercy*" are the words chosen by the Romish Inquisition, as forming the maxims of that court, in proceeding against heretics. But the tortures inflicted falsify the profession. No court of judgment, in any age or nation, was ever found so utterly at variance with these principles, or conducted in a manner so manifestly opposed to equity and humanity. A few selected cases of their tortured victims will still further illustrate the diabolical savageness of the inquisitors: these cases are given from the most undoubted authorities.

1. JUAN DE SALAS.—This victim was a young man, and it appears an officer of the Inquisition in Spain. He had been charged with employing the language of heresy, and therefore immured in the dungeon. The Inquisition transgressed their own rules in relation to him, refusing to hear the witnesses whom he wished to be examined in his favour. He positively denied having used the words attributed to him; on which account he was subjected to the torture, to compel his confession. The particulars of his sufferings under the inquisitors, Moriz and Dr. Alvarado, are contained in the following record, drawn up by the notary of the Inquisition :—

"At Valladolid, on the 21st of June, 1527, the licentiate Moriz, inquisitor, caused the licentiate Juan de Salas to appear before him. After the reading, the said licentiate Salas declared that *he had not said that of which he was accused;* and the said licentiate Moriz immediately caused him to be conducted to the chamber of torture, where, being stripped to his shirt, Salas was put by the shoulders into the *chevalet*, where the executioner, Pedro Porras, fastened him by the arms and legs with cords of hemp, of which he made eleven turns round each limb. Salas, during the time that the said Pedro was tying him thus, was several times warned to speak the truth; to which he always replied that *he had never said what he was accused of.* He recited the creed '*Quicumque vult,*' and several times gave thanks to God and our Lady; and, the said Salas being still tied as before men-

M

tioned, a fine wet cloth was put over his face, and
about a pint of water was poured into his mouth
and nostrils from an earthen vessel, with a hole at
the bottom, and containing about two quarts;
nevertheless, Salas persisted in denying the accusation. Then Pedro Porras tightened the cord
on the right leg, and poured a second measure of
water on the face; the cords were tightened a
second time on the same leg, but Juan de Salas
still persisted in denying that he had ever said any
thing of the kind; and, although pressed to tell the
truth several times, he still denied the accusation.
Then the said licentiate Moriz having declared
that *the torture was begun, but not finished,* commanded that it should cease. The accused was
withdrawn from the *chevalet,* or *rack,* at which I,
Henry Paz, was present from the beginning to the
end.—*Henry Paz,* Notary."

Juan de Salas was condemned, notwithstanding
his denial; and Llorente makes the following remarks on the whole case of shocking injustice and
cruelty:—

"We may form an idea of the humanity of the
Inquisition at Valladolid from the definitive sentence
pronounced by the licentiate Moriz and his colleague,
Dr. Alvarado, without any other formality, after
they had taken (if we may believe them) the advice
of persons noted for their learning and virtue, but
without the adjournment which ought to have
preceded it, and without the concurrence of the
diocesan in ordinary. They declared that the fiscal
had not entirely approved the accusation, and that

the prisoner had succeeded in destroying some of the charges; but that, on account of the suspicion arising from the trial, Juan de Salas was condemned to the punishment of the public *auto da fé*, in his shirt, without a cloak, his head uncovered, and with a torch in his hand; that he should abjure heresy publicly; and that he should pay ten ducats of gold to the Inquisition, and fulfil his penance in the church assigned. It is seen, by a certificate afterwards given in, that Juan de Salas performed his *auto da fé* on the 24th of June, 1528, and that his father paid the fine. The trial offers no other peculiarity. This affair, and several others of a similar nature, caused the supreme council to publish a decree, in 1558, commanding that the torture should not be administered without an order from the council."

2. DONNA JOHANNA BOHORQUES.—Limborch, from Gonsalvius, gives the following account of this noble young lady, who was really murdered by the inquisitors in their tortures of her, about A.D. 1569.

"At the same time almost, they apprehended, in the Inquisition at Seville, a noble lady, Johanna Bohorques, the wife of Don Francis de Vargos, a very eminent man, and Lord of Heguera, and daughter of Peter Garsia Xeresius, a wealthy citizen of Seville. The occasion of her imprisonment was, her sister, Maria Bohorques, a young lady of eminent piety, who was afterwards burnt for her pious confession, had declared, in her torture, that she had several times conversed with her sister concerning her doctrine. When she was first imprisoned she was about six

months gone with child, upon which account she
was not so straitly confined, nor used with that
cruelty which the other prisoners were treated with,
out of regard to the infant she carried. Eight days
after her delivery they took the child from her, and
on the fifteenth shut her up close, and made her
undergo the fate of the other prisoners, and began
to manage her cause with their usual arts and
rigour. In so dreadful a calamity she had only this
comfort, that a certain pious young woman, who
was afterwards burnt for her religion by the inquisitors, was allowed her for her companion. This
young creature was, on a certain day, carried out to
her torture; and being returned from it into her
gaol, she was so shaken, and had her limbs so
miserably disjointed, that when she was laid upon
her bed of rushes, it rather increased her misery
than gave her rest, so that she could not turn
herself without the most excessive pain. In this
condition, as Bohorques had it not in her power to
show her any, or but very little outward kindness,
she endeavoured to comfort her mind with great
tenderness. The girl had scarcely begun to recover
from her torture, when Bohorques was carried out
to the same exercise, and was tortured with such
diabolical cruelty upon the rack, that the rope
pierced and cut into the very bones in several
places; and in this manner she was brought back
to prison, just ready to expire, the blood running
out of her mouth in great plenty. Undoubtedly
they had burst her bowels, insomuch that the
eighth day after her torture she died. And when,

after all, they could not procure sufficient evidence
to condemn her, though sought after and procured
by all their inquisitorial arts—yet as the accused
person was born in that place, where they were
obliged to give some account of the affair to the
people, and, indeed, could not, by any means, dis-
semble it—in the first act of triumph appointed
after her death, they commanded her sentence to
be pronounced in these words :—' Because this lady
died in prison (without doubt suppressing the cause
of it), and was found to be innocent upon inspecting
and diligently examining her cause, therefore the
holy tribunal pronounces her free from all charges
brought against her by the fiscal, and absolving her
from any further process, doth restore her, both as
to her innocence and reputation, and commands all
her effects, which had been confiscated, to be restored to those to whom they of right belonged.'
And thus, after they had murdered her, by torture,
with savage cruelty, they pronounced her innocent! "

Llorente adds, " Under what an overwhelming
responsibility will these monsters appear before the
tribunal of the Almighty !"

This instance of refined barbarity in the inquisitors strikingly displays their hypocrisy as professors
of the benevolent religion of Christ, and their malignity against those who dared to listen to the
doctrines of the Scriptures, then condemned under
the name of LUTHERANISM.

3. DONNA MARIA BOHORQUES.—This lady was
sister of Johanna, who had been murdered in the

Inquisition. She perished in the flames at Seville. The account of her states, " She had completed her twenty-first year when she was arrested on suspicion of being a Lutheran. Under the instruction of D. Juan Gil, bishop of Tortosa, she was perfectly acquainted with the Latin language, and had made considerable progress in Greek. She knew the Gospel by heart, and was deeply read in those commentaries which explain, in a Lutheran sense, the text referring to justification by faith, good works, the sacraments, and the characteristics of the true church.

" Donna Maria was confined in the secret prisons of the Inquisition, where she avowed the doctrines imputed to her, defended them against the arguments of the priests who visited her, and boldly told the inquisitors, that instead of punishment for the creed which she held, they would do much better to imitate her example. With regard to the depositions of her accusers, though she allowed the principal points, she persisted in denying some things which related to the opinions of other individuals ; and this denial gave the inquisitors an opportunity of putting her to the rack. By this torture they only procured a confession that her sister, Johanna Bohorques, knew her sentiments, and had not disapproved of them ; and, as she persisted in her confession of faith, sentence was passed upon her as an obstinate heretic. In the interval between her condemnation and the *auto da fé*, at which she was to suffer, the inquisitors made every exertion to bring her back to the Romish faith. They sent to her, successively, two Jesuits and two Dominican priests, who laboured with great zeal for her conversion; but they returned without having effected their object, full of admiration of the talents she displayed, and regretting the obstinacy with which she persisted in what they supposed a damnable heresy. The evening before the *auto da fé*, two Dominicans joined in the attempt, and were followed by several theologians of other orders. Donna Maria received them with civility, but dissuaded them from attempting the hopeless task. To the professions which they made of being interested in the welfare of her soul, she answered, that she believed them to be sincere, but that they must not suppose that she, being the party chiefly concerned, felt a less interest in the matter than they did. She told them, that she came to prison fully satisfied of the orthodoxy of the creed which she held, and that she had been confirmed in her belief by the evident futility of the arguments brought against it.

"At the stake, Don Juan Ponce de Leon, who had abjured the Lutheran doctrines, exhorted Donna Maria to follow his example. The weakness of this apostate for a moment overcame her, and she silenced him by language rather of contempt than of pity. Recollecting herself, however, she told him that the time for controversy was past, and that their wisest plan would be, to occupy the few minutes which remained to them, in meditating on the death of their Redeemer, in order to confirm that faith by which alone they could be justified. All that poor Juan Ponce de Leon gained by his apostacy was, that he was not burnt alive, but first strangled, and then burnt. On this occasion, the attendant priest, moved by the youth and talents of Donna Maria, offered her this milder death, if she would merely repeat the Creed. With this offer she readily complied; but having finished it, she began immediately to explain its articles, according to the sense of the reformers. This confession of faith was immediately interrupted. Donna Maria was strangled by the executioner, and her body was afterwards reduced to ashes!"

4. MELCHIOR HERNANDEZ.—This victim was a merchant of Toledo, whence he removed to settle, A.D. 1564, in Murcia, where he was arrested by the officers of the Inquisition, charged with Judaism. Witnesses, known to be his enemies, appeared against him, but their evidence was contradictory; yet he was detained in prison. Being dangerously ill, he demanded an audience of the inquisitors, to whom he said that he had been present at a meeting, a year before, where the subject of conversation was the law of Moses. Some days after, at his re-examination, he declared that what was said at the meeting was in jest, and he did not recollect the particulars of the conversation. Having said to the visitor of the tribunal that the things which he had declared, he had been induced to utter before his judges by the fear of death, he was put to the torture, to compel him to confess what he knew respecting certain persons; but he bore the cruel infliction without uttering a word.

On the 18th of October, 1565, he was declared, as
a Jewish heretic, to be guilty of concealment in his
confession, and condemned to be burnt. His
execution was fixed for the 9th of December; and
on the 7th he was exhorted to a full confession.
He replied, that he had confessed all he knew; and
the next day, being desired to prepare for death,
he declared that he had seen the persons whom he
had mentioned, and some others at the meeting;
that they conversed respecting the law of Moses,
but that he regarded their communications as mere
pastime. Between this and the commencement of
the *auto da fé*, next day, he made several communications, in hope of escaping death, giving the
names of various parties as his accomplices. This
disclosure being unavailing to induce the inquisitor
to suspend his execution, Melchior stated that he
had really believed, for a year, what had been
preached in the synagogue, though he had not confessed the fact, because he thought there was no
proof of heresy in the depositions of the witnesses.
His execution was suspended, and he was subjected
to new examinations, at which he made extraordinary and contradictory statements, perplexing
to his judges; three of whom voted for his punishment and two for his reconciliation. The council
decreed that Melchior should be burnt on the 8th
of June, 1567; and on each of the three preceding
days he was called up, and exhorted to declare his
accomplices. The habit of a prisoner to be burnt
was put upon him, when he declared that he could
name other accomplices, and an inquisitor went to

receive his confession. He gave another synagogue, and seven other places, with the names of
fourteen persons who frequented them. This not
being deemed satisfactory, he was led, with others,
to the place of execution, where he mentioned two
more houses, and twelve heretics; in a *second*
audience, he gave seven more persons; and in a
third audience, two more houses, and six persons.
He was again remanded, as he hoped; but on the
23rd of June, despairing of success, he appealed
to his judges, "What more could I do than accuse
myself falsely? Know that I have never been
summoned to any assembly; that I never attended
any but for the purposes of commerce." After
many audiences, he was for the third time sentenced for execution, and he again succeeded in
escaping the fire. In five subsequent audiences he
denounced various persons; but he was declared
"*still guilty of concealment, in not mentioning several
persons not less distinguished and well known than
those already denounced, and that he could not be
supposed to have forgotten them.*"

Overcome by this malignant suggestion, Melchior
delivered an indignant invective against the inquisitors, and all who appeared on the trial, and then
said, "What can you do to me?—burn me?
Well, then, be it so. I cannot confess what I do
not know. All that I have said of myself is true,
but what I have declared of others is entirely
false. I invented it, *because I perceived that you
wished me to denounce innocent persons; and being
unacquainted with the names and quality of these*

unfortunate people, I named all whom I could think of, in the hope of finding an end to my misery. I now perceive that my situation admits of no relief, and I therefore retract all my depositions; and now, having fulfilled this duty, proceed to burn me as soon as you please." The papers relating to the trial were sent to the supreme council, which confirmed the sentence of burning, and reprimanded the inquisitors for the delay. Instead of submitting to this decision, the inquisitors called Melchior again before them, representing to him that his declarations contained many contradictions, and that, for the good of his soul, it was necessary that he should finally make a confession, respecting himself and all his guilty acquaintances. This artful appeal did not shake his constancy. Melchior affirmed that they would find all the truth in the declaration that he had made before the visitor, Senor Ayora. It was found in this that Melchior had stated, that "*he knew nothing of the subject on which he was examined.*" The inquisitor then said, "How can this declaration be true, when you have several times declared that you have attended the Jewish assemblies, believed in their doctrines, and persevered in the belief for the space of one year, until you were undeceived by a priest?" Melchior replied, "I spoke falsely when I made a declaration against myself." "But how is it," said the inquisitor, "that what you have confessed of yourself, and many other things, which you now deny, are the result of the depositions of a great many witnesses?" "I do not know," replied Melchior, "if that is true or false, for I have not seen the writings of the trial; but if the witnesses have said that which is imputed to them, it was *because they were placed in the same situation as I am.* They do not love me better than I love myself; and I have certainly declared against myself both truth and falsehood." "What motive had you, then," asked the inquisitor, "in declaring things injurious to yourself, if they were false?" Melchior declared, "I expected to derive great advantage from them, because I saw that if I did not confess anything, I should be considered as impenitent, and the truth would lead me to the scaffold. I thought that falsehood would be most useful to me, and I found it so in two *autos da fé.*"

Nothing was now to be expected but death, and he was desired, on the 6th of June, 1568, to prepare for it by the next day. At two o'clock in the morning he desired an audience with the inquisitor, who, with his notary, went to his cell. Melchior then said to him, "That at the point of appearing before the tribunal of the Almighty, and without any hope of escaping from death by new delays, he thought himself bound to declare that he had never conversed with any person on the Mosaic law; that all he had said on this subject was founded on the wish to preserve life, and the belief that his confessions were pleasing to the inquisitors; that he asked pardon of the persons implicated, that God might pardon him, and that no injury might be done to their honour and reputation."

Melchior Hernandez was, therefore, sacrificed to the bigotry of the inquisitors, first being strangled and then burnt. As to his inventions and false accusations of others, nothing can justify him; but such endeavours to escape from the dreadful tribunal appear to be common among the unhappy prisoners of that horrid court which knows no mercy.

5. LEWIS PEZOA.—About the year 1650, Lewis Pezoa, a new Christian, his wife, and two sons, and one daughter, besides some relations living with him, were all thrown into the gaol of the Inquisition in Portugal. They were accused by some of their enemies of being Jews. Pezoa denied the charge, and refuted it, but in vain; he demanded that his accusers might be discovered to him, that he might convict them of falsehood. He was condemned, as a negative heretic, to be delivered over to the secular court to be burnt. This was made known to him fifteen days before the sentence was pronounced by the court.

Pezoa being a man of wealth, the Duke de Cadaval knew him, and desired to know, from his intimate friend, the Duke d'Aviera, inquisitor-general, how he would be treated; and understanding that unless he confessed before his going out of prison, he would not escape the fire, because he had been convicted according to the laws of the Inquisition, he entreated, and obtained from the inquisitor-general a promise, that if he could persuade Pezoa to confess, even after sentence was pronounced, and his procession in the act of faith,

he should not die, though it was contrary to the
laws.   Upon that solemn day, therefore, on which
the act of faith was held, he went with some of his
own friends, and some of Pezoa's, to the Inquisition, to prevail on him, if possible, to confess.   He
was led forth in the procession, wearing the infamous attire and the mitre, indicating the sacrifice
of his life.   His friends, with many tears, besought
him, in the name of the Duke of Cadaval, and by all
that was dear to him, that he would preserve his
life, and intimated to him, that if he would confess
and repent, the duke would give him more than he
had lost, as he obtained his life on that condition
from the inquisitor-general.   But all in vain; Pezoa
continually protesting himself innocent, and that
the accusation was the contrivance of his enemies,
who sought his destruction, as guilty of crimes.
When the procession was ended, and the act of
faith almost finished, the sentences of those who
were condemned to certain penances having been
read, and, on the approach of evening, the sentences
of those who were to be delivered over to the
secular court being begun to be read, his friends
repeated their entreaties, by which they overcame
his constancy at last; so that, desiring an audience,
and rising up, that he might be heard, he said,
" Come, then, let us go and confess the crimes I am
falsely accused of, and thereby gratify the desires
of my friends."

Having made confession, he was remanded to
gaol.   But, two years after, he was sent to Evora,
and walked in procession in another act of faith,

wearing the infamous garment, on which was painted the fire inverted, according to the usual custom of the Portuguese Inquisition; and after five years more, in which he was detained in the gaol of the Inquisition, he was condemned to the galleys, as a slave, for five years.

CHAPTER XV.

ACTS OF FAITH OF THE INQUISITION.

The *Auto da Fé*—Act of Faith at Madrid—Act of Faith at Lisbon—Testimony of Rev. Mr. Wilcox.

THE *auto da fé*, or *act of faith*, in the Romish church, is a grand ceremony performed by the Inquisition, for the punishment of heretics, and the absolution of those who have been declared innocent. It is usually contrived to fall on great festivals of the church, that the whole procedure may strike the spectators with the utmost awe. The *auto da fé* may be called *the last act of the inquisitorial tragedy*. It is a kind of gaol delivery, as often as a competent number of prisoners in the Inquisition are convicted of heresy, either by their own voluntary or extorted confession, or on the testimony of certain witnesses. The process is generally as follows:—

In the morning, the prisoners are brought into a great hall, where they put on certain habits, which

are to be worn in the procession, and from which
they know their doom. The procession is led forth
by Dominican friars, after whom come the penitents,
being all in black coats without sleeves, and bare-
footed, with wax candles in their hands. These are
followed by those penitents who have narrowly
escaped being burnt, and who, over their black
coats, have flames painted, with their points turned
downwards. Next come the *negative* and *relapsed*,
who are doomed to be burnt, having flames on their
habits pointing upwards. After these come such
as profess doctrines contrary to the faith of Rome,
who, besides flames pointing upwards, have their
pictures painted on their breasts, with dogs, serpents, and devils, as in a fury. Each prisoner is
attended by a familiar of the Inquisition; and those
to be burnt, have also a Jesuit on each hand urging
them to abjure. After the prisoners, there follow
a troop of familiars on horseback, and then the
inquisitors and other officers of the court, on mules:
last of all, the inquisitor-general on a white horse,
led by two men with black hats and green hat-
bands.

On the occasion, a scaffold is erected large enough
for two or three thousand persons; at one end of
which are the prisoners, at the other the inquisitors.
After a sermon, made of encomiums on the Inquisition, and invectives against heretics, a priest ascends
a desk near the scaffold, and having taken the abjuration of the penitents, he recites the final sentence
of those who are to be put to death, and delivers
them to the secular arm, earnestly beseeching the

authorities not to touch their blood, nor to put
their lives in danger! The prisoners, being thus
in the hands of the civil magistrate, are presently
loaded with chains, and carried first to the secular
gaol, and thence, in an hour or two, brought before
the civil judge; who, after asking in what religion
they intend to die, pronounces sentence on such as
declare they die in the communion of the church of
Rome, that they shall be first strangled, and then
burnt to ashes! or such as die in any other faith,
that they be burnt alive! Both are immediately
carried to a place of execution, where there are as
many stakes set up as there are prisoners to be
burnt, with fuel of dried furze. The stakes for the
professed, or such as reject the Romish faith, are
about four yards high, having a small board near
the top for the prisoner to be seated on. The
negative and relapsed being first strangled and
burnt, the professed mount their stakes by a ladder,
and the Jesuits, after several repeated exhortations
to be reconciled to the church, retire, telling them
that they leave them to the devil, who is standing
at their elbow to receive their souls, and carry them
to the flames of hell. On this, a great shout is
raised, the cry being "Let the dogs' beards be
made;" that is done by thrusting flaming furzes,
fastened on long poles, against their faces, till they
are scorched, and every feature destroyed; and
this is accompanied with the loudest exclamations
of savage joy. At last, fire is set to the furze at
the bottom of the stake, over which the victim is
chained so high that the flame can scarcely reach

N

the seat, and the sufferer is thus made to endure a
roasting.   There cannot be a more lamentable
spectacle ; the sufferers cry out, as long as they are
able, "Pity, for the love of God!" or such-like
appeals for mercy and sympathy ; yet it is beheld,
by both sexes of the superstitious populace, with
transports of joy and satisfaction, illustrating the
genuine spirit of Popery.

ACT OF FAITH AT MADRID, A.D. 1680.

Spain and Portugal, more than any other countries, have been governed on the principles of
Popery.   To learn its true genius, we must look at
the horrid ceremony of burning dissenters, under the
designation of heretics.   The following account
relates to the act of faith celebrated in honour of
Charles II., on the occasion of his public entry into
Madrid, after his marriage, A.D. 1680.

Charles II., of Spain, was born A.D. 1662, and
ascended the throne at nearly the age of four years,
October 7, 1665.   In February, 1680, he married
Maria Louise of Orleans.   This was publicly celebrated under the direction of the priesthood, with
all possible magnificence at Madrid, and an *act of
faith* by the Inquisition, May 3, 1680.

A month before the general execution, the officers
of the Inquisition, preceded by their standard, rode
with great solemnity from the palace of the Holy
Office to the open square, where, in the presence of
crowds of people, they proclaimed, by sound of
trumpet and kettle-drums, that on that day month,

an act of faith, or general execution of the heretics, would be exhibited. The proclamation being over, extensive preparations were made for the dreadful solemnities, under pretence that the horrid sacrifice was in honour of the blessed Jesus and his religion, the Gospel of peace. Previous to this bloody solemnity, a scaffold, fifty feet long, was erected in the great square, and raised to the same height, with a balcony upon it with seats for the king and queen and royal family. At the end, and along the sides, seats were placed, as an amphitheatre, in view of the king, for the council of the Inquisition. On one side, under a splendid canopy, a rostrum was elevated for the grand-inquisitor; and at the opposite side was an elevated platform, on which the prisoners were required to stand. In the centre of the scaffold were erected two enclosures, or cages, open at the top, enclosing the prisoners while sentence of death was pronounced on them. Three pulpits also were erected, two of which were for the use of those who read the sentence, and the third for the preacher; and, lastly, an altar was erected near the rostrum, where the several counsellors sat. The seats, on which their Catholic majesties sat, were ranged so that the queen was at the king's left hand, and on the right the queen-mother. The rest of the whole scaffold was filled with the ladies of honour of both queens; balconies were likewise erected for the foreign ambassadors, and for the lords and ladies of the court, and scaffolds also for the people.

On the solemn day, a month after the proclamation, the ceremony opened in the following order. The march was preceded by a hundred coal-merchants, armed with pikes and muskets, indicating their being under obligation to furnish fuel for the burning of the criminals. These were followed by Dominican friars, before whom a white cross was carried. Behind them came the Duke of Mendini Celi, carrying the standard of the Inquisition, a privilege hereditary in his family. The standard was of red damask, on one side of which was represented a drawn sword in a crown of laurels, and the arms of Spain on the other. Then was brought forward a green cross, covered with black crape, which was followed by several grandees and other persons of quality, familiars of the Inquisition, wearing black cloaks, marked with black and white crosses, edged with gold wire. The march was closed by fifty halbardiers or guards, belonging to the Inquisition, clothed with black and white garments, and commanded by the Marquis of Ponar, hereditary protector of the Inquisition in the province of Toledo.

The procession having marched in this order before the palace, proceeded to the square, when the standard and the green cross were placed on the scaffold, where none but the Dominicans remained, the rest having retired. These Dominican friars had spent the night in chanting psalms, and several masses were celebrated on the altar from day-break until six in the morning. About an hour after, the king, the queen, and the queen-mother, with all the royal family, the lords, ladies and officers of the court, made their appearance, and at eight o'clock ascended the scaffold. The coal-merchants placed themselves on the left of the king's balcony, and his guards stood on the right. Afterwards came thirty men carrying images of pasteboard, as large as life, some representing those who had died in prison, and whose bones were brought in chests, with flames painted on them, and the rest those who had escaped and were outlawed.

These figures were placed at one end of the amphitheatre, and then came twelve men and women with ropes about their necks, torches in their hands, and pasteboard caps on their heads, three feet high, on which were written their crimes. These were followed by fifty others, having also torches in their hands, and clothed with yellow great coats, on which were crosses of St. Andrew X., behind and before. These were Jews, who had repented of their crimes, and desired to be admitted into the church as believers in Jesus Christ. Next came twenty Jews of both sexes, who had relapsed thrice into their former errors, and were condemned to the flames. Those who had given some tokens of repentance were to be strangled before they were burnt; but the rest, for having persisted in their errors, were to be burnt alive. These last wore linen garments, with devils and flames painted on them, and caps after the same manner. Five or six among them, who were more obstinate than the rest, were gagged, to prevent their uttering what the Roman Catholics call blasphemous tenets.

Such as were condemned to die, were surrounded each by four Dominicans and two familiars of the Inquisition. These unhappy creatures passed, in the manner above related, under the king of Spain's balcony, and after having walked round the scaffold, were placed in the amphitheatre that stood on the left, and each of them surrounded by the monks and familiars who had attended them. Some of the grandees of Spain were among these familiars, and they, consistently with their usual national pride, seated themselves on high benches erected for the purpose. The clergy of St. Martin's parish, coming forward, placed themselves near the altar; the officers of the supreme council of the Inquisition, the inquisitor, and several other persons of distinction, both regulars and seculars, all on horseback, with great solemnity, arrived afterwards, and placed themselves on the right hand of the amphitheatre, and on both sides of the rostrum in which the grand-inquisitor was to seat himself. The grand-inquisitor came last, dressed in a purple habit, accompanied by the president of the council of Castile, and several other officers, who, on this occasion, would have been reckoned among the number of heretics, had they not become the more than obsequious slaves of the priests.

Then they began to celebrate mass; in the midst of which, the priest who officiated went down from the altar and seated himself in a chair, which had been placed for him. The grand-inquisitor came down from his seat, and having saluted the altar, and put the mitre on his head, he advanced towards

the king's balcony. Then he went up the steps
that stood at the end of the balcony, with several
officers, who carried the cross and Gospels, and a
book containing the oath by which the kings of
Spain obliged themselves to protect the Catholic
faith, to extirpate heretics, and to support the holy
Inquisition to the utmost of their power.

The king, standing up bareheaded, having on one
side of him a grandee of Spain, holding the royal
sword with the point upward, swore to observe the
oath which a counsellor of the Inquisition had just
read to him. The king continued in this posture
till such time as the grand-inquisitor was returned
back to his seat, where he took off his pontifical
vestments. Then one of the secretaries of the
Inquisition ascended a pulpit appointed for that
purpose, and read an oath to the same purport,
which he administered to all the grandees who were
then present; and this part of the ceremony was
followed by that of a Dominican going up into the
pulpit, and delivering a sermon full of flattery in
praise of the Inquisition.

About two o'clock in the afternoon they began
to read the sentences of the condemned criminals ;
and they began with those who had died in prison,
or who had been outlawed. Their figures in pasteboard were carried up to the little scaffold, and put
into the cages, and then they read the sentences to
each of the criminals who were alive, and they
were, one by one, put into the cages, in order that
every person present might know them. There
were, in all, twenty persons, of both sexes, con-

demned to the flames; and of these, six men and two women could not be prevailed on either to confess or repent of their errors. A young woman was remanded to prison because she had always made the strongest protestations of her innocence, and therefore they thought it would be proper to re-examine the evidence that had been produced against her. Lastly, they read the sentences of those who had been found guilty of bigamy, or witchcraft, with several other crimes, and this lasted till about nine in the evening, when mass was finished.

Mass being finished, the grand-inquisitor, clothed in his pontifical vestments, pronounced a solemn absolution on all those who would repent; and then, the king being withdrawn, the criminals who had been condemned to be burnt, were delivered over to the civil power, and, being mounted upon asses, were carried in this manner through the gate called Foncural. About three hundred paces from it they were chained to stakes, and executed a little after midnight. Those who persisted in their errors were burnt alive; but such as repented, were first strangled before the fire was lighted. Those condemned to lesser punishments were remanded to prison, and the inquisitors returned home to their palace!

To us, in our enlightened times, it must appear very astonishing, that proceedings so inhuman and shocking could be witnessed and sanctioned by a great monarch and his mighty nobles. Yet these outrages continued, but not without complaints against the Inquisition from some of the nobility and statesmen, so that no less than 9,216 victims of that court are reckoned in the reign of Charles II., from A.D. 1666 to A.D. 1700: of these, 1,728 were burnt to death; 576 were burnt in effigy; and 6,912 were subjected to severe penances, in Spain.

ACT OF FAITH AT LISBON, A.D. 1682.

Dr. Michael Geddes, an eminent English divine, and chaplain to the factory at Lisbon for several years, until he was apprehended by the Inquisition in 1686, when he was interdicted from officiating in his ministerial capacity, and returned to England, witnessed an *auto da fé*, in 1682, and he describes it as follows:—

"In the morning of the day, the prisoners are all brought into a great hall, where they have the habits put on they are to wear in the procession, which begins to come out of the Inquisition about nine of the clock in the morning. The first in the procession are the Dominican friars, who carry the standard of the Inquisition, which on the one side hath their founder Dominic's picture, and on the other side, a cross between an olive leaf and a sword, with this motto, *Justitia et Misericordia*. Next after the Dominicans come the penitents, some with *benitos*, some without, according to the nature of their crimes; they are all in black coats without sleeves, and bare-footed, with a wax candle in their hand. Next come the penitents who have narrowly escaped being burnt, who, over their black coat, have flames painted, with their points turned downwards, to signify their having been saved, but so as by fire: this habit is called by the Portuguese *fuego revolto*, or flames turned upside down. Next come the negative and relapsed, that are to be burnt, with flames upon their habit, pointing upward; and next come those who profess doctrines contrary to the faith of the Roman church, and who, besides flames on their habit, pointing upward, have their picture, which is drawn two or three days before, upon their breasts, with dogs, serpents, and devils, all with open mouths, painted upon it. Pequa, a famous Spanish inquisitor, calls this procession, *Horrendum ac tremendum spectaculom;* and so it is in truth, there being some things in the looks of all the prisoners, besides those that are to be burnt, that is ghastly and disconsolate, beyond what can be imagined; and in the eyes and countenance of those that are to be burnt, there is something that looks fierce and eager.

"The prisoners that are to be burnt alive besides a familiar, which all the rest have, have a Jesuit on each hand of them, who are continually preaching to them to abjure their heresies; but if they offer to speak anything in defence of the doctrine, for professing which they are going to suffer death, they are immediately gagged, and not suffered to speak a word more. This I saw done to a prisoner presently after he came out of the gates of the Inquisition, upon his having looked up to the sun, which he had not seen before for several years, and cried out in rapture, 'How is it possible for people to behold that glorious body, to worship any being but Him that created it?' After the prisoners come a troop of familiars on horseback, and after them the inquisitors, and other officers of the court, upon mules, and last of all comes the inquisitor-general, upon a white horse, led by two men, with a black hat and a green hatband, and attended by all the nobles that are employed as familiars in the procession.

"In the *Terceiro de Paco*, which may be as far from the Inquisition as Whitehall is from Temple Bar, there is a scaffold erected, which may hold two or three thousand people; at the one end sit the inquisitors, and at the other end the prisoners, and in the same order as they walked in the procession, those that are to be burnt being seated on the highest benches behind the rest, and which may be ten feet above the floor of the scaffold. After some prayers, and a sermon, which is made up of encomiums on the Inquisition, and invectives against heretics, a secular priest ascends a desk, which stands near the middle of the scaffold, and who, having first taken all the abjurations of the penitents, who kneel before him, one by one, in the same order as they walked in the procession, at last he recites the final sentence of the Inquisition upon those who are to be put to death, in the words following :—

"'We, the inquisitors of heretical pravity, having, with the concurrence of the most illustrious *N.*, lord archbishop of Lisbon, or of his deputy, *M.*, called on the name of his Lord Jesus Christ, and of His glorious mother, the Virgin Mary, and sitting on our tribunal, and judging with the holy Gospels lying before us, that so our judgment might be in the sight of God, and our eyes might behold what is just in all matters between the magnific Doctor *N.*, advocate-fiscal, on the one part, and you, *N.*, now before us, on the other; we have ordained that in this place, and on this day, you should receive your definitive sentence. We do, therefore, by this our sentence, put in writing, define, pronounce, declare, and sentence thee, *N.*, of the city of Lisbon, to be a convicted, confessing, affirmative, and professed heretic, and to be delivered by us as such to the secular arm; and we, by this sentence, do cast thee out of the ecclesiastical court, as a convicted, confessing, affirmative, and professed heretic, and we do leave and deliver thee to the secular arm, and to the power of the secular court, but at the same time do *most earnestly beseech that court so to moderate its sentence as not to touch thy blood, or to put thy life in any danger.'*

"Is there in all history," asks Dr. Geddes, "an instance of so gross and confident a mockery of God and the world as this of the inquisitors, earnestly beseeching the civil magistrates not to put the heretic they have condemned and delivered to them to death? For were they in earnest when they make their solemn petition to the secular magistrates, why do they bring their prisoners out of the Inquisition, and deliver them to those magistrates, in coats painted over with flames? Why do they teach that all heretics, above all other malefactors,

ought to be punished with death? And why do
they never resent the secular magistrates having
so little regard to their earnest and joint petition
as never to fail to burn all the heretics which are
delivered to them by the Inquisition, within an
hour or two after they have them in their hands?
And why, in Rome, where the supreme civil and
ecclesiastical authority are lodged in the same person, is this petition of the Inquisition, which is made
there as well as in other places, never granted?
Certainly, not to take any notice of the old canon,
which forbids the clergy to have any hand in the
blood of any person whatsoever, would be a much
less dishonour to the Inquisition, than to pretend to
go on observing that canon, by making a petition
which is known to be so contrary to their principles
and desires.

"The prisoners are no sooner in the hands of
the civil magistrate than they are loaded with
chains, and before the eyes of the inquisitors; and,
being first carried to the secular gaols, are within
an hour or two brought thence before the lord
chief-justice, who, without knowing any thing of
their particular crimes, or of the evidence that was
against them, asks them, one by one, *in what religion do they intend to die?* If they answer that they
will die in the communion of the Roman church,
they are condemned by him to be *carried forth to
the place of execution, and there to be first strangled,
and then burnt to ashes.* But if they say that they
will die in the Protestant or any other faith that
is contrary to the Roman, they are sentenced by

him to be *carried to the place of execution, and there
to be burnt alive.* At the place of execution, which,
at Lisbon, is in the Ribera, there are so many stakes
set up as there are prisoners to be burnt, with a
good quantity of dry furze about them. The stakes
of *the professed,* as the inquisitors call them, may
be about four yards high, and have a small board
whereon the prisoner is to be seated, within half
a yard of their top. The negative and relapsed
being first strangled and burnt, the professed go
up a ladder between the two Jesuits, who have
attended them all day, and when they are come
even with the fore-mentioned board, they turn
about to the people, and the Jesuits do spend near
a quarter of an hour in exhorting the professed to
be reconciled to the church of Rome ; which, if the
professed refuse to be, the Jesuits come down, and
the executioner ascends, and, having turned the
professed off the ladder upon the seat, and chained
their bodies close to the stake, he leaves them, and
the Jesuits go up to them a second time, to renew
their exhortation to them, and at parting tell them
that they leave them to the devil, who is standing
at their elbow to receive their souls, and carry
them with him into the flames of hell-fire, so soon
as they are out of their bodies. Upon this a great
shout is raised, and as soon as the Jesuits are off
the ladder, the cry is, *'Let the dogs' beards be made !
Let the dogs' beards be made !'* which is done by
thrusting of flaming furzes, fastened to a long pole,
against their faces ; and this inhumanity is commonly continued until their faces are burned to a

coal, and is always accompanied with such acclamations of joy as are not to be heard on any other occasion; a bull fight or a farce being but dull entertainments to the using of a professed heretic thus inhumanly.

"The beards of the professed having been thus made, as they call it in jollity, fire is set to the furze which is at the bottom of the stake, and above which the professed are chained so high that the top of the flame seldom reacheth higher than the seat they sit upon; and if there happen to be a wind, and to which that place is much exposed, it seldom reacheth so high as their knees; so that though there be a calm, the professed are commonly dead in half an hour after the furze is set on fire; yet, if it prove windy, they are not after that dead in an hour and a half, or two hours, and so are really roasted, and not burnt to death. But though out of hell there cannot be a more lamentable spectacle than this, being joined with the sufferers, so long as they are able to speak, crying out, '*Misericordia, por amos de Dios,*' (*Mercy, for the love of God,*) yet it is beheld by people of both sexes and of all ages with such transports of joy and satisfaction, as are not on any other occasion to be met with. And that the reader may not think that this inhuman joy may be the effect of a natural cruelty that is in those people's disposition, and not of the spirit of their religion, he may rest assured that all public malefactors, besides heretics, have their violent deaths nowhere more tenderly lamented than among the same people, and even when there is nothing in the manner of their deaths that appears inhuman or cruel.

"Within a few days after the execution, the pictures of all that have been burnt, and which were taken off their breasts when they were brought to the stake, are hung up in St. Domingo's church, whose west end, though very high, is all covered over with such trophies of the Inquisition, hung up there in honour to Dominic, who, to fulfil his mother's dream, was the first inventor of that court. Dominic's mother, when she was about to be delivered, having dreamed that she was delivered, not of a human creature, but of a fierce dog, with a burning torch in his mouth!"

Enormities of cruel bigotry so truly shocking might well require to be authenticated by the most unquestionable testimony. This has been given. That of the Rev. Mr. Wilcox, chaplain to the English factory of Lisbon in the reign of Queen Anne, and afterwards Bishop of Rochester, wrote in reply to the inquiry of Bishop Burnet, confirming the statements of Dr. Geddes, June 15, 1706. Part of his letter is as follows:—

"My Lord,—In obedience to your lordship's commands of the 10th ultimo, I have here sent all that was printed concerning the last *auto da fé*. I saw the whole process, which is agreeable to what is published by Limborch and others upon that subject. Of the five persons condemned, there were but four burnt; Antonio Tavances, by an unusual reprieve, being saved after the procession. Heytor Dias and Maria Pinteyra were burnt alive, and the other two first strangled. The execution was very cruel. The woman was alive in the flames half an hour, and the man above an hour. The present king and his brothers were seated at a window so near as to be addressed, for a considerable time, in very moving terms, by the man as he was burning. But though the favour he begged was only a few more faggots, yet he was not able to obtain it. Those who are burnt alive here are seated on a bench twelve feet high, fastened to a pole, and above six feet higher than the faggots. The wind being a little fresh, the man's hinder parts were perfectly wasted; and as he turned himself, his ribs opened before he left speaking, the fire being recruited as it wasted, to keep him just in the same degree of heat. But all entreaties could not procure him a larger allowance of wood to shorten his misery and dispatch him!"

CHAPTER XVI.

MODERN VICTIMS OF THE INQUISITION.

Galileo—Dr. Orobio de Castro—Count of Olavides—A Beata
—Joseph da Costa.

"POPERY is unchangeable." Such is the profession of its greatest advocates. They declare that "the Holy Roman Catholic Apostolic Church" is ever

o

the same in its divine foundation, its principles of faith, and its ecclesiastical order. But history, as we have seen, records a long series of changes in its doctrines and institutions, adapted to the varying policy of its hierarchy, which is antichristian; and the advancement of society in knowledge and religion has compelled the observance of far more respect than formerly to the dictates of humanity. Hence the abolition of the horrid custom of publicly burning men for their religious opinions. The spirit of intolerance and bigotry, however, is essential to Romanism, as a system of priestly claims; but even this spirit has been restrained, as will appear from the following examples of its modern victims.

1. GALILEO TORTURED IN THE INQUISITION.— Galileo Galilei, son of a Florentine nobleman, was born A.D. 1564. He became a famous mathematician and astronomer at Pisa and Padua, and by his newly invented telescope he made valuable discoveries, so that, A.D. 1615, he taught that the sun, not the earth, is the centre of our system. This was considered by the Pope and cardinals a heresy, and he was seized by the Inquisition, and condemned as a heretic. He recanted, and was released under promise not to offend again; but being confident in the correctness of his science, he published, A.D. 1632, his "Dialogues on the Ptolemaic and Copernican System of the World," when he was again arrested and condemned by that court to imprisonment for life, while his books were burnt, as if science could injure religon. Torture in the prison

compelled him to sign the following abjuration; and, lest his death should endanger the Inquisition, he was banished to Florence. " I, Galileus, son of the late Vincentius Galileus, a Florentine, aged *seventy*, being here personally upon my trial, and on my knees before you, the most eminent and reverend the lord cardinals, inquisitors-general of the universal Christian commonwealth against heretical pravity, having before my eyes the most Holy Gospels, which I touch with my proper hands, do swear that I always have believed, and do now believe, and by the help of God hereafter will believe all that which the holy Catholic and apostolic Roman church doth hold, preach, and teach. But because, after I had been juridically enjoined and commanded by this Holy Office, that I should wholly forsake that false opinion, which holds that the sun is the centre, and immoveable; and that I should not hold, defend, nor by any manner, neither by word or writing, teach the aforesaid false doctrine; and after it was notified to me that the aforesaid doctrine was contrary to the Holy Scripture, I have written and printed a book, in which I treat of the said doctrine already condemned, and produce reasons of great force in favour of it, without giving any answer to them, I am, therefore, judged by the Holy Office as vehemently suspected of heresy, *viz.*, that I have held and believed that the sun is the centre of the world, and immoveable, and that the earth is not the centre, but moves.

" Being, therefore, willing to remove from the minds of your eminences, and of every Catholic

Christian, this vehement suspicion legally conceived
against me, I do, with a sincere heart and faith
impressed, abjure, curse, and detest the abovesaid
errors and heresies, and, in general, every other
error and sect contrary to the aforesaid holy church;
and I swear, that for the future I will never more
say or assert, either by word or writing, anything
to give occasion for the like suspicion; but that if
I know any heretic, or person suspected of heresy,
I will inform against him to this Holy Office, or to
the inquisitor or ordinary of the place in which I
shall be. Moreover, I swear and promise that I
will fulfil and wholly observe all the penances which
are, or shall be, enjoined me by this Holy Office.
But if, what God forbid, it shall happen that I
should act contrary, by any words of mine, to my
promises, protestations, and oaths, I do subject myself to all the penalties and punishments which have
been ordained and published against such offenders
by the sacred canons and other constitutions general
and particular. So help me God and His Holy
Gospels, which I touch with my own proper hands.

"I, the abovesaid Galileus Galilei, have abjured,
sworn, promised, and obliged myself as above; and
in testimony of these things have subscribed, with
my own proper hand, this present writing of my
abjuration, and have repeated it word for word at
Rome, in the convent of Minerva.

"I, Galileus Galilei, have abjured as above, with
my own proper hand." July 22nd, 1633.

Galileo, indignant against his oppressors for com-
pelling him to swear to an error, as he rose from

his knees, said, "It still moves!" His tortures left him afflicted, but he lived seven years, and died in January, A.D. 1642.

2. DR. BALTHASAR OROBIO DE CASTRO.—Limborch gives the following account "of the method of torturing, and the degree of tortures now used in the Spanish Inquisition," as he received it from Dr. Orobio de Castro, a Jew, about A.D. 1680. This eminent man was born at Seville, and became professor of metaphysics at Salamanca and at Seville, where he was accused to the Inquisition, as of the Jewish religion. This accusation was made by his servant, a Moor, who had before been convicted, and whipped by his order, for thieving; and afterwards, he was again accused before that tribunal by a certain enemy for another fact, which would have proved him to be a Jew. But Orobio obstinately denied his Jewish opinions, and he was, therefore, immured in the gaol of the Inquisition.

"I will here give the account of his torture," says Limborch, "as I had it from his own mouth. After three whole years which he had been in gaol, and several examinations, and the discovery of his crimes to him of which he was accused, in order to his confession, and his constant denial of them, he was at length carried out of his gaol, and through several turnings brought to the place of torture, towards the evening. This was a large underground room, arched roof, and the walls covered with black hangings. The candlesticks were fastened to the wall, and the whole room enlightened with candles placed in them. At one end of it

there was an enclosed place like a closet, where the
inquisitor and notary sat at a table, so that the place
seemed to him as the very mansion of death, every
thing appearing so terrible and awful. Here the inquisitor again admonished him to confess the truth,
before his torments began. When he answered he
had told the truth, the inquisitor gravely protested,
that since he was so obstinate as to suffer the torture, the Holy Office would be innocent, if he should
shed his blood, or even expire in his torments.
When he had said this, they put a linen garment
over his body, and drew it so very close on each
side, as almost squeezed him to death. When he
was almost dying, they slackened the sides of the
garment, and after he began to breathe again, the
sudden alteration put him to the most grievous
anguish and pain. When he had overcome this
torture, the same admonition was repeated, that he
would confess the truth in order to prevent further
torment. And as he persisted in his denial, they
tied his thumbs so very tight with small cords, as
made the extremities of them to swell, and caused
the blood to spurt out from under his nails. After
this, he was placed with his back against a wall, and
fixed upon a bench. Into the wall were fastened
little iron pulleys, through which there were ropes
drawn, and tied round his body, in several places,
and especially his arms and legs. The executioners,
drawing these ropes with great violence, fastened
his body with them to the wall, so that his hands
and feet, and especially his fingers and toes, being
bound so straitly with them, put him to the most

exquisite pain, and seemed to him just as though he had been dissolving in flames. In the midst of these torments the torturer, on a sudden, drew the bench from under him, so that the miserable wretch hung by the cords without anything to support him, and by the weight of his body drew the knots yet much closer. After this, a new kind of torture succeeded. There was one instrument like a small ladder, made of two upright pieces of wood, and five cross ones sharpened before. This the torturer placed over against him, and by a certain proper motion struck it with great violence against both his shins, so that he received upon each of them at once five violent strokes, which put him to such intolerable anguish that he fainted away. After he came to himself, they inflicted upon him the last torture. The torturer tied ropes about the wrists of Orobio, and then put the ropes about his own back, which was covered with leather to prevent his hurting himself. Then falling backwards, and putting his feet up against the wall, he drew them with all his might, till they cut through Orobio's flesh, even to the very bones; and this torture was repeated thrice, the ropes being tied about the distance of two fingers' breadth from the former wound, and drawn with the same violence. But it happened, that as the ropes were drawing the second time, they slid into the first wound, which caused so great an effusion of blood that he seemed to be dying. Upon this the physician and surgeon, who are always ready, were sent for out of a neighbouring apartment, to ask their advice, if the torture could be continued without danger of death, lest the ecclesiastical judges should be guilty of an irregularity if the criminal should die in his torments. They, who were far from being enemies to Orobio, answered, that he had strength enough to endure the rest of the torture; and hereby preserved him from having the tortures that he had already endured, repeated on him; because his sentence was, that he should suffer them all at one time, one after another, so that, if at any time they are forced to leave off through fear of death, all the tortures that have already been suffered must be successively inflicted, to satisfy the sentence of the inquisitors. Upon this decision of the physician, the torture was repeated the third time, and then ended. After this he was bound up in his own clothes, and carried back to his prison; and he was scarcely healed of his wounds in seventy days. And inasmuch as he made no confession under his torture, he was condemned, not as one convicted, but suspected of Judaism, to wear, for two whole years, the infamous habit called *San-benito*, and after that term to perpetual banishment from the kingdom of Seville. On regaining his liberty he settled at Amsterdam, professed himself a Jew, and was circumcised, taking the name of Isaac, and died A.D. 1687."

3. Count D'Olavides. — Don Paul, Count d'Olavides, was an extraordinary person. He undertook the fertilising Sierra Morena, or the Black Mountain, on which he planted colonies of Germans. These being Protestants, he was apprehended as a heretic, A.D. 1776. Limborch says,

"The victim which marks this period was the celebrated Olavides, whose arrest suspended the progress of colonisation in the Sierra Morena. This incident was derived from the same causes which contributed to the removal of his protector (d'Aranda). With a similar spirit of free-thinking, which he imbibed from the fashionable philosophers of the day, he was equally offended by the obstacles which he experienced in his beneficial designs, from the prejudices and institutions of Spain. As most of the colonists were Protestants, he resisted all endeavours for their conversion, and opposed the attempt to enforce their attendance on the rites of the Catholic worship. Having established a law to permit no monks in the vicinity of the settlement, he obtained an order for the removal of a convent, and built his own house on the site. He frequently indulged himself in expressions of ridicule against the idleness and licentiousness of the monks, and spoke with too great freedom of the depopulation and other mischiefs occasioned by the celibacy of the clergy.

"Olavides' imprudence awakened the jealousy of the Spanish church. His conduct was closely scrutinised; his works and actions were noted and exaggerated; and a formal accusation was preferred against him for heresy, before that tribunal which is considered as the bulwark of religion. The removal of his protector gave full scope to the machinations of his enemies. He was summoned to Madrid, under the pretence of rendering an account of the establishment under his care. Apprised of his danger, he made some ineffectual attempts to obtain the royal protection, and to soothe the guardians of the faith; but after a residence of a twelvemonth in the capital, he was suddenly arrested, and conveyed to the prisons of the Inquisition; his papers were seized, and his effects sequestrated." After two years of impenetrable seclusion, his process was closed, and his sentence was publicly announced. We give an account of this ceremony in the words of an eye-witness :—

"The *autos da fé* are still celebrated at the tribunal of the Inquisition, with more or less publicity, according to the impressions intended to be made. A great number of persons, of all ranks, civil, military, and ecclesiastical, were invited, I should rather say summoned, to attend at the Holy Office, at eight o'clock in the morning, on the 24th of the last month. They were all totally ignorant of the reason of their being called on. After waiting some time, in an apartment destined for their reception, they were admitted to the tribunal—a long, darkish room, with the windows near the ceiling, and furnished with a crucifix, under a black canopy; a table, with two chairs for the inquisitors; a stool for the prisoner; two chairs for his guards; and benches for the spectators. The familiars of the Inquisition, Abrantes, Mora, and others, grandees of Spain, attended as servants, without hats or swords.

"Olavides soon appeared, attended by his brothers in black, his looks quite cast down, his hands closed together, and holding a green taper. His dress was an olive-coloured coat, white canvas breeches, and thread stockings, and his hair was combed back into a bag. He was seated on the stool prepared for him. The secretaries then read, during three hours, the accustomed accusations and proceedings against him. They consisted of above one hundred articles, such as his possession of free books, loose pictures, letters of recommendation from Voltaire, his having neglected some external duties of devotion, uttering hasty expressions, his inattention to images, together with every particular of his life, birth, and education, were all noted. It concluded with declaring him guilty of heresy. At that moment he fainted away, but was brought to the recovery of his senses, that he might hear the sentence pronounced against him. It was no less than this:—Deprivation of all his offices, incapacity of holding any hereafter, or of receiving any royal favour, confiscation of his property, banishment to thirty leagues from Madrid, from all places of royal residence, from Seville, the new colony, and Lima, the place of his birth; prohibition from riding on horseback, or wearing gold, silver, or silk; and eight years' confinement and monastic discipline in a convent. From respect to St. Jago, his wearing the cross of that order was not mentioned, and he was excused from putting on the *San-benito*.

"The sentence being read, he was led to the table, where, on his knees, he recanted his errors, and acknowledged his implicit belief in the articles of the Roman Catholic faith. Four priests in surplices, and with wands in their hands, then came in. They repeatedly laid their wands across his shoulders while a *Miserére* was sung. He then withdrew from the inquisition.

"However rigorous this punishment may appear, yet it is mild when compared with the severity with which the Inquisition formerly visited similar offences. Nothing less than the personal inter- ference of the monarch himself, and the clemency of the grand-inquisitor, could probably have pre- vented a repetition of those dreadful scenes which have rendered this formidable tribunal an object of universal horror; for the confessor, and many of the subordinate members, insisted on the necessity of an *auto da fé*, in which Olavides would have been infallibly committed to the flames."

Olavides made his escape from the convent in which he had been confined, and retired to France. There he wrote a book, entitled, "The Gospel Triumphant; or, the Converted Philosopher," for which he obtained pardon and permission to return to Spain.

4. SUFFERINGS OF A BEATA.—*Beatas*, or *blessed females*, are devotees in the Romish church. One of this class, a lady of extraordinary piety and courage, perished at the stake of the Inquisition in Seville, about the year 1780. She had adopted the principles of Michael de Molinos, a Romish priest, of a noble family in Spain, founder of the *Quietists*. They placed religion in spiritual feeling, in opposi- tion to ceremonies, deducing his principles from the Scriptures. Molinos having published a book, entitled "Spiritual Guide," at Rome, A.D. 1675, he

was imprisoned in the Inquisition, condemned as a heretic, and died under torture.

In a " Letter to the Spanish Inquisition," about 1810, the writer says of this lady :—" The confinement of the Beata lasted three or four years, during which time there was scarcely a graduate of any order, who did not, in turn, undertake the conversion of the heretic. The assessors to the inquisitors exhausted the syllogistic art, but hardened as she was, she would not yield to their powerful arguments and authorities. The poor wretch was not aware of her danger in not being convinced, and the cause was drawing towards a conclusion. This arrived, and she insisted in arguing. The tribunal declared her an obstinate heretic, and appointed a time for the *auto da fé*. Scarce an inhabitant of Seville but went to see this solemn act. It lasted from the early part of the morning until night. The criminal was conducted, gagged, and mounted on an ass, in the midst of divines, who endeavoured to subdue her obstinacy by new arguments, and vie with the multitude in stunning her with repeated shouts of *Viva la fé* (long live the faith). Her cause was read from the pulpit, in the principal church of the Dominicans, intermixed with obscenities expressed in the grossest terms. Nothing now remained but to deliver her up to the secular judge, that she might be punished with death. A retraction, previous to this act, might have saved her life, but the unfortunate fanatic persisted in not making it, and was delivered up. The approaching punishment, and depression of spirits, occasioned by the

fatigues of the day, made her desist from her obstinacy when it was too late. She was converted, to
the satisfaction of the monks who were present;
but the punishment could not even be deferred.
She alone obtained as a favour to be burnt after
death; and was *strangled* in the evening, amidst the
tears of all devout souls, who admired the pious
artifice by which this opportunity was taken of
sending her to heaven, to prevent her falling again
into heresy."

"You will have no difficulty," says the writer,
"in persuading yourself, that this happened only
thirty years ago. But remember, that the same
laws now exist in all their force, and that it is scarce
a year since the famous *Quemadero*, [the pile on
which criminals are burnt,] where this scene was
represented, was destroyed at Seville, because it
stood in the way of the fortifications which were
erecting against the French. A *Quemadero*, on
which many thousands have perished, and which,
doubtless owing to the frequent call for it, was constructed of solid materials, unlike other scaffolds,
which are erected merely as occasion requires.
Imagine to yourself that the greater part of the
people are still disposed to look quietly on the
repetition of such scenes; and tell me then, whether
the Inquisition can be viewed in the light in which
you place it?

"The time has gone by, it is true, when these
scenes were exhibited daily; when the victims
groaned in subterraneous dungeons, and made the
hall of the tribunal resound at night with the cries

which torture wrung from them; the time has passed, though not long since. It has passed, though it depends on the will of three men to restore it. It has passed:—then why all this declamation? Leave this question to those, who, forced by the circumstances of the times to conceal their inclinations and their opinions, clothe themselves in sheep-skins, anxiously awaiting the day when they may wreak their vengeance on those who have constrained them to show a mildness and forbearance. You strangers, who have lately visited Spain, have no means of forming a correct idea of the slow and endless oppression which this tribunal occasions, even in its actual state of slumber."

5. JOSEPH DA COSTA, PEREIRA FURTADO DE MENDONIA.—Da Costa was a native of *Colonia da Sacramenta*, on the river La Plata; but he suffered from the Inquisition in Portugal. In his "Narrative," he says, "Three or four days had elapsed, after my arrival at Lisbon from England, in July, 1802, when a magistrate abruptly entered my apartments, and telling me who he was, informed me that he had orders to seize all my papers, and to conduct me to prison, where I was to be rigorously kept aloof from all communication. I doubted whether he were the person he represented himself to be, not only on account of his unpolished manners, but also because he had neither his official staff, nor any other sign of power; and though I knew that this was an error of essential consequence in a magistrate, that it justified me in impugning his authority, and considering him as a mere intruder

upon the sacred asylum of my abode, I invited him civilly to sit down, and entreated that he would show me the order he pretended to possess, or tell me by whose authority it had been issued. He then showed me a letter from the intendant-general of police, which directed my imprisonment, the seizure of my papers, and that endeavours should be made to find, upon or about me, some masonical decorations. The motive of this proceeding, as stated in the *order*, was, that I had been to England without a previous passport.

" When I had read this fatal note, all the sorrowful consequences of an imprisonment rushed upon my mind, sensible that the fury of my persecutor would know no limits. I had sufficient coolness, however, to represent to this myrmidon of justice, that the harsh treatment of the intendant-general, without having any previous information of my case, was not a little surprising, since, so far from having gone to England without a passport, I had previously procured one from his Royal Highness the Prince Regard, which leave I had solicited, in consequence of being employed in the royal service as one of the literary directors of the royal printing-office, and my not deeming it proper to leave the kingdom without my sovereign's permission; that I had not only obtained leave of absence, in writing, from the secretary of state's office, and procured a formal passport from the minister of foreign affairs, but that the minister of finance had charged me, by the sovereign's command, to transact some business relative to the royal service in London;

and that, in proof of this, I could show him the official letters, some of which were directed to me in Lisbon, before my departure, and others were forwarded to London after my arrival in that city. I pleaded, therefore, my right to expect that the intendant-general of police should have been informed of all this, before he proceeded against me with such severity, or alleged, as a cause of his proceedings against me, that I had gone to England without a passport.

"The corregidor, willing to show me that there had been no precipitation in his way of proceeding, accused me of rashness for thinking that so excellent a magistrate as the intendant-general, whose probity was equal to his knowledge and learning, would have proceeded in a case of such importance without mature deliberation; and he showed me another letter. In this he was ordered by the intendant of police to take care of every thing that I might have brought from England belonging to the royal service, such as a collection of books I had purchased for the public library of Lisbon, some instruments directed to be made in England, and some books and other things belonging to the royal printing-office.

"The reading of this second letter produced in me sentiments at variance with those which I had entertained of the first; for, if the idea of the misfortunes I was about to suffer had impressed my mind with a natural dejection, I now reflected on the meanness of the souls that could prescribe orders so manifestly contradictory. This reflection

P

inspired me with such a contempt for the orders, and for those who had sanctioned and were to carry them into execution, that the recollection of it proved no small consolation to me during my troubles.

" Enclosed, then, in a solitary cell, in the prison called Limoeiro, without any other company than that of sorrowful thoughts, labouring under uncertainty as to my fate, and sustaining every possible inconvenience attendant on such prisons, I remained for eight days ; until one night the gaoler came to my dungeon, and told me that he had orders to take me before the corregidor, my judge, who wished to proceed in the necessary interrogatories, preparatory to my trial. I appeared before the judge, in a small room of the gaol; when I requested him to order that I should be released from my solitary confinement. He stated, that the intendant-general of police was in the habit of detaining his prisoners in solitary confinement for days, months, and years—indeed, so long as he thought convenient ; and that the magistrates were left to their own discretion, with unlimited powers to investigate crimes, and to bring the culprits to punishment.

" Six months had I passed in solitary confinement, when one night the gaoler came to the cell, accompanied by four or six men. This mysterious and absurd way of proceeding rendered it apparent to me that I was going to the prison of the Inquisition ; an event which I had long anticipated. I was taken in chains to a carriage, where I found a silent companion ; and being surrounded by con-

stables, officers of the Inquisition, who walked by
the side of the carriage, I was conveyed to St.
Anton Gate. There, to prevent any person from
guessing my destination, I was ordered to alight,
and led through an alley, to the gate of the palace
of the Inquisition, which communicates with the
prison. I was then conveyed to a room, where
they entered my name in the books, made an
inventory of the few clothes I had, and asked me
if I had any knife, razor, or scissors, or any other
instrument; also, if I had any gold, silver, or
jewels; and, on their saying that they would rely
on my word in this respect, I produced some pieces
of gold coin, most stupidly relying on their asser-
tion; but as soon as they obtained this, and found
that I had nothing else to produce, they began
the most scrupulous search over every part of my
body.

"The gaoler, who for greater dignity has the
name of *alcaide*, that is, keeper of the castle,
addressed to me almost a little sermon, recommending me to behave in this respectable house
with great propriety; stating also, that I must not
make any noise in my room, nor speak loud, lest
the other prisoners might happen to be in the
neighbouring cells and hear me, with other similar
instructions. He then took me to my cell, a small
room, 12 feet by 8, with a door to the passage: in
this door were two iron grates, far from each other,
and occupying the thickness of the wall, which was
three feet, and outside of these grates there was,
besides, a wooden door; in the upper part of this

P 2

was an aperture that let into the cell a borrowed
light from the passage, which passage received its
light from the windows fronting a narrow yard, but
having opposite, at a very short distance, very high
walls. In this small room were a kind of wood
frame without feet, whereon lay a straw mattress,
which was to be my bed; a small water-pot; and
another utensil for various purposes, which was
emptied only once every eight days, when I went to
mass in the prisoners' private chapel. This was
the only opportunity I had of taking fresh air
during such a period; and they contrived seven
divisions in the chapel in such a manner that the
prisoners could never see each other, or know how
many were granted the favour of going to mass.
The cell was arched above, and the floor was brick,
the wall being formed of stone, and very thick.
The place was consequently very cold in winter,
and so damp, that very frequently the grates were
covered with drops of water like dew; and my
clothes, during the winter, were in a state of perpetual moisture. Such was my abode for the period
of nearly three years!

"The day following my entrance into these
prisons, the gaoler came at nine o'clock, with
another turnkey, and said that I must accompany
him to the hearing of my case by the lord-inquisitor,
appointed by the holy tribunal to be my judge, and
what they call reporter of the cause, who happened
to be the first inquisitor and president of the small
board, Manoel Stanislao Fragoso. The affability
with which this priest treated me, when I first

spoke to him, knew no abatement during the time
of my imprisonment, except in one or two instances,
when his temper was ruffled.

"I must acknowledge, as a warning to others,
that my childish credulity, in entertaining the hope
of finding in the Holy Office meekness, clemency,
or despatch in my trial, had no other ground, except
the popular rumour in every corner of Portugal,
that the Holy Office is very much altered, and does
not now practise those cruelties which it before
committed. The inquisitor was in the audience
room, with another priest, who acted as clerk, or,
as they call it, notary, and he commenced the
interrogatories, first, by inquiring my name, parent-
age, and place of birth; next, if the familiar, who
brought me to the prisons of the Holy Office, had
done me any violence; or if I knew the cause that
had subjected me to the notice of the Inquisition.
He then observed to me, that I was before the
most just and merciful tribunal on earth; but to
obtain its mercy and pardon for my crimes, it was
necessary that I should, of my own free will and
accord, confess all crimes of which I had been
guilty, without concealing my accomplices, frauds,
or any other circumstances, and that this confession must be immediate; because the present time
was the most favourable moment a prisoner in the
Inquisition could have—for, should I confess afterwards what I might deny in the beginning, the
lenity of the tribunal would be very different.

"I replied to the inquisitor, that having been
first imprisoned by the police, on the ground of

having gone to England without passports, although
I was not interrogated about this subject, but only
with respect to my having entered into the order of
freemasonry, I was led to conjecture that my being
a freemason was the cause of my trial by the Inquisition. If, indeed, this was the crime of which I
was accused, I was disposed to confess it, not only
because it was true that I was a freemason, but
with a view that I might obtain the mercy he, the
inquisitor, had promised me; but if I was mistaken
in my conjecture, and the crime I was accused of
was different, I begged that its nature might be
disclosed to me, and I would reply to the accusation as should be necessary. The inquisitor replied,
that he could do no otherwise than praise my laud-
able resolution to confess my crimes; but it was
his duty again to admonish me (and he said this
with a great deal of apparent charity), that I ought
to examine my conscience thoroughly, and not leave
anything untold of all that I had done in any
period of my life; that I had committed crimes
whose cognisance belonged to that holy tribunal,
and that I was accused of them, and informed
against on that account; that I should remember
his recommendation, that to confess my crimes was
highly important to the clearing of my conscience,
to the salvation of my soul, and to the successful
issue of my cause; and that he, to do me a favour,
would send me back to my solitary prison, that I
might have time to examine my conscience. I told
him, that the greatest possible favour he could confer upon me was that of accelerating my cause; for

having been more than six months in prison without
being allowed to communicate with any one, my
health was so seriously injured, that all I wished
was to have a sentence, in order to get free from
my painful situation and suspense; and, however
rigorous that sentence might be, it would always
be preferable, in my estimation, to being in a solitary prison, under circumstances that could only
lead to an inevitable ruin, which was the more to
be feared, as I was literally dying by inches in slow
torments.

"I was then immediately remanded to my prison;
and the gaoler came to inform me that the goodness
of the lords inquisitors extended so far as to order
that I should have, besides the ordinary allowance,
some coffee for breakfast, and, in consideration of
the state of my health, a daily allowance of wine.
The ordinary allowance he spake of was half a pound
of boiled meat—the bones enter into the weight of
this half pound, and, on some days, this allowance
is very scanty—a few spoonfuls of rice, a cup of
gravy, and some bread. The only persons who are
allowed to have any access to the prisoner, or who
can see and speak to him, are the gaoler, and four
guards, called the 'faithful of the prisoner,' who
convey the prisoner backwards and forwards to the
audiences, and are at the same time the executioners who administer the tortures. These guards
also wait upon the prisoners, and bring them what
they want,—such as food, water, &c. But it is
necessary to observe here, that these guards are,
properly speaking, spies set upon the prisoner, to

observe everything in the prisons, and to relate it to the inquisitors, not only what they can gain by listening to the conversation of the prisoners, but also what they can see through small holes they make in the ceiling, just at the corners of the cells."

Da Costa was kept thus in prison for three years, during which period he was tormented by repeated examinations, without sentence being passed upon him. Finding his health decline, he formed the desperate resolution of attempting his escape from prison; and, happily, he succeeded, and at length reached England. The relation of his sufferings in the Inquisition occasioned his friends to request his giving an account of them to the public; and, therefore, he published in London the "Narrative of his Persecutions," in 1811.

CHAPTER XVII.

BRITISH VICTIMS OF THE INQUISITION.

William Lithgow—Elizabeth Vasconellos—John Coustos—Mr. Bower.

SPANISH and Portuguese bigotry could not be satisfied with the sacrifice of native subjects. The vengeance of the Inquisition had been wreaked on the helpless of other nations, whom Providence,

from time to time, brought within its grasp.
To prevent their sufferings had not always been
in the power of foreign governments; and even
British subjects have been sufferers by this horrid
court. The terror of the name of Oliver Cromwell,
the Lord Protector of England, compelled the
inquisitors to liberate and to honour the English
consul, Thomas Maynard. (See Chapter XI.) But
how many have been tortured and murdered in the
concealment of the Inquisition cannot be ascertained
by us before the day of judgment. A few cases of
such sufferers may, however, be given, still further to
illustrate the intolerance and cruelty of the papacy.

1. WILLIAM LITHGOW.—William Lithgow was
a gentleman of Scotland, and while travelling on
foot over Europe he came to Malaga, in Spain, in the
year 1620, when he was apprehended as a spy connected with the English fleet then in that port. His
cruel treatment by the governor and his sufferings
in the Inquisition will best appear from his own
words, as follows:—

"Upon the knowledge that I was secretly to be
incarcerate in the governor's palace, entered the
Mr. Sergeant and begged my money, and license to
search it; and liberty granted, he found in my
pockets eleven phillipoes or ducatoons; and then
unclothing me before their eyes, even to my shirt,
and searching my breeches, he found in my doublet-
neck, fast shut between two canvasses, a hundred
and thirty-seven double pieces of gold. Whereat
the corregidor arose, and counting my gold, being
five hundred and forty-eight ducats, he said to the

sergeant, ' Clothe him again, and enclose him there
in the cabinet till after supper.' Meanwhile, the
sergeant got the eleven ducatoons of silver; and
my gold, which was to take me to Ethiopia, the
governor seized upon; giving afterwards two hundred crowns of it to supply the new foundation of a
Capuchin monastery there, reserving the rest, being
three hundred and forty-eight ducats, for his own
avaricious ends.

"This done, and midnight come, the sergeant
and two Turkish slaves, releasing me from the
inferior room, brought me through certain ascending
passages to a chamber right above his summer
kitchen ; where, and then, the sergeants and the
two slaves thrust on every ancle a heavy bolt, my
legs being put to a full stride, by a strong gad of
iron, far above a yard long ; upon the ends of which
the two bolts depended that were fastened about
my legs; insomuch that I could never sit up, nor
walk, nor stand, nor turn me, but lay continually
on my back, the two irons being thrice heavier than
my body. They left me with solacious words, and
straight returned with victuals, being a pound of
boiled mutton, a wheat bread, and a small pint of
wine, which was the first, the best, and the last of
this kind that ever I got in that woeful mansion.
The sergeant leaving me, never seeing him more till
a more unwelcome sight, he directed the slaves that
after I had contented my discontented appetite,
they should lock the door and carry the keys to
Areta, a Spaniard, and keeper of the silver plate.
The day following, the governor entered my prison

alone, entreating me to confess that I was a spy,
and he would be my friend, and procure my pardon;
neither in the meantime should I lack any needful
thing. But I still attesting my innocence, he wrath-
fully swore that I should see his face no more till
grievous torments should make me do it; and leaving
me in a rage he observed too well his condition.

"But withal, in my hearing, he commanded
Areta that none should come near me, except the
slave, nor any food be given me but three ounces of
musted brown bread every second day, and a fuleto,
or English pint of water, neither any bed, pillow, or
coverlet to be allowed me. 'And close up,' said he,
'this window in his room, with lime and stone;
stop the holes of the doors with double mats,
hanging another lock on it; and to withdraw visible
and sensible comfort from him, let no tongue nor
feet be heard near him till I have my designs
accomplished. And thou, Hazier, I charge thee, at
thy incomings to have no conference with him, nor at
thy outgoings abroad to discover him to the English
factors, as thou wilt answer upon thy life, and the
highest tortures that can be devised.' These directions delivered, and, alas! too accessory to me in
the performance, my room was made a dark drawn
dungeon, my body the anatomy of merciless hunger,
my comfortless hearing the receptacle of sounding
bells, my eye wanting light, a loathsome languishing
in despair, and my ground-lying body the woeful
mirror of misfortunes, every hour wishing another's
coming, every day the night, and every night the
morning. My body grew weak and infirm, insomuch

that the governor, after his answers received from
Madrid, made haste to put in execution his bloody
and merciless purpose before Christmas holyday;
lest, ere the expiring of the twelfth day, I should
be utterly famished, and unable to undergo my
trial without present perishing. By God's permission, the forty-seventh day after my first imprisonment, and five days before Christmas, about
two o'clock in the morning, I heard the noise of a
coach in the street; within a while I heard the locks
of my prison door opening; whereupon, bequeathing
my soul to God, I humbly implored his gracious mercy
and pardon for my sins; for neither in the former
night, nor in this, could I get any sleep, such was
the force of my gnawing hunger, and the portending
heaviness of my presaging soul.

"Meanwhile, nine sergeants, accompanied with
the scrivan, entered the room without speaking, and
carrying me thence, they laid me on my back in the
coach, where two of them sat beside me. Baptista,
the coachman, an Indian negro, arriving, I was
brought westward, almost a league from the town,
to a vine-press house, standing alone, where they
enclosed me in the room till daylight; for hither the
rack had been brought the night before. All this
secrecy was used, that neither English, French, or
Flemings, should see or get any knowledge of my
trial, my grievous tortures, and dreadful despatch.
At the break of day the governor, Don Francisco,
and the alcaide came, and I, invited to their presence,
pleaded for an interpreter, the which they absolutely
refused; neither would they suffer or grant me an

appellation to Madrid. After new examinations from morning till dark night, finding my first and second confessions run into one, the governor swore, 'Is it possible he can, in such distress, and so long a time, observe, so strictly, in every manner, the points of his first confession?'

"The governor's interrogation and my confession being mutually subscribed, he and Don Francisco besought me earnestly to confess my guiltiness in time, saying, 'Thou art as yet in my power, and I may spare or pardon thee, providing thou wilt confess thyself a spy, and a traitor against our nation.' But finding me stand fast to the mark of my spotless innocency, he, invective and malicious he, after many tremendous threatenings, commanded the scrivan to draw up a warrant for the chief-justice; which being done, he set his hand to it, and, taking me by the hand, delivered me and the warrant into the alcaide-major's hands, to be tortured, broken, and cruelly tormented. Whence being carried along to the end of a stone gallery, where the rack was placed, the encarnador, or tormentor, began to disburden me of my irons, which he could not unloose for a long time, whereat the chief-justice being offended, the malicious villain struck away above an inch of my heel with the bolt; whereupon I grievously groaning, being exceeding faint, and without my three ounces of bread and a little water for three days together, the alcaide said, 'O, traitor, all this is nothing, but the earnest of a greater bargain you have in hand!'

"After this, the alcaide and scrivan, being both

chair-set, the one to examine, the other to write
down my confession and tortures, I was stripped
to the skin, brought to the rack, and mounted to
the top of it; where, soon after, I was hung by
the bare shoulders, with two small cords, which
went under my arms, running on two rings of iron
that were fixed to the wall above my head. Then
being hoisted to the appointed height, the tormentor
descended below, and, drawing my legs through
the two sides of the three-planked rack, he tied a
cord about each of my ancles; and then ascending
upon the rack, he drew the cord upward, and
bending forward with main force my two knees
against the two planks, the sinews of my two hams
burst asunder, and the lids of my knees being
crushed, and the cords made fast, I hung so for a
large hour. At last, the encarnador informing the
governor that I had the mark of Jerusalem on my
right arm, joined with the name and crown of King
James, and done upon the holy grave, the corregidor gave direction to tear asunder the name and
crown, as he said, of that heretic king, and arch
enemy of the holy Catholic church. Then the tormentor, laying the right arm above the left, and
the crown upmost, did cast a cord over both arms,
seven distinct times; and then lying down upon his
back, and setting both his feet upon my hollow
pinched belly, he charged and drew violently with
his hands, making my womb support the force of
his feet, till the several cords combined in one place
of my arm; and cutting the crown, sinews, and
flesh to the bare bones, did pull in my fingers close

to the palm of my hands; the left hand of which is lame so still, and will be for ever.

"Now mine eyes began to startle, my mouth to foam and froth, and my teeth to chatter like to the doubling of drumsticks. O strange inhumanity of monster men-manglers! surpassing the limits of their national law; threescore tortures being the trial of treason, which I had, and was to endure; yet thus to inflict a sevenfold surplusage of more intolerable cruelties; and, notwithstanding of my shivering lips in this fiery passion, my vehement groaning, and blood springing forth from my arms, broke sinews, hams, and knees, yea, and my depending weight on flesh-cutting cords, yet they struck me on the face with cudgels, to abate and cease the thundering noise of my wrestling voice. At last, being loosed from these pinnacles of pain, I was, handfast, set on the floor, with this their imploration, 'Confess, confess, confess in time, for thine inevitable ensue;' when, finding nothing from me but still innocent, 'O, I am innocent; O Jesus! the Lamb of God, have mercy upon me, and strengthen me with patience to undergo this barbarous murder.'

"Then, by command of the justice, was my trembling body laid above and long, upon the face of the rack, with my head downward, inclosed within a circled hole, my belly upward toward the top of the rack; my legs and arms being drawn asunder, were fastened with pins and cords to both sides of the outward planks, for now was I to receive my greatest torments.

"Now, the alcaide giving commission, the executioner laid fast a cord over the calf of my leg, then another in the middle of my thigh; and the third cord over the great part of my arm, which was severally done on both sides of my body, receiving the ends of the cords from the six several places, through the holes made in the outward planks, which were fastened to pins, and the pins made fast with a device: for he was to charge on the outside of the planks with as many pins as there were holes and cords, the cords being first laid next to my skin; and on every one of these six parts of my body I was to receive seven several tortures, each torture consisting of three winding throws of every pin, which amounted to twenty-one throws in every one of those six parts. Then the tormentor, carrying a pot full of water, in the bottom whereof was a hole, stopped by his thumb till it came to my mouth, he did pour it into my belly; the measure being an English pottle. The first and second services I gladly received, such was the scorching drought of my tormenting pain, and I had drunk none for three days before. But at the third charge, perceiving these measures of water to be inflicted upon me as tortures, I closed my mouth; whereat, the alcaide, enraged, set my teeth asunder with a pair of iron cadges, whereupon my hunger-charged belly waxing great, grew drum-like; for it being a suffocating pain, in regard of my head hanging downward, and the water re-ingorging itself in my throat with a struggling force, it strangled and swallowed up my breath from yowling and groaning.

"Between each one of these seven circular charges I was always re-examined half an hour; each half hour a hell of infernal pain; and between each torment a long distance of life-quelling time. Thus lay I six hours upon the rack, between four o'clock in the afternoon and ten o'clock at night, having had inflicted upon me threescore and seven torments. Nevertheless, they continued me a large half hour, after all my torture, at the full bending, my body being all begored with blood, and cut through, in every part, to the crushed and bruised bones; I pitifully roaring, howling, foaming, and gnashing my teeth, with insupportable cries, before the pains were undone and my body loosed. True it is, it passeth the capacity of man either sensibly to conceive, or I patiently to express, the intolerable anxiety of mind and affliction of body, in that dreadful time I sustained. At last, my head being by their arms advanced, and my body taken from the rack, the water regushed abundantly from my mouth; then they, reclothing my broken, bloody, cold, and trembling body, being all this time stark naked, I fell twice in a sounding trance; which they again refreshed with a little wine, and two warm eggs—not done out of charity, but that I should be reserved for further punishment; and if it were not well known that these sufferings are true, it would almost seem incredible to many, that a man, being brought so low with starving hunger and extreme cruelties, could have subsisted any longer, reserving life.

"And now, at last, they charged my broken legs

Q

with my former eye-frighting irons, and carried me
to the coach, being after brought secretly to my
former dungeon, without any knowledge of the
town, save to my lawless and merciless tormentors.
I was laid, with my head and heels alike high, on
my former stones. The latter end of this woeful
night, poor mourning Hazier, the Turk, was sent to
keep me; and on the morrow the governor entered
my room, threatening me with still more tortures,
to confess; and so he caused every morning, to
make me believe I was going to be racked again,
to make me confess an untruth; and thus they
continued every day of five days to Christmas.

"Upon Christmas-day, Marina, the ladies' gen-
tlewoman, got permission to visit me, and with
her licence she brought abundance of tears, presenting me also with a dish of honey, sugar, some
confections, and raisins in great plenty, to my no
small comfort, besides using many sweet speeches,
for consolation's sake. The twelfth day of Christmas expired, they began to threaten me on still
with more tortures, even till Candlemas. In all
which comfortless time I was miserably afflicted
with the beastly plague of gnawing vermin, which
lay crawling in lumps, within, without, and about
my body; yea, hanging in clusters about my beard,
my lips, my nostrils, and my eye-brows, almost
inclosing my sight. And for my greater satisfaction to their merciless minds, the governor called
Areta, his silver-plate keeper, to gather and sweep
the vermin upon me twice in eight days, which
tormented me almost to death, being a perpetual

punishment; yet the poor infidel, some few times, and when opportunity served, would steal the keys from Areta, and about midnight would enter my room, with sticks and burning oil, and sweeping them together in heaps, would burn the greatest part, to my great release; or, doubtless, I had been miserably eaten up and devoured by them."

Cruelty more diabolical it appears difficult to imagine, than that exercised upon this unhappy Scotchman. Yet he was preserved for still greater suffering. For being now in the power of the inquisitors, they pretended to be anxious for his soul's salvation; and therefore they implored him to be converted to the Roman Catholic faith, that he might escape condemnation to the flames as a heretic. When the inquisitor interrogated him as to his difficulties, errors, and misbelief, Lithgow replied, like a North Briton taught by the Bible, that "he was confident in the promises of our Saviour, believing the revealed doctrines of the Gospel, professed by the reformed Catholic church; that these being confirmed by grace, he possessed an infallible assurance in his own soul of the true word of Christ." "To these words," as Lithgow observes, "he answered, 'Thou art no Christian, but an absurd heretic, and, without conversion, a member of perdition.' Whereupon I replied, 'Reverend Sir, the nature of charity and religion does not consist in opprobrious speeches: wherefore, if you would convert me, as you say, convince me by argument; if not, all your threatenings of fire, death, or torments, shall not make me shrink from

the truth of God's word in Sacred Scriptures.'
Whereupon the mad inquisitor clapt me on the
face with his foot, abusing me with many railings;
and if the Jesuits had not intercepted him, he had
stabbed me with a knife; where, when dismissed, I
never saw him more."

Lithgow was as little affected by another interview with an inquisitor; he made no confession,
and he was sentenced to be again tortured. He says,
therefore, "I was condemned to receive that night
eleven strangling torments in my dungeon; and
then, after Easter holidays, I should be transported
privately to Granada, and there, about midnight, to
be burnt, body and bones, into ashes, and my ashes
to be flung into the air. Well, that same night,
the scrivan, sergeants, and the young English
priest entered my melancholy prison, where the
priest, in the English tongue, urging me all he
could, though little it was he could do, and not
prevailing, I was disburdened of mine irons, un-
clothed to my skin, set on my knees, and held up
fast with their hands; where, instantly setting my
teeth asunder with iron cadges, they filled my belly
full of water, even gorging to my throat; then with
a garter they bound fast my throat, till the white of
mine eye turned upward; and being laid on my side,
I was tumbled by two sergeants to and fro seven
times through the room, till I was almost strangled.
This done, they fastened a small cord about each of
my great toes, and hoisting me therewith to the
roof of a high loft (for the cords ran in two rings
fastened above), they cut the garter, and there I

hung, with my head downward, in my tormented weight, till all the gushing water dissolved. This done, I was let down from the loft, quite senseless, lying a long time cold dead among their hands; whereof the governor being informed, came running up stairs, crying, 'Is he dead? O fie, villains, go fetch me wine!' which they poured in my mouth, regaining thereby a slender spark of breath.

"These strangling torments closed, and I re-clothed and fast bolted again, they left me lying on the cold floor, praising my God, and singing of a psalm. The next morning, the pitiful Turk visiting me with bread and water, brought me also secretly, in his shirt sleeve, two handfuls of raisins and figs, laying them on the floor, amongst the crawling vermin; for having no use of arms, I was constrained by hunger and impotency of time to lick one up with another with my tongue. This charity of figs the slave did once every week or fortnight, or else I had long or then famished."

Mr. Lithgow's case became known, by some means, to the English factors at Malaga; and they, therefore, at once united with the consul in an application to the king and council of Spain. Their petition was granted, and the release of the wretched prisoner was ordered, in a warrant to the governor. His generous friends received the injured confessor, treated him with kindness, and procured for him a passage to England in a ship-of-war, in 1621. His case being made known at court, he was visited by many of the nobility, and by King James I., who commanded him to be sent to the Spanish ambassador, then in London. That grandee promised that restitution should be made to him of the money and valuables that had been taken from him at Malaga, and compensation for the injuries that he had sustained in prison. These assurances were not, however, honoured; and Mr. Lithgow, reproaching the ambassador with having deceived him, and, as some say, striking him, under the provocation, he was imprisoned for some months in the Marshalsea, London.

2. ELIZABETH VASCONELLOS.—This lady, having been released from the Inquisition at Lisbon, made the following deposition, in December, 1706 :—

"Elizabeth Vasconellos, now in the city of Lisbon, doth on the 10th day of December, Anno 1706, in the presence of John Milner Esq., her majesty's consul-general of Portugal, and Joseph Willcocks, minister of the English factory at Lisbon, declare and testify,

"That she was born at Arlington, in the county of Devon, and a daughter of John Chester, Esq., bred up in the church of England; and in the eleventh year of her age, her uncle, David Morgan, of Cork, intending to go and settle in Jamaica, as a physician, by her father's consent, he having several children, took her with him to provide for her.

"In 1685, they went in an English ship, and near the island they were attacked by two Turkish ships; in the fight her uncle was killed, but the ship got clear into Madeira, and she, though left destitute, was entertained by Mr. Bedford, a merchant, with whom, and other English, she lived as a servant till 1696. In that year she was married, by the chaplain of an English man-of-war, to Cordoza Vasconellos, a physician of that island, and lived with him eight years, and never in the least conformed to the Romish church.

"In 1704, her husband being gone on a voyage to Brazil, she fell dangerously ill, and, being lightheaded, a priest gave her the sacrament, as she was told afterwards, for she remembered nothing of it. It pleased God she recovered, and then they told her she had changed her religion, and must conform to the Romish church, which she denied, and refused to conform; and thereupon, by the bishop of that island, she was imprisoned nine months, and then sent prisoner to the Inquisition at Lisbon, where she arrived the 19th of December, 1705. The secretary of the house took her effects, in all above £500 sterling; she was then sworn that that was all she was worth, and then put into a strait dark room, about five feet square, and there kept nine months and fifteen days.

"That the first nine days she had only bread and water, and a wet straw bed to lie on. On the ninth day, being examined, she owned herself a Protestant, and would so continue; she was told she had conformed to the Romish church, and must persist in it or burn; she was then remanded to her room, and after a month's time brought out again, and persisting in her answer as to her religion, they bound her hands behind her, stripped her back naked, and lashed her with a whip of knotted cords a considerable time, and told her afterwards that she must kneel down to the court, and give thanks for their merciful usage of her, which she positively refused to do.

"After fifteen days she was again brought forth and examined, and a crucifix being set before her, she was commanded to bow down to it and worship it, which she refusing to do, they told her that she must expect to be condemned to the flames and to be burnt with the Jews, at the next *auto da fé*, which was nigh at hand; upon this she was remanded to her prison again for thirty days, and being brought out, a red-hot iron was got ready, and brought to her in a chafing-dish of burning coals, and her breast being laid open, the executioner, with one end of the red-hot iron, which was about the bigness of a large seal, burnt her to the bone in three several places on the right side, one hard by the other, and then sent her to her prison, without any plaister, or other application, to heal the sores, which were very painful to her.

"A month after this, she had another severe whipping as before; and, in the beginning of August, she was brought before the table, a great number of inquisitors being present, and was questioned, whether she would profess the Romish religion or burn. She replied, she had always been a Protestant, and was a subject of the queen [Anne] of England, who was able to protect her, and she doubted not would do it, were her condition known to the English residing in Lisbon; but as she knew nothing of that, her resolution was to continue a

Protestant, though she were burnt for it. To this
they answered, that her being the queen of England's subject signified nothing in the dominions of
the king of Portugal; that the English residing in
Lisbon were heretics, and would certainly be
damned; and that it was the mercy of that tribunal to endeavour to rescue her out of the flames
of hell; but if her resolution were to burn, rather
than profess the Romish religion, they would give
her a trial of it beforehand. Accordingly, the officers were ordered to seat her in a fixed chair, and
to bind her arms and her legs, that she could make
no resistance nor motion; and the physician being
placed by her, to direct the court how far they
might torture her without hazard of life, her left foot
was made bare, and an iron slipper red-hot being
immediately brought in, her foot was fastened into
it, which continued on burning her to the bone, till
such time as, by extremity of pain, she fainted
away, and the physician declaring her life was in
danger, they took it off, and ordered her again to
her prison.

"On the 19th of August she was again brought
out, and whipped after a cruel manner, and
her back was all over torn; and being threatened
with more and greater tortures, and on the other
hand being promised to be set at liberty, if she
would subscribe such a paper as they should give
her, though she could have undergone death, yet not
being able to endure a life of so much misery, she consented to subscribe as they would have her, and
accordingly, as she was directed, wrote at the bottom

of a large paper, which contained she knew not what; after which they advised her to avoid the company of all English heretics, and not restoring to her anything of all the plate, goods, or money, she brought in with her, and engaging her by oath to keep secret all that had been done to her, turned her out of doors, destitute of all relief, but what she received from the help and compassion of charitable Christians.

"The abovesaid Elizabeth Vasconellos did solemnly affirm and declare the above-written deposition to be true, the day and year above written.

"John Milner,

"Joseph Willcocks.

"*Lisbon, January* 8, 1707, N. S."

3. John Coustos.—Mr. Coustos having escaped from the Inquisition, published the narrative of his sufferings, shortly after his return to England in 1744. From his account the following is abridged:—

"I am a native of Berne in Switzerland, and a lapidary. In 1716, my father came and settled in London; and after living twenty-two years in that city, I went to Paris, to work in the galleries of the Louvre. Five years after I removed to Lisbon, in hopes of going to Brazil, to make my fortune; but the king of Portugal being informed of the skill I might have in diamonds, refused my petition, as improper for a foreign lapidary to be allowed in a country abounding with immense treasures.

"I got acquainted with several jewellers and other persons of credit in Lisbon, whose generous offers I accepted, having a prospect of supporting my family and of a competency, could I but have escaped the cruel inquisitors. They have assumed so formidable a power in Spain and Portugal, as to encroach on the privilege of kings, and stop, at the post-office, the letters of all whom they suspect. In this manner I was served a year before the inquisitors ordered me to be seized, in order to discover the secrets of freemasonry. They did not find that it struck at the Romish religion, or tended to disturb the government—still they concluded to seize one of the chief freemasons of Lisbon; and I was pitched upon as master of a lodge, and Mr. A. J. Mouton, a diamond cutter, born at Paris, and a Romanist. He had been six years at Lisbon, a housekeeper in the city, where his integrity gained him the approbation of all.

"We did not know that our art was forbidden in Portugal, and we were discovered by the barbarous zeal of a lady at confession. The officers of the Inquisition engaged a jeweller, a familiar of the Holy Office, to send for Mr. Mouton on pretence of mending a diamond weighing four carats. This was a mere pretence to know the person of Mouton. I happened to be with him, which gave the jeweller the highest joy. He made his report to the inquisitors; and, two days after, Mr. Mouton went alone to fetch the diamond, computed to be worth a hundred moidores. This familiar had five subalterns of the Inquisition with him; and having led him into the back shop, they seized him as a prisoner in the king's name.

" Being sensible that he had not committed any crime, so as to incur his Portuguese majesty's displeasure, he gave up his sword, when several familiars fell upon him, and declared that they arrested him in the name of the Inquisition. Forbidding him to murmur, they dragged him to a small chaise at the back-door, and conveyed him to prison in the Inquisition, and spread a report that he was gone off with the diamond. His friends, shocked at the slander, went and offered full payment to the jeweller, who declined the amount, pretending that the owner was very wealthy.

" Four days after, I was betrayed by a Portuguese friend, and nine officers of the Inquisition seized me, March 5, 1743, pretending I had passed my word for the diamond which Mr. Mouton had taken. In vain was my attempt at justification: the wretches took away my sword, handcuffed me, and forced me into a chaise. They commanded me not to open my lips ; but I called aloud to a friend. They forced me into the prison, and delivered me to one of the officers of the pretended holy place. This officer bid the guards to search me, and take away all the gold, silver, papers, knives, scissors, buckles, &c., about me. They then led me into a lonely dungeon, expressly forbidding me to speak loud. It was then that, struck with all the horrors of the place, I plunged into the blackest melancholy. I passed a whole day and two nights in these terrors, heightened at every interval by the complaints, the dismal cries, and hollow groans, echoing through these dreadful mansions, of several other prisoners, my neighbours, and which the silence of the night made infinitely more shocking. These threescore hours appeared to me like so many years. However, I endeavoured to arm my soul with patience. I considered that, being a Protestant, I should inevitably feel all that rage and barbarous zeal could infuse into the breast of monks, who cruelly gloried in committing to the flames great numbers of ill-fated victims, whose only crime was differing from them in religious opinions.

" In a few days, after having been shaved, and had my hair cut by their order, I was led, bareheaded, to the president and four inquisitors, who bid me kneel and swear to speak truly to all questions they should ask. They informed me that the diamond was only a pretence to get an opportunity of seizing me. I now besought them to let me know the true cause of my imprisonment; that having been born and educated in the Protestant religion, I had been taught to confess myself to God and not to man. They declared that a confession would be forced from me. They gave orders for my being conveyed into another deep dungeon; I was overwhelmed with grief, and gave myself up entirely for lost.

"During my stay in this dungeon I was taken three times before the Inquisition, and I fell sick. A physician visited me, and another prisoner was sent to attend me in another dungeon, into which some glimmerings of daylight were admitted. Having recovered, I was sentenced to suffer the tortures

employed by the Holy Office. I was conveyed to
the torture room, where no light appeared but what
two candles gave; and, to prevent the dreadful
cries and shocking groans of the unhappy victims
from reaching the ears of the other prisoners, the
doors are lined with a sort of quilt.

"I was seized with horror, when, at my entering
this infernal place, I saw myself surrounded by
six wretches, who stripped me naked all to my
drawers, and laid me on my back. First, they put
round my neck an iron collar, which was fastened
to the scaffold; they then fixed a ring to each foot;
and this being done, they wound two ropes, the
thickness of one's little finger, round each arm,
and two round each thigh, passing under the
scaffold, through holes, and drawn tight by four
men. My pains were intolerable; the ropes pierced
through my flesh quite to the bone, making the
blood gush out of eight different places. I persisted in refusing to discover any more; the ropes
were drawn together four times; but suspended at
intervals, by order of the physician and surgeon in
attendance.

"While thus suffering, they barbarously declared that, if I died under torture, I should be
guilty of self-murder. And the last time of suffering I fainted, and was carried to my dungeon
unperceiving it. Finding that the more they made
me suffer, the more I supplicated patience from
heaven, these barbarians exposed me to another
kind of torture. They made me stretch my arms
so that the palms of my hands were turned out-

wards; when, by a rope that fastened them together
at the wrist, and which they turned by an engine,
they drew them in such a manner that the back of
each hand touched; both my shoulders were dislocated, and a considerable quantity of blood issued
from my mouth. This torture was repeated
thrice, after which, the physician and surgeons,
in setting my bones, put me to exquisite pain in my
dungeon.

"Two months after, being a little recovered, I
was again conveyed to the torture room, where they
turned round my body a thick iron chain, which,
crossing my stomach, terminated at my wrists.
They next set my back against a thick board, at
each extremity of which was a pulley, through
which there was a rope run, that caught the ends
of the chains at my wrists. These ropes, by means
of a roller, pressed or bruised my stomach, so that
my wrists and shoulders were put out of joint.
The surgeons set my bones presently, and the barbarians made me undergo this torture a second
time, which I bore with equal constancy. I was
remanded to my dungeon, attended by the surgeons, who dressed my bruises; and here I continued till their *auto da fé*.

"Nine different times they put me to the torture, when most of my limbs were put out of joint,
and bruised in such a manner that I was unable,
during some weeks, to lift my hand to my mouth.
I fear that I shall feel the effect of this cruelty so
long as I live; being seized from time to time with
thrilling pains, with which I never was afflicted till

I fell into the merciless and bloody hands of the inquisitors.

"The day of the *auto da fé* being come, I was made to walk in the procession with the other victims of this tribunal. At St. Dominic's church my sentence was read, of being condemned to the galleys during four years. Four days after I was conveyed to the galleys; and joined, the next day, in the occupation of my fellow-slaves. However, the liberty I had of speaking to my friends, after having been deprived of the sight of them during my wretched abode in the prison of the Inquisition, the open air, and being freed from the apprehensions which always overspread my mind, made me find the toil of the galley more supportable.

"By the tortures inflicted on me in the Inquisition, I was unfit for the painful labour allotted me, viz., the carrying water to the prisons of the city; but fear of the inhumanity of the overseers caused me to exert myself, and I fell sick. I was then sent to the infirmary for two months; when I was visited by the first friars of the convent of Corpo Santo, who offered to get my release, provided I would turn Roman Catholic. I assured them that I expected my enlargement from the Almighty; and having leisure, I desired a friend to write to my brother-in-law, Mr. Barber, informing him of my deplorable state, and entreating him to address the Earl of Harrington in my favour, he having the honour to live in his lordship's family. This nobleman spoke to his grace the Duke of Newcastle, secretary of state, supplicating leave from our sovereign that his minister at Lisbon might demand me, as a subject of Great Britain.

"His majesty was so gracious as to interpose in my favour. Mr. Compton, the British minister at Lisbon, demanded my liberty of the king of Portugal, in the name of his Britannic majesty; and I obtained it in the latter end of October, 1744. The officer took me from the galley by order of the inquisitors, and brought me before them, when the president told me that Cardinal de Cunha had ordered my release, but I must return in three days.

"I could perceive that the spies of the Inquisition followed me. I waited upon our envoy, and our consul; and five days after I returned to the inquisitors, when the president declared that the tribunal would not permit me to continue any longer in Portugal, and that I must name the city and kingdom whither I intended to retire. I replied that, ' as my family is in London, I design to go thither;' and they bid me embark in the first ship that should sail for England."

Mr. Coustos was kindly received by the Dutch admiral on board his ship, then in the port of Lisbon, and he permitted him to send for his friend, Mr. Mouton, being affected with the relation of their sufferings. They arrived in London, December 15th, 1744. He adds,

"I here return thanks, with all the power of my soul, to the Almighty, for his having so visibly protected me from that infernal band of friars,

R

who employed their various tortures to force me
to apostatise from my holy religion. I return our
sovereign, George II., the most dutiful and respect-
ful thanks for his so graciously interposing in
favour of an ill-fated galley-slave. I shall retain,
so long as I have breath, the deepest sensation of
affection and loyalty for his sacred person, and will
ever be ready to expose my life for his majesty and
his august family."

MR. BOWER.—Mr. Archibald Bower was not so
much a victim as to be subjected to the torture, as
he was enabled to escape from the power of the
inquisitors; but his biography illustrates the character of the Inquisition. He was born in 1686,
near Dundee, in Scotland. His parents being Roman Catholics, sent him, at the age of five years,
to an uncle in Italy, for education. First at Douay,
and then at Rome, his progress was uncommon.
He became a Jesuit, and was appointed professor of
rhetoric and logic, in the college of Macerata, in
Italy. In this city he became intimate with the
inquisitor-general of the Holy Office, from whom
he received preferment as a counsellor to the Inquisition. There were twelve counsellors, each of
whom had a residence, with about £200 per annum,
besides extensive privileges.

On being installed into office, he received a manuscript book of directions for inquisitors, for his
private guidance. These rules required the ex-
tremes of inhumanity; and his attendance on the
trials of the Holy Office he found most agonising, so
that he frequently uttered exclamations of horror.

Though not suspected, the inquisitor-general, on one occasion, in great warmth, striking the table, remarked, " Mr. Bower, you always object to the evidence." At another time, looking on the face of a wretched victim undergoing the torture, he perceived symptoms of death, and fainted, when he was carried out of the hall ; and on his return he was reproved by the chief-inquisitor, alleging that " what is done to the body is for the good of the soul." Mr. Bower excused himself, urging " the weakness of his nature, which he could not help." "Nature !" exclaimed the inquisitor, "you must overcome nature by grace !" But the colloquy ceased, as the miserable victim died at that moment under the torment !

While considering how he might escape from this horrid office, Mr. Bower was required to " conquer nature," by the arrest of a nobleman, who was a personal friend. His alleged crime was some trifling expression regarding the particular garb of two friars, one of whom denounced him to the Inquisition. Being ordered to arrest his best friend in Macerata, he remonstrated with the inquisitor-general, urging, " My lord, you know the connexion— ;" when the inquisitor, with all the sternness of his official character, interrupted him,— " Connexion ! what, talk of *connexion* when the holy faith is concerned ?" And, as he withdrew, he ordered, " See that it be done ; the guards shall wait without ;" adding, " this is the way to conquer nature, Mr. Bower." Unable to save or to warn his friend, he proceeded with the guards, obtained admittance to his residence and to his bed-room, and found both the nobleman and his lady asleep. The lady awaking, shrieked on seeing the strangers, when one of the ruffian officers gave her a blow on the head, which was followed by blood. The nobleman was astonished at being thus arrested by his friend, but dared not to reproach him; while Bower could not look him in the face, in performing so shameful an act.

Mr. Bower announced the arrest, next morning, as he delivered the key to the chief-inquisitor, who commended him,—" This is done like one who is desirous of conquering the weakness of nature." The nobleman was soon subjected to torture by the pulley, and died in three days after its infliction. His estates were then confiscated to the Inquisition, a small pension only being allowed to his widow, to whom the inquisitor wrote, desiring her to pray for the soul of her deceased husband, at the same time warning her against complaining of injustice or cruelty against the Holy Office.

Mr. Bower could endure his situation no longer, and he resolved on attempting his escape from Italy. He, therefore, solicited permission to make a pilgrimage to the house of the Virgin Mary, at Loretto; and this being granted by the inquisitor-general, he proceeded with his portmanteau, on horseback, concealing his valuable papers. He took his course through the Adriatic States for Switzerland; but the papers that he had taken with him were soon missed by the inquisitor-general, who offered a reward for his head of about £600 in

English money, or £800, if brought alive to the Inquisition. His danger became imminent through this proclamation; as he found in a post-house a copy of it, and two of his countrymen, to one of whom he was known. He challenged the man, and threatened him; and mounting his horse, escaped, so that after many difficulties he reached Calais. At the hotel he found two Jesuits, who wore the red cross of the Inquisition; when he hastily left the room, and found that the packet would be three days before it sailed for England. He applied to a fisherman, who dared not venture to cross the Channel; and he was in agony, especially when on his return he was told by his hostess, in reply to his inquiry for the Jesuits, " Oh, Sir, I am sorry to inform you that they are upstairs, searching your portmanteau." At that moment he heard voices talking loudly in another room, and, supposing them to be English, he entered, and recognised in one Lord Baltimore, whom he had seen at Rome. He entreated his protection, but that nobleman exclaimed, " Mr. Bower, you are undone; I cannot protect you: they are searching your apartment." However, he and his friends guarded him to their boat; and, with four pairs of oars, soon reached a yacht that was taking a short cruise; and the wind being fair, they conveyed him safely to Dover

Mr. Bower now relinquished his former religion, conformed to the church of England, and married. He became tutor in the family of Lord Aylmer, and found a generous patron in Lord Lyttleton. Numerous enemies from among the Catholics

brought grievous accusations against him; but he
vindicated himself from their slanders, and gained
himself a high reputation by several literary works,
especially his "Lives of the Popes," in seven
volumes quarto.   He died in England, in the year
1766, as is believed, a sincere Protestant.

CHAPTER XVIII.

THE INQUISITION IN GOA.

State of the Inquisition of Goa—Dr. Dellon's sufferings in the
Inquisition—Dr. Buchanan's visit to Goa.

PORTUGUESE bigotry completely triumphed in
Goa.   In its prosperity, nothing in India could be
compared with it in grandeur.   The capital was a
city of churches: one of which was erected with
extraordinary magnificence, in honour of Francis
Xavier, "the Apostle of the Indies," as he is called
by the Romanists, as he died there, A.D. 1552.

This once celebrated city is now nearly deserted
by all except the priests; and the country, once
populous, is reduced to a few thinly inhabited
villages.   Their inhabitants are mostly baptised
into the Romish faith: and a pagan native, or
Mohammedan, is not suffered to live in the city;
but the wretched people, sunk in superstition, are
deplorably ignorant of Christianity.

Already we have seen (Chap. VIII.) how the

Inquisition was established at Goa, by Cardinal Henry, at the request of Francis Xavier, under John III., king of Portugal. Its operations, in cruelty and terror, were like those of kindred establishments in Europe, sacrificing multitudes of its victims in prison, and many in public, by the *auto da fé*. But these will appear best in their true character, from the account given by Dellon.

Dr. Dellon was a French physician, who travelled in India. For some time, in the year 1673, he resided at Damuan, a city of Goa, belonging to the Portuguese. From his conversation, he was found to be not a strict Catholic; and he was, therefore, accused to the inquisitors. Apprehending that a process would be issued against him, he waited on the commissary, accused himself, and professed his desire to conform to the wishes of the holy court. He was known to that officer, and treated by him with courtesy; so that he was led to suppose that he was in no danger; but the priests contrived his ruin, through jealousy of him, in visiting a lady of that place, a favourite of the governor of Damuan, and also of the black priest, the secretary to the Inquisition.

Dellon was arrested by the inquisitors, and thrown into prison. In vain he made application to be informed of the cause of his arrest, or to obtain release, or a trial. No attention would be paid to his case until after the *auto da fé*, then about to be celebrated. He was designed for the next horrid festival, in about three months; and accordingly he was kept in the damp and loathsome

prison, which was destitute of conveniences, and
swarmed with vermin. From this place he was
taken on board of a galley, loaded with irons, and
conveyed to Goa, where he was secured in the
prison of the Inquisition, which is thus described
by Dellon:—

"The Palace of the Inquisition, called by the
Portuguese, ' *Santa Casa*,' or ' *The Holy House*,'
is situated on one side of the great square, opposite
to the cathedral dedicated to St. Catherine. It is
extensive and magnificent; in the front are three
entrances, of which the centre is the largest, and
opens upon the grand staircase ascending to the
hall. The two other portals severally lead to the
apartments of the inquisitors, which are sufficiently
commodious for considerable establishments.
Within are various apartments for the officers of
the house, and passing through the interior there
is a vast edifice, divided into distinct masses, or
squares of buildings, of two stories each, separated
by small courts. In each story is a gallery, resembling a dormitory, containing seven or eight small
chambers, ten feet square; the whole number of
which is about two hundred. In one of these
dormitories the cells are dark, being without windows, and smaller and lower than the rest; as I had
occasion to know, from the circumstance of having
been taken to see them, on complaining that I was
too rigorously treated, in order to satisfy me that I
might fare worse. The rest of the cells are square,
vaulted, whitewashed, clean, and lighted by a small
grated window, placed at a height above the reach

of the tallest man. All the walls are five feet thick. Every chamber is secured by two doors, one opening inwards, and the other without; the inner door is made in two divisions, is strong, well-fitted, and opened by the lower half, in the manner of a grate; in the upper part there is a little window, through which the prisoners receive their food, linen, and other things. There is a door to this opening, guarded by strong bolts. The outer door is neither so thick nor so strong as the other, but it is entire, and without any aperture. It is usually left open from six o'clock in the morning till eleven, in order to ventilate the chamber through the crevices of the inner doors."

Dellon, on entering the Inquisition, had his irons taken off; and shortly after he was called before the inquisitor, seated at a table with his secretary, in the audience chamber; at the end of which was a large crucifix, reaching to the ceiling. Dellon cast himself at the feet of the dread officer, to move his pity, but in vain. He bid him rise, and take his seat; and then inquired his name and profession, and whether he knew the cause of his imprisonment? Dellon stated that he supposed he knew the cause, and would acknowledge it; but the inquisitor put him off for a more leisure season, as matters of greater consequence claimed his present regard. He was led to his cell; and his chest being brought, an inventory was made of the several articles of his property. Everything was taken from him, except his clothes, and a few pieces of gold, which he had sewed up in his garters; but he was assured that all would be restored on his release. In his cell he was not allowed the use of any book, or any means of amusement; though he was supplied with sufficient food, and the guards, who watched by day and night, sleeping in the galleries, were ready to attend at his calls.

After a considerable time, he was brought up again to the audience chamber, having his head, feet, and legs naked. Being sworn to declare the truth, and urged to confess all his errors, he made confession of all that he had spoken against the Catholic forms of religion. He signed this confession, as it had been written down, and then was led back to his cell. Twice more was he brought before the tribunal, but without any advantage to him; and he attempted suicide, by abstinence from food. Recollecting some other expressions that he had used respecting the Holy Office, he obtained permission to declare them; but this not satisfying the inquisitors; he was remanded again to his dungeon. He sunk into despair, and again attempted suicide by various means. Having feigned illness, he was bled by a native doctor; but the black physician having left him, he tore off the bandages for the blood to escape, and sunk almost to death. Of this he repented, and made confession; but he then broke one of his pieces of gold, and, having sharpened it, he opened an artery with it, that he might bleed fatally. This failed; when they put a collar on his neck, and heavily ironed his arms and legs, to prevent such attempts in future. In despair, he dashed his head against the ground; but his guards kept watch over him, and soothed him with kind expressions and the hope of speedy release.

Dellon waited in hope of the next *auto da fé*; and, after a length of time, he was roused one night by the gaolers, bearing lights. Having dressed himself, and put on a black garment striped with white lines, and a pair of drawers, which they had brought for him, he was led into the galleries, where he joined about two hundred other prisoners, all ranged against the walls. They were mostly coloured men, there being only about twelve white persons among them. There were female prisoners in another gallery; and several men in a cell, with their confessors exhorting them to return to the true faith, as they were to be burnt as heretics. The *San-benitoes* and pasteboard hats were then brought for the several prisoners, each carrying a yellow wax-light. Some bread and figs being supplied to the prisoners while they sat waiting for the procession, but Dellon refusing them, as not being hungry, he was urged by the officer to put them in his pocket, as he would need them before he returned to his cell. By this he was somewhat comforted; as he inferred that he was not doomed to suffer in the fire.

At day-break, the citizens of Goa were summoned to assist in the *auto da fé*, by the tolling of the great bell in the cathedral; and these being assembled, the prisoners were marched singly through the hall, where each was given in charge to an inhabitant, who was responsible for his safety, as his "*godfather*." The procession, headed by the Dominicans, was led through the principal streets of the city; and the ceremonies of this shocking exhibition were similar to those which were used in Portugal and Spain.

Dellon being pronounced guilty of having denied the efficacy of baptism, and of asserting that images ought not to be worshipped, he was sentenced to excommunication, to forfeiture of his goods, to banishment from the Indies, and to slavery in the Portuguese galleys for five years, besides penances at the pleasure of the Inquisition.

Two persons, a black man and woman, native Christians, but accused of sorcery, were burnt on this occasion, besides effigies and the bones of *four* others; of whom, one had died in the Inquisition, and another had closed his life in his own house, but having left large property, the inquisitors had his bones disinterred for a trial, when he was brought in guilty of Judaism; so that his property was confiscated. The victims were burnt on the banks of the river, and the rest were conducted back again to prison, to be disposed of in various punishments, by those pretended ministers of the merciful Redeemer.

Dellon, being sentenced, was sent the next day to a religious house for instruction. Penances were prescribed for him by the inquisitors, and he was sent to Portugal, where he was made a galley-slave; but having met with a French gentleman of consequence, he obtained his services in seeking his liberty, which was procured by the government, and he succeeded in escaping back to France.

Dellon's testimony regarding himself indicates nothing of his being tortured in the prison at Goa; but he states that he could frequently hear the cries of those who were made so to suffer in that horrid Inquisition.

DR. C. BUCHANAN AT THE INQUISITION OF GOA.

Dr. Claudius Buchanan, chaplain to the East India Company, and vice-provost of the college of Fort William, in Bengal, visited Goa in 1808. His objects were,—"1. *To ascertain whether the Inquisition actually refused to recognise the Bible among the Romish churches in British India.* 2. *To inquire into the state and jurisdiction of the Inquisition, particularly as it affected British subjects.*" On account of his high character, and as a friend of Colonel Adams, the British resident, he was received politely by the Portuguese viceroy, Count de Cabral, and by the Archbishop of Goa. Colonel Adams thought he exposed himself to danger; since everything relating to that court was kept so secretly, that the most respectable of the Portuguese laity were held in ignorance of its proceedings; while the viceroy had no authority over its officers.

Dr. Buchanan proceeded to fulfil his intention; and he was received, January 19, 1808, very courteously, at the convent of the Augustinians, by Josepha Doloribus, the second in dignity of the

inquisitors. "Apartments were assigned to me,"
he remarks, "in the college adjoining the convent,
next to the rooms of the Inquisition. Next day
after my arrival I was introduced to the Archbishop
of Goa. We found him reading the Latin letters
of St. Francis Xavier. On my adverting to the
long duration of the city of Goa, while other cities
of Europeans in India had suffered from war or
revolution, the archbishop observed, that the preservation of Goa was owing to the prayers of St.
Francis Xavier.

"On the same day I received an invitation to
dine with the chief-inquisitor, at his house in the
country. The second inquisitor accompanied me,
and we found a respectable company of priests and
a sumptuous entertainment. In the library of the
chief-inquisitor I saw a register, containing the
present establishment of the Inquisition at Goa,
and the names of all the officers. On my asking
the chief-inquisitor whether the establishment was
as extensive as formerly, he said it was nearly the
same. I had hitherto said little to any person concerning the Inquisition, but I had indirectly gleaned
much information concerning it, not only from
the inquisitors themselves, but from certain priests,
whom I had visited at their respective convents;
particularly from a father in the Franciscan convent,
who had himself witnessed an *auto da fé*.

"January 27th, 1808. On the second morning
after my arrival, I was surprised by my host, the
inquisitor, coming into my apartment clothed in
black robes from head to foot, for the usual dress

of his order is white. He said he was going to
sit on the tribunal of the Holy Office. 'I presume, father, your august office does not occupy
much of your time?' 'Yes,' answered he, 'very
much. I sit on the tribunal three or four days
every week.'

"In the evening he came in as usual, to pass an
hour in my apartment. After some conversation,
I took the pen in my hand to write a note in my
journal; and, as if to amuse him, while I was
writing, I took Dellon's book, which was lying with
some others on the table, and, handing it across to
him, asked him whether he had ever seen it. It
was in the French language, which he understood
well. 'RELATION DE L'INQUISITION DE GOA,'
pronounced he, with a slow and articulate voice.
He had never seen it before, and he began to read
it with eagerness. He had not proceeded far, before
he betrayed evident symptoms of uneasiness. He
turned hastily to the middle of the book, and then
to the end, and then ran over the table of contents
at the beginning, as if to ascertain the full extent
of the evil.

"It was on this night that a circumstance happened which caused my first alarm at Goa. My
servants slept every night at my chamber door, in
the long gallery which is common to all the apartments, and not far distant from the servants of the
convent. About midnight I was awaked by loud
shrieks and expressions of terror, from some person
in the gallery. In the first moment of surprise, I
concluded it must be the *alguazils* of the Holy

Office, seizing my servants to carry them to the Inquisition. But, on going out, I saw my own servants standing at the door, and the person who had caused the alarm (a boy of about fourteen), at a little distance, surrounded by some of the priests, who had come out of their cells on hearing the noise. The boy said he had seen a *spectre;* and it was a considerable time before the agitation of his body and voice subsided. Next morning, at breakfast, the inquisitor apologised for the disturbance, and said the boy's alarm proceeded from a '*phantasma animi,*' a phantasm of the imagination.

"After breakfast we resumed the subject of the Inquisition. The inquisitor admitted that Dellon's descriptions of the *dungeons,* of the *torture,* of the *mode of trial,* and of the *auto da fé,* were, in general, just; but he said the writer judged untruly of the motives of the inquisitors, and very uncharitably of the character of the holy church; and I admitted that, under the pressure of his peculiar sufferings, this might possibly be the case. The inquisitor was now anxious to know to what extent Dellon's book had been circulated in Europe. I told him that Picart had published to the world extracts from it, in his celebrated work called 'Religious Ceremonies,' together with plates of the system of torture and burnings at the *auto da fé.* I added, that it was now generally believed in Europe that these enormities no longer existed, and that the Inquisition itself had been totally suppressed; but that I was concerned to find that this was not the case. He now began a grave narration, to show that the

Inquisition had undergone a change in some respects, and that its terrors were mitigated.

"I had already discovered, from written or printed documents, that the Inquisition of Goa was suppressed by royal edict in the year 1775, and established again in 1779. The Franciscan father before mentioned witnessed the annual *auto da fé*, from 1770 to 1775. 'It was the humanity and tender mercy of a good king,' said the old father, 'which abolished the Inquisition.' But, immediately on his death, the power of the priests acquired the ascendant under the queen dowager, and the tribunal was re-established, after a bloodless interval of five years. It has continued in operation ever since. It was restored in 1779, subject to certain restrictions, the chief of which are the two following :—

" ' *That a greater number of witnesses should be required to convict a criminal than were before necessary; and,*

" ' *That the* auto da fé *should not be held publicly as before; but that the sentences of the tribunal should be executed privately, within the walls of the Inquisition.'*

"In this particular, the constitution of the new Inquisition is more reprehensible than that of the old one; for, as the old father expressed it, ' *Nunc sigillum non revelat Inquisitio.*' Formerly, the friends of those unfortunate persons who were thrown into its prison, had the melancholy satisfaction of seeing them once a year walking in the procession of the *auto da fé;* or, if they were condemned to die, they witnessed their death, and

N

mourned for the dead. But now they have no means of learning, for years, whether they be dead or alive. The policy of this new mode of concealment appears to be this,—to preserve the power of the Inquisition, and at the same time to lessen the public odium of its proceedings, in the presence of British dominion and civilisation. I asked the father his opinion concerning the nature and frequency of the punishments within the walls. He said he possessed no certain means of giving a satisfactory answer; that everything transacted there was declared to be *sacrum et secretum*. But this he knew to be true, that there were constantly captives in the dungeons; that some of them are liberated after long confinement; but that they never speak afterwards of what passed within the place. He added, that of all the persons he had known, who had been liberated, he never knew one who did not carry about with him what might be called 'The mark of the Inquisition;' that is to say, who did not show, in the solemnity of his countenance, or in his peculiar demeanour, or his terror of the priests, that he had been in that dreadful place.

"The chief argument of the inquisitor to prove the melioration of the Inquisition was the *superior humanity* of the inquisitors. I remarked, that I did not doubt the humanity of the existing officers; but what availed humanity in an inquisitor? He must pronounce sentence according to the *laws of the tribunal*, which are notorious enough; and a *relapsed heretic* must be burnt in the flames, or confined for life in a dungeon, whether the inquisitor be humane or not. 'But if,' said I, 'you would satisfy my mind completely on this subject, show me the Inquisition.' He said, it was not permitted to any person to see the Inquisition. I observed, that mine might be considered as a peculiar case ; that the character of the Inquisition, and the expediency of its longer continuance, had been called in question ; that I had myself written on the civilisation of India, and might possibly publish something more upon that subject ; and that it could not be expected that I should pass over the Inquisition without notice, knowing what I did of its proceedings ; at the same time, I should not wish to state a single fact without his authority, or at least his admission of its truth. I added, that he himself had been pleased to communicate with me very fully on the subject, and that in all our discussions we had both been actuated, I hoped, by a good purpose. The countenance of the inquisitor evidently altered on receiving this intimation, nor did it ever after wholly regain its wonted frankness and placidity. After some hesitation, however, he said he would take me with him to the Inquisition, the next day. I was a good deal surprised at this acquiescence of the inquisitor, but I did not know what was in his mind.

"When I left the forts, to come up to the Inquisition, Colonel Adams desired me to write to him ; and he added, halfway between jest and earnest, 'If I do not hear from you in three days, I shall march down the 78th and storm the Inquisition.' This I promised to do. But having been so well entertained by the inquisitors I forgot my promise. Accordingly, on the 26th of January, I was surprised by a visit from Major Broomcamp, aide-de-camp to his excellency the viceroy, proposing that I should return every evening and sleep at the forts, on account of the *unhealthiness* of Goa.

"This morning, the 28th, after breakfast, my host went to dress for the Holy Office, and soon returned in his inquisitorial robes. He said he would go half an hour before the usual time, for the purpose of showing me the Inquisition. I fancied that his countenance was more severe than usual; and that his attendants were not so civil as before. The truth was, the *midnight scene* was still on my mind. The Inquisition is about a quarter of a mile distant from the convent, and on our arrival at the place the inquisitor said to me, as we were ascending the steps of the outer stair, that he hoped I should be satisfied with a transient view of the Inquisition, and that I would retire whenever he should desire it. I took this as a good omen, and followed my conductor with tolerable confidence.

"He led me first to the great hall of the Inquisition. We were met at the door by a number of well-dressed persons, who, I afterwards understood, were the familiars and attendants of the Holy Office. They bowed very low to the inquisitor, and looked with surprise at me. The great hall is the place in which the prisoners are marshalled for the procession of the *auto da fé*. At the procession described by Dellon, in which he himself walked barefoot, clothed

with the painted garment, there were upwards of
one hundred and fifty prisoners. I traversed this
hall for some time with a slow step, reflecting on its
former scenes; the inquisitor walked by my side in
silence. I thought of the fate of the multitude of
my fellow-creatures who had passed through this
place, condemned by a tribunal of their fellow-
sinners—their bodies devoted to the flames, and
their souls to perdition; and I could not help
saying to him, ‘Would not the holy church wish,
in her mercy, to have those souls back again, that
she might allow them a little further probation?’
The inquisitor answered nothing, but beckoned me
to go with him to a door at one end of the hall.
By this door he conducted me to some small rooms,
and thence to the spacious apartments of the chief-
inquisitor. Having surveyed these, he brought me
back again to the great hall, and I thought he
seemed now desirous that I should depart. ‘Now,
father,’ said I, ‘lead me to the dungeons below; I
want to see the captives.’ ‘No,’ said he, ‘that
cannot be.’ I now began to suspect that it had
been in the mind of the inquisitor, from the beginning, to show me only a certain part of the Inquisition, in the hope of satisfying my inquiries in a
general way. I urged him with earnestness, but
he steadily resisted, and seemed to be offended, or
rather agitated, by my importunity. I intimated
to him plainly, that the only way to do justice to
his own assertions and arguments, regarding the
present state of the Inquisition, was to show me
the prisons and the captives. I should then des-

cribe only what I saw; but now the subject was left in awful obscurity. 'Lead me down,' said I, 'to the inner building, and let me pass through the two hundred dungeons, ten feet square, described by your former captives. Let me count the number of your present captives, and converse with them. I want to see if there be any subjects of the British government to whom we owe protection. I want to ask how long they have been here—how long it is since they beheld the light of the sun, and whether they ever expect to see it again. Show me the chamber of torture; and declare what modes of execution or of punishment are now practised within the walls of the Inquisition, in lieu of the public *auto da fé*. If, after all that has passed, father, you resist this reasonable request, I shall be justified in believing that you are afraid of exposing the real state of the Inquisition in India'. To these observations the inquisitor made no reply, but seemed impatient that I should withdraw. 'My good father,' said I, 'I am about to take my leave of you, and to thank you for your hospitable attentions, (it had been before understood that I should take my final leave at the door of the Inquisition,) and I wish always to preserve on my mind a favourable sentiment of your kindness and candour. You cannot, you say, show me the captives and the dungeons; be pleased, then, merely to answer this question, for I shall believe your word:—' How many prisoners are there now below, in the cells of the Inquisition?' The inquisitor replied, 'That is a question which I cannot answer.'

On his pronouncing these words I retired hastily towards the door, and wished him farewell. We shook hands with as much cordiality as we could at the moment assume; and both of us, I believe, were sorry that our parting took place with a clouded countenance.

"From the Inquisition I went to the place of burning, in the *Campo Santo Lazaro*, on the river-side, where the victims were brought to the stake at the *auto da fé*. It is close to the palace, that the viceroy and his court may witness the execution; for it has ever been the policy of the Inquisition to make these spiritual executions the executions of the state. An old priest accompanied me, who pointed out the place, and described the scenes. As I passed over this melancholy plain, I thought of the difference between the pure and benign doctrine, which was first preached to India in the apostolic age, and that bloody code which, after a long night of darkness, was announced to it under the same name. And I pondered on the mysterious dispensation, which permitted the ministers of the Inquisition, with their racks and flames, to visit these lands before the heralds of the Gospel of peace. But the most painful reflection was, that this tribunal should yet exist, unawed by the vicinity of British humanity and dominion.

"I was not satisfied with what I had seen or said at the Inquisition, and I determined to go back again. The inquisitors were now sitting on the tribunal; and I had some excuse for returning, for I was to receive from the chief-inquisitor a letter, which he said he would give me, before I left the place, for the British resident in Travancore, being an answer to a letter from that officer.

"When I arrived at the Inquisition, and had ascended the outer stairs, the door-keepers surveyed me doubtingly, but suffered me to pass, supposing that I had returned by permission and appointment of the inquisitor. I entered the great hall, and went up directly towards the tribunal of the Inquisition, described by Dellon, in which is the lofty crucifix. I sat down on a form, and then desired one of the attendants to carry in my name to the inquisitor. As I walked up the hall, I saw a poor woman sitting by herself, on a bench by the wall, apparently in a disconsolate state of mind. She clasped her hands as I passed, and gave me a look expressive of her distress. This sight chilled my spirits. The familiars told me she was waiting there to be called up before the tribunal of the Inquisition. While I was asking questions concerning her crime, the second inquisitor came out in evident trepidation, and was about to complain of the intrusion, when I informed him I had come back for the letter from the chief-inquisitor. He said it should be sent after me to Goa; and he conducted me with a quick step towards the door. As we passed the poor woman, I pointed to her, and said, with some emphasis, 'Behold, father, another victim of the holy Inquisition!' He answered nothing. When we arrived at the head of the great stair, he bowed, and I took my last leave of Joseph à Doloribus, without uttering a word!"

Dr. Buchanan makes various reflections on his detail of the visit which he paid to this dreadful institution. He states, "The foregoing particulars concerning the Inquisition at Goa, are detailed chiefly with this view—that the English nation may consider, whether there be sufficient ground for presenting a remonstrance to the Portuguese government, on the longer continuance of that tribunal in India; it being notorious, that a great part of the Romish Christians are now under British protection. 'The Romans,' says Montesquieu, 'deserved well of human nature, for making it an article in their treaty with the Carthaginians, that THEY SHOULD ABSTAIN FROM SACRIFICING THEIR CHILDREN TO THEIR GODS!' It is surely our duty to declare our wishes, at least, for the abolition of these inhuman tribunals (since we take an active part in promoting the welfare of other nations), and to deliver our testimony against them in the presence of Europe!"

CHAPTER XIX.

LICENTIOUSNESS OF THE INQUISITORS.

Corruptions predicted—Licentiousness of celibate Priests— Splendour of the Chief-inquisitor at Madrid—Inquisitors' seraglios at Saragossa—Case of a Victim—Number of the Ladies of three Inquisitors.

DIVINE Inspiration, describing the papal apostacy, gives various striking particulars, illustrations

of which are given variously in the foregoing
history. Among those shocking practices, the
Holy Spirit declares that its ministers "speak lies
in hypocrisy; having their conscience seared with
a hot iron; forbidding to marry."—1 Tim. iv. 2, 3.

Every one acquainted with the manners of the
people in popish countries is aware of the prevalence
of impurity, even among the priests. It is too
notorious to be denied. All classes, from the popes
downward, are known to be guilty. Many papal
bulls have condemned unchastity, with characteristic
hypocrisy, which may be illustrated by a single
fact. Pope Pius IV., A.D. 1561, issued a bull,
directed to the Inquisition, the commencement of
which is as follows:—"Whereas certain ecclesiastics in the kingdom of Spain, and in the cities
and dioceses thereof, having the cure of souls, or
exercising such cure for others, or otherwise deputed
to hear the confessions of penitents, have broken
out into such heinous acts of iniquity as to abuse
the sacrament of penance in the very act of hearing
the confessions, nor fearing to injure the same
sacrament, and Him who instituted it, our Lord
God and Saviour Jesus Christ, by *enticing and pro-
voking, or trying to entice and provoke females to
lewd actions, at the very time when they were making
their confessions,*" &c., &c.

Upon the publication of this bull in Spain, the
Inquisition issued an edict requiring all females,
who had been thus abused by the priests at the
confessional, and all who were privy to such acts,
to give information, within thirty days, to the holy

tribunal; and very heavy censures were attached
to those who should neglect or despise this injunc-
tion. When this edict was first published, as
Catholic authors of credit state, such a considerable
number of females went to the palace of the Inquisition, in the single city of Seville, to reveal the
conduct of their base confessors, that twenty
notaries, and as many inquisitors, were appointed
to minute down their several informations against
them; but these being found insufficient to receive
the depositions of so many witnesses, and the
inquisitors being thus overwhelmed, as it were, with
the pressure of such affairs, thirty days more were
allowed for taking the accusations; and this lapse of
time also proving inadequate for the intended
purpose, a similar period was granted for a *third*
and a *fourth* time. Maids and matrons of every
rank and station, dreading the excommunication,
crowded to the Inquisition. Modesty, shame, and
the desire of concealing the facts from their
husbands, induced many to go veiled. But the
multitudes of depositions, and the odium which the
discovery drew on auricular confession and on the
priesthood, caused the Inquisition to quash the
prosecutions, and to consign the depositions to
oblivion!

From the enormous hypocrisy and unparalleled
cruelty that we have seen recorded of the inquisitors, every one will be prepared to believe that
they must have been guilty of the most atrocious
personal immoralities. Many of them were priests;
and the celibacy of the clergy, as enjoined by the

Romish religion, was the occasion of the most
shocking violations of the laws of God. These
crimes are testified by papal historians of the
highest character, and proved by laws of the popes
made against them; but the records of the lives of
the priests exhibit the most disgusting and dreadful
crimes.

Elevation in office generally rendered the inquisitors above all law; and the peculiarity of their
stations shielded them from accusation, rendering
it dangerous in the extreme for any one to breathe
a whisper against them. They, therefore, commonly rolled in luxury, and indulged in licentiousness that would appear incredible, were it not for
their other enormities and abominations recorded
on the faithful pages of history.

The translator of Limborch's history remarks,
therefore :—"The licentious character so largely
applied to the Romish clergy has not been wanting
in those deputed to the office of inquisitors.
Whilst by the very constitution of their authority
they are placed in a great degree above the laws,
they possess, in addition to their ecclesiastical
revenues, opportunities of amassing enormous
wealth from the wreck of those whom they condemn; and, besides, such unbounded power as to
command any object of desire, or to gratify any
purpose of revenge. With such temptations,
therefore, it is no wonder if the inquisitor should
become voluptuous, and that, possessing the authority, he should assume the vices of the oriental
monarchs." M. Lavallée, in his "Histoire des

Inquisitions Religieuses," relates the following circumstance :—

" A gentleman, who was then (1809) residing at Paris, having business in Lisbon some years before the French revolution, and being about to go thither, took with him, from a nobleman at Versailles, a letter to the chief-inquisitor at Madrid, through which he passed. On his arrival in that city, being fatigued, and at the same time unwilling to impede his journey, he fulfilled the ceremony of delivering the letter to the inquisitor by the hands of his servant, excusing himself, on those grounds, from doing himself the honour of a personal attendance. The grand-inquisitor, however, came himself to his hotel, and, with great politeness, prevailed on him to spend the evening at his residence. The gentleman repaired to his apartment, and was lost in astonishment at the splendour of the saloons, furniture, and attendants. After some noblemen who were present had withdrawn, the inquisitor offered his guest a sight of his bed-chamber; this surpassed anything that he had ever seen for sumptuous elegance. The walls were hung with most exquisite paintings, from the heathen mythology; the floor of the finest marble, and so constructed as to admit the growth of orange trees, and a crystal stream, which, imparting a delicious coolness, rolled off through basons of porphyry, in subterranean channels, whilst the bed was adorned with such tasteful drapery as to give to the whole the air of royalty. As soon as the visitor had inspected with admiration the various embellish-

ments of this splendid retreat, which he was the
more surprised to find where he had rather expected to have seen the rigid tokens of inquisitorial
devotion, he prepared to withdraw. But the inquisitor prevented him, expressing surprise that he
should so soon appear fatigued; then making a
signal, a Dominican appeared (his confidential
minister), who conducted the traveller into a
splendid saloon, lighted by a profusion of wax
candles; here a magnificent supper was prepared,
to which sat down the grand-inquisitor, his visitor,
six ladies of great beauty and accomplishments, and
some monks, who were peculiar favourites. The
evening was spent with the greatest gaiety, whilst
music, poetry, singing, and agreeable conversation
protracted the stay of the company until sunrise.
At length the traveller took his leave, greatly
pleased with the courtesy of his highness, and
admiring the method of relaxation he had chosen,
after the studies and fatigue devolving on him from
the Holy Office!"

Rev. D. A. Gavin, a Spanish priest, but, since
1715, a clergyman in the Church of England, in
his "Master-Key to Popery," vol. i., p. 192–205,
gives the following account by a lady, daughter of
Counsellor Balabriga, of Saragossa. She had been
seized by the familiars of the Holy Office, and
confined there, with others, as a victim of the
abominable licentiousness of the inquisitors; but
delivered from her degradation by the French army,
when part of the troops were quartered at Saragossa,
after the great battle of Almanza, in 1706. M. de

Legal, the lieutenant-general, having been excommunicated by the inquisitors, on account of his making an assessment upon them for the support of his troops, sent four regiments of soldiers to eject the inquisitors, and release the prisoners. Among these, amounting to about *four hundred*, he found *sixty* young women, who had formed the seraglios of the three inquisitors. On learning this event, the Archbishop of Saragossa, fearing the disgrace that would arise from the discovery of such atrocious wickedness, desired the general to send the young women to his palace, that he might take care of them. But M. de Legal replied, that he would gladly oblige his grace, but that it was not in his power, for the ladies were taken care of by the French officers. One of these ladies, whose family was known to Gavin, being married by a French officer, her deliverer, gave her history to her friend, some time after, when he met her in his travels in France.

"I went one day," said this lady, "with my mother, to visit the Countess of Attaress, and I met there Don Francisco Torrejon, her confessor, and second inquisitor of the Holy Office. After we had drunk chocolate he asked me my age, and my confessor's name, and so many intricate questions about religion that I could not answer him. His serious countenance did frighten me; and, as he perceived my fear, he desired the countess to tell me that he was not so severe as I took him to be; after which he caressed me in the most obliging manner in the world, gave me his hand, which I kissed with great respect and modesty; and when he went away, he told me, ' My dear child, I shall remember you till the next time.' I did not mind the sense of the words, for I was inexperienced in matters of gallantry, being only fifteen years old at that time. Indeed, he did remember me; for the very night following, when we were in bed, hearing a hard knocking at the door, the maid that lay in the same room where my bed was, went to the window, and asking, ' Who is there?' I heard say, ' The Holy Inquisition!'

"I could not forbear crying out, ' Father! father! I am ruined for ever!' My dear father got up, and inquiring what the matter was, I answered him, with tears, ' The Inquisition!' and he, for fear that the maid should not open the door so quick as such a case required, went himself, as another Abraham, to open the door, and to offer his dear daughter to the fire of the inquisitors; and as I did not cease to cry out, as if I was a mad girl, my dear father, all in tears, did put in my mouth a bridle, to show his obedience to the Holy Office, and his zeal for the Catholic faith; for he thought I had committed some crime against religion. So the officers, giving me but time to put on my petticoat and a mantle, took me down into a coach, and, without giving me the satisfaction of embracing my dear father and mother, they carried me into the Inquisition. I did expect to die that very night; but when they carried me into a noble room, well furnished, and an excellent bed in it, I was quite surprised. The officers left me there,

and immediately a maid came with a silver salver of
sweetmeats and cinnamon-water, desiring me to
take some refreshment before I went to bed.   I
told her I could not, but that I should be obliged
to her if she would tell me whether I was to die
that night or not?   'Die!' said she, 'you did not
come here to die, but to live like a princess; and
you shall want nothing in the world but the liberty
of going out.   And now, pray mind nothing, but go
to bed and sleep easy, for to-morrow you shall see
wonders in this house; and, as I am chosen to be
your waiting-maid, I hope you will be very kind to
me.   I have not leave to tell you anything else
till to-morrow, only that nobody shall come to
disturb you, for my bed is in the closet near your
bed.'

    "The great amazement that I was in took away
all my senses, or the free exercise of them; for I
had not liberty to think of my parents, nor of my
grief, nor of the danger that was so near me.   So,
in this suspension of thought, the waiting-maid
came, and locked the chamber-door after her, and
told me, 'Madam, let us go to bed, and only tell
me at what time in the morning will you have the
chocolate ready?'   'Mary! for heaven's sake,' said
I, as she had told me her name, 'tell me whether I
am to die or not.'   'I told you, madam, that you
come,' said she, 'to live as one of the happiest
creatures in the world.'   And as I observed her
reservedness, I did not ask her any more questions;
so recommending myself to God Almighty, and to
our Lady of the Pillar, and preparing myself to die,

T

I went to bed, but could not sleep. I was up with
the day, but Mary slept till six of the clock. She
left me half an hour alone, and came back with a
silver plate, with two cups of chocolate and some
biscuits. I drank one cup and desired her to drink
the other. 'Well, Mary,' said I, 'can you give me
any account of the reason of my being here?'
'Not yet, madam,' said she, 'but only have patience
for a little while.' With this answer she left me,
and an hour after came again with two baskets,
with a fine Holland shift, a Holland under-petticoat,
with fine lace round about it; two silk petticoats,
and a little Spanish waistcoat with a gold fringe all
over it; with combs and ribbons, and everything
suitable to a lady of higher quality than I. But
my greatest surprise was to see a gold snuff-box,
with the picture of Don Francisco Torrejon on it.
Then I soon understood the meaning of my confinement. So I considered with myself that to
refuse the present would be the occasion of my
immediate death, and to accept of it was to give
him, even on the first day, too great encouragement
against my honour. But I found, as I thought
then, a medium in the case; so I said, 'Mary, pray
give my service to Don Francisco Torrejon, and tell
him that, as I could not bring my clothes with me
last night, honesty permits me to accept of these
clothes, which are necessary to keep me decent;
but, since I take no snuff, I beg his lordship to
excuse me if I do not accept this box.' Mary went
to him with this answer, and came again with a
picture nicely set in gold, with four diamonds at

the four corners of it, and told me that his lordship
was mistaken, and that he desired me to accept
that picture, which would be a great favour to him;
and while I was thinking with myself what to do,
Mary said to me, 'Pray, madam, take my poor
advice; accept the picture, and everything that he
sends to you; for consider, that if you do not
consent and comply with everything he has a mind
for, you will soon be put to death, and nobody will
defend you; but if you are obliging and kind to him,
he is a very complaisant and agreeable gentleman,
and will be a charming lover; and you will be here
like a queen, and he will give you another apartment with a fine garden, and many young ladies
shall come to visit you. So I advise you to send a
civil answer to him, and desire a visit from him, or
else you will soon begin to repent yourself.' 'O
dear me!' said I, 'must I abandon my honour
without any remedy? If I oppose his desire, he
will obtain it by force;' and, full of confusion, I
bid Mary to give him what answer she thought fit.
She was very glad of my humble submission, and
went to give Don Francisco my answer. She came
back, in a few minutes after, all overjoyed to tell
me that his lordship would honour me with his
company at supper, and that he could not come
sooner on account of business that called him
abroad; but, in the meantime, he desired me to
divert myself, and to give Mary my measure for a
suit of new clothes, and order her to bring me
everything that I could wish for. Mary added to
this, 'Madam, I may now call you *my mistress*; and

must tell you, that I have been in the Holy Office these fourteen years, and I know the customs of it very well; but because silence is imposed upon me under pain of death, I cannot tell you anything but what concerns your person. So, in the *first* place, do not oppose the holy father's will and pleasure; *secondly,* if you see some young ladies here, never ask them the occasion of their being here, nor anything of their business; neither will they ask you anything of this nature; and take care not to tell them anything of your being here. You may come and divert yourself with them, at such hours as are appointed; you shall have music and all sorts of recreations. Three days hence you shall dine with them; they are all ladies of quality, young and merry, and this is the best of lives. You will not long for going abroad, you will be so well diverted at home; and when your time is expired, then the holy fathers will marry you to some nobleman. Never mention the name of Don Francisco, nor your name, to any one. If you see here some young ladies of your acquaintance in the city, they will never take notice of your formerly knowing each other, though they will talk with you of indifferent matters; so take care not to speak anything of your family.'

"All these things together stupified me, and the whole seemed to me a piece of enchantment; so that I could not imagine what to think of it. With this lesson she left me, telling me she was going to order my dinner; and every time she went out she locked the door after her. There were but two high windows in my chamber, and I could see nothing through them; but, examining the room all over, I found a closet with all sorts of historical and profane books. So I spent my time till the dinner came in, reading some diverting amorous stories, which was a great satisfaction to me. Mary came with the things for the table, but I was inclined to sleep; so she asked me when she should wake me, and I proposed two hours. My sleep was a great refreshment to me; and at the time fixed she waked me to dinner, which consisted of every thing that could satisfy the nicest appetite. After dinner she left me alone, directing me to ring the bell to call her, if I needed anything; so I went again to my closet, and spent three hours in reading. I really think I was under some enchantment; for I was in a perfect suspension of thought, so as to remember neither father nor mother; and what was most in my mind I do not know. Mary, at length, came and told me that Don Francisco was come home, and she thought he would come to see me very soon; and begged of me to prepare myself to receive him with all manner of kindness. At seven in the evening Don Francisco came in his night-gown and night-cap, not with the gravity of an inquisitor, but with the gaiety of an officer. He saluted me with great respect and civility, and told me he had designed to keep me company at supper, but could not that night, having some business of consequence to finish in his closet; and that his coming to see me was only out of the respect he had for my family, and to tell me, at the same time, that some of my lovers had procured my ruin for me, accusing me in matters of religion; that the informations were taken, and the sentence pronounced against me was, to be burnt alive in the dry-pan with a gradual fire; but that he, out of pity and love to my family, had stopped the execution of it. Each of these words was a mortal stroke on my heart, and knowing not what I was doing, I threw myself at his feet, and said, 'Seignior, have you stopped the execution for ever?' 'That belongs only to you to stop it or not,' said he; and with this he wished me a good night. As soon as he went away, I fell a crying; but Mary came and asked me what could oblige me to cry so bitterly. 'Ah! good Mary,' said I, 'pray tell me what is the meaning of the dry-pan, and gradual fire? for I am in expectation of nothing but death, and that by it.' 'O! madam, never fear, you will see the dry-pan and gradual fire another day; but they are made for those that oppose the holy fathers' will, but not for you that are so ready to obey them. But pray, was Don Francisco very civil and obliging?' 'I do not know,' said I, 'for his discourse has put me out of my wits; this I know, that he saluted me with respect and civility, but he left me very abruptly.' 'Well,' said Mary, 'you do not know his temper; he is the most obliging man in the world, if people are civil with him; and if not, he is as unmerciful as Nero. And so, for your preservation, take care to oblige him in all respects. Now pray go to supper, and be easy.'

"I was so much troubled in mind with the

thoughts of the dry-pan and gradual fire, that I could neither eat nor sleep that night. Early in the morning, Mary got up, and told me that nobody was yet up in the house, and that she would show me the dry-pan and gradual fire, on condition that I should keep it a secret for her sake, and my own too, which I having promised her, she took me along with her, and showed me a dark room with a thick iron door, and within it an oven and a large brass pan upon it, with a cover of the same, and a lock on it—the oven was burning at that time, and I asked Mary for what use that pan was there ?   And she, without giving me any answer, took me by the hand out of that place, and carried me into a large room, where she showed me a thick wheel, covered on both sides with thick boards, and opening a little window in the centre of it, desired me to look with a candle on the inside of it, where I saw all the circumference of the wheel set with sharp razors. After that, she showed me a pit full of serpents and toads.   Then she said to me, ' Now, my good mistress, I will tell you the use of these three things. The dry-pan and gradual fire are for heretics, and those that oppose the holy fathers' will and pleasure ; for they are put all naked and alive into the pan, and the cover of it being locked up, the executioner begins to put in the oven a small fire, and by degrees he augments it, till the body is reduced to ashes! The second is designed for those who speak against the pope and the holy fathers ; for they are put within the wheel, and the little door being locked, the executioner turns the wheel till the person is dead. And the third is for those who condemn the images, and refuse to give the due respect and veneration to ecclesiastical persons; for they are thrown into the pit, and they at once become the food of serpents and toads!'

"Then Mary said to me that another day she would show me the torments for public sinners and transgressors of the five commandments of our holy mother the church; so I, in deep amazement, desired her to show me no more places; for the very thoughts of those three which I had seen were enough to terrify me to the heart. So we went to my room, and she charged me again to be very obedient to all the commands Don Francisco should give me, or to be assured, if I did not, that I was to undergo the torment of the dry-pan. Indeed, I conceived such a horror of the gradual fire, that I was not mistress of my senses, nay, nor of my thoughts. So I told Mary that I would follow her advice, and grant Don Francisco everything he would desire of me. 'If you are in that disposition,' said she, 'leave off all your fears and apprehensions, and expect nothing but pleasure and satisfaction, and all manner of recreation; and you shall begin to experience some of these things this very day. Now let me dress you, for you must go and wish a good-morrow to Don Francisco, and breakfast with him.' I really thought this was a great honour to me, and some comfort to my troubled mind; so I made all the haste I could, and Mary conveyed me through a gallery into Don Francisco's apartment. He was still in bed, how-

ever, and desiring me to sit down by him, told
Mary to bring the chocolate two hours after; and
with this she left me alone with Don Francisco,
who immediately ardently declaring his inclinations,
I had not the liberty to make any excuse, and so,
by extinguishing the fire of his passion, I was freed
from the gradual fire and dry-pan, which was all
that then troubled my mind. When Mary came
with the chocolate, kneeling by the bed, she paid
me homage as if I had been a queen, and served me
first with a cup of chocolate, still on her knees, and
bade me to give another cup to Don Francisco myself, which he received mighty graciously. Having
drunk up the chocolate, she went out, and we dis-
coursed for a while of various things, but I never
spoke a word except when he desired me to answer
him. So, at ten of the clock, Mary came again, and
dressing me, she desired me to go along with her;
and leaving Don Francisco in bed, she carried me
into another chamber, very delightful, and better
furnished than the first, for the windows of it were
lower, and I had the pleasure of seeing the river
and gardens on the other side out of it. Then
Mary told me, 'Madam, the young ladies of this
house will come before dinner to welcome you, and
make themselves happy in the honour of your company, and will take you to dine with them. Pray
remember the advice I have given you already, and
do not make yourself unhappy by asking useless
questions.' She had not finished these words, when
I saw entering my apartments—which consisted of a
large anti-chamber, and a bed-chamber with two

large closets—a troop of young, beautiful ladies,
finely dressed, who all, one after another, came to
embrace me, and to wish me joy. My senses were
in a perfect suspension, and I could not speak a
word, nor answer to their kind compliments. But
one of them, seeing me so silent, said to me,
'Madam, the solitude of this place will affect you
in the beginning; but when you are sometime in
our company, and feel the pleasures of our amuse-
ments and recreations, you will quit your pensive
thoughts. Now we beg of you the honour to come
and dine with us to-day, and henceforth three days
in a week.' I thanked them, and we went to dinner. That day we had all sorts of exquisite meats,
and were served with delicate fruits and sweetmeats. The room was very long, with two tables
on each side, and another at the front of it, and I
reckoned in it, on that day, *fifty-two* young ladies,
the oldest of them not exceeding *twenty-four* years
of age. Six maids did serve the whole number of
us; but my Mary waited on me alone that day.
After dinner, we went up stairs into a long gallery,
all round about with lattice windows, where some
of us playing on instruments of music, others playing at cards, and some walking about, we spent
three hours together. At last, Mary came up ringing a small bell, which was the signal to retire into
our rooms, as they told me: but Mary said to the
whole company,—'Ladies, this is a day of recreation; so you may go into what room you please till
eight of the clock, and then you are to go into your
own chambers.' So they all desired leave to go

with me to my apartment to spend the time there; and I was very glad that they preferred my chamber to another.   All going down together, we met in my anti-chamber, where we found a large table with all sorts of sweetmeats upon it, iced cinnamon-water, almond-milk, and the like.   Every one did eat and drink, but nobody spoke a word touching the sumptuousness of the table, nor mentioned anything concerning the inquisition of the holy fathers.   So we spent our time in merry, indifferent conversation till eight of the clock.   Then every one retired to her own room, and Mary told me that Don Francisco did wait for me; so we went to his apartment, and supper being ready, we both alone sat to table, attended by my maid only.

" After supper Mary went away, and we to bed; and next morning she did serve us with chocolate, which we drank in bed, and then slept till ten of the clock.   Then we got up, and my waiting-maid carried me into my chamber, where I found ready two suits of clothes of a rich brocade, and every thing else suitable to a lady of the first rank.   I put on one, and when I was quite dressed, the young ladies came to wish me a good-morrow, all dressed in different clothes, and better than the day before; and we spent the second and third days in the same recreation, Don Francisco continuing also with me in the same manner.   But the fourth morning, after drinking chocolate in bed, as the custom was for Don Francisco and me, Mary told me that a lady was waiting for me, in her own room, and desired me to get up, with an air of command; and Don Francisco saying nothing against it, I got up and left him in bed. I thought really that this was to give me some new comfort and diversion; but I was very much mistaken; for Mary conveyed me into a young lady's room, not eight feet long, which was a perfect prison, and there, before the lady, told me, 'Madam, this is your room, and this young lady your bed-fellow and comrade;' and left me there with this unkind command.

"I was in a most desperate condition; but my new sister, Leonora,—this was her name,—prevailed so much upon me, that I overcame my vexation before Mary came again to bring our dinner. Then she began to say, 'My dear sister, you think it a hard case that has happened to you; I assure you, all the ladies here in this house have already gone through the same, and in time you shall know all their stories, as they hope to know yours. I suppose that Mary has been the chief instrument of your fright, as she has been of ours; and I warrant she has shown to you some horrible places, though not all, and that, at the very thought of them, you were so much troubled in your mind, that you have chosen the same way that we did, to get some ease in our hearts. By what has happened to us, we know that Don Francisco has been your Nero; for the three colours of our clothes are the distinguishing tokens of the three holy fathers: the *red* silk belongs to Don Francisco, the *blue* to Guerrero, and the *green* to Aliaga. For they give, for the first three days, these colours to those ladies that they bring for their use. We are strictly commanded to make all demonstrations of joy, and to be very merry three days, when a young lady comes here, as we did with you, and you must do with others. But, after it, we live like prisoners, without seeing any living soul but the six maids and Mary, who is the housekeeper. We dine all of us in the hall three days a week, and three days in our rooms. When any of the holy fathers has a mind for one of his slaves, Mary comes for her at nine of the clock, and conveys her to his apartment. If one of us happens to be with child, she is removed into a better chamber, and she sees nobody but the maid, till she is delivered. The child is taken away, and we do not know where it is carried. We are at present fifty-two young ladies, and we lose every year six or eight; but we do not know where they are sent. At the same time we get new ones; and I have sometimes seen here *seventy-three* ladies. All our continual torment is to think, and with great reason, that when the holy fathers are tired of one, they put her to death; for they never will run the hazard of being discovered in these misdemeanours, by sending out of the house any of our companions.'

"We lived together eighteen months, in which time we lost eleven ladies, and got nineteen new ones. After the eighteen months, one night Mary came and ordered us to follow her. On our going down stairs, she bade us go into a coach, and this we thought the last day of our lives. We went out of the house, but where we did not know, till

we were put in another house and room, worse than
the first, where we were confined above two months,
without seeing any of the holy fathers, or Mary, or
any of our companions. And in the same manner
we were removed from that house to another,
where we continued till we were miraculously delivered by the French officers. Mr. Faulcaut,
happily for me, did open the door of my room;
and, as soon as he saw me, he began to show me
very much civility, and took me and Leonora along
with him into his lodgings; and after he heard my
whole story, and fearing that things would turn to
our disadvantage, he ordered the next day to send
us to his father. We were dressed in men's clothes,
to go the more safely; and so we came to this
house, where I was kept for two years as the
daughter of the old man, till Mr. Faulcaut's regiment being broken, he came home, and in two
months after married me. Another officer married
Leonora."

CHAPTER XX.

ABOLITION OF THE INQUISITION IN SPAIN.

Modern operations of the Inquisition in Spain—Effects of the
French revolution—The Chevalier de St. Gervais—
Napoleon decrees the abolition of the Inquisition—Its
demolition by Colonel Lehmanowsky—Its revival by
Ferdinand VII.—Its final overthrow by the Cortes—Its
victims.

LIGHT and knowledge continued to advance in
Europe during the eighteenth century. Every

intelligent mind perceived by this means the enormous superstitions and cruelty of the papacy; but these advantages, without the blessed principles of the Scriptures, leaving men ignorant of true Christianity, generated infidelity. The papal priesthood, therefore, by whom the sacred books had been taken from the people, suffered a fearful retribution from the infidels in France, in the revolution at the close of the century. The whole Continent was scourged by this event, in the order of Divine Providence. Still the Inquisition carried on its pernicious operations in several countries, particularly in Spain, though its doom was sealed and its overthrow determined. Its deeds, however, were less shocking; but its modern character may be learned from a few facts.

Concerning the Drama in Spain, Sismondi remarks, that "the Lives of the Saints were represented publicly, with the approbation and applause of the Inquisition, in the eighteenth century. But whilst the taste of the people was so eager for this kind of spectacle, and whilst it was encouraged by the clergy, and supported by the Inquisition, the Court, enlightened by criticism and by a better taste, was desirous of rescuing Spain from the scandalous reproach which these pretended pious representations excited among strangers. Charles III., in 1765, prohibited the further performance of religious plays and *autos sacramentales;* and the house of Bourbon had already deprived the people of another recreation, not less dear to them—the *autos da fé.* After the extinction of the Spanish branch of the house of Austria, the Inquisition was no longer allowed to destroy its victims in public; but it has continued, even to our days, to exercise the most outrageous cruelties on them in its dungeons."

While many wretched beings were sacrificed in private, perishing in the horrid prisons, those who were liberated carried marks of their fearful treatment all through life. Every prisoner, before being dismissed, was bound, under a dreadful curse, to observe the most profound silence as to all that he had seen, and heard, and uttered in the Inquisition. Mr. Townsend relates, that the Dutch consul, with whom he became acquainted during his travels in Spain, in 1787, could never be prevailed on to give an account of his imprisonment in the Inquisition at Barcelona, which happened thirty-five years before, and betrayed the greatest agitation when pressed to say anything about the treatment he had received. His fellow-prisoner, Mr. Falconet, who was but a boy, turned grey-headed during his short confinement; and to the day of his death, though retired to Montpelier, observed the most tenacious silence on the subject.

Inquisitorial domination, however, was at length overthrown by the French Catholic soldiers under Buonaparte. While the troops of France made progress in Spain, in 1807, the Chevalier de St. Gervais, a French officer, was seized and imprisoned by the inquisitors of Barcelona. One day, "after dinner," he says, "I went to take a walk on that beautiful terrace, which extends along the

port in that part called *Barcelonette*. The sides
of this walk, which is named the *Longa*, are
adorned with fine buildings. I was tranquilly en-
joying this delightful place, and the serene evening
of the fine day, when, suddenly, six men surrounded
and commanded me to follow them. I replied by
a firm refusal; whereupon one of them seized me
by the collar. I instantly assailed him with a
violent blow on the face, which caused him to
bellow with pain; but in an instant the whole band
pressed on me so closely, that I was obliged to
draw my sword. I fought as long as I was able;
but not being possessed of the strength of Antæus
or Hercules, I was at last compelled to yield. The
ruffians endeavoured to inspire me with respect
and dread, by saying that they were familiars of the
Holy Office. I submitted to force, and was taken
to the prisons of the Inquisition.

"As soon as I found myself within the talons of
these vultures, I began to ask myself what was my
crime, and what I had done to incur the censure of
this hateful tribunal. 'Have these Jacobin monks,'
said I, 'succeeded to the Druids, who called themselves the agents of the Deity, and arrogated to
themselves the right of excommunicating and
putting to death their fellow-citizens?' My complaints were lost in empty air.

"On the following day, a Dominican, shrouded
in hypocrisy, and with a tongue of deceit, came to
conjure me, by the bowels of Jesus Christ, to confess my faults, in order to the attainment of my
liberty. 'Confess your own faults first,' said I to

U

him; 'ask pardon of God for your hypocrisy and injustice. By what right do you arrest a gentleman, a native of France, who is exempted from the jurisdiction of your infernal tribunal, and who has done nothing in violation of the laws of this country?' 'Oh! holy Virgin!' said he, 'you make me tremble! I will go and pray to God in your behalf, and I hope he will open your eyes and turn your heart!' 'Go, pray to the devil,' said I to myself; 'he is your only divinity.' However, on that same day, M. Aubert, having in vain waited for me at the dinner-hour, sent to my hotel to inquire about me. The landlord informed him that I had disappeared on the preceding evening; that my luggage still remained in his custody, but that he was entirely ignorant of what had become of me. This obliging gentlemen, uneasy for my fate, made inquiries concerning me over the whole city, but without being able to gain the smallest intelligence. Astonished at this circumstance, he began to suspect that some indiscretion on my part had drawn down upon me the vengeance of the Holy Office. He begged of the captain-general to demand my enlargement. The inquisitors denied the fact of my detention with the utmost effrontery of falsehood; but M. Aubert, not being able to discover any other probable cause for my disappearance, persisted in believing me to be a prisoner in the Holy Office.

"Next day, the familiars came to conduct me before the three inquisitors; they presented me with a yellow mantle to put on, but I disdainfully rejected this Satanic livery. However, they persuaded me that submission was the only means by which I could hope to recover my liberty. I appeared, therefore, clad in yellow, with a wax-taper in my hand, before these three priests of Pluto. In the chamber was displayed the banner of the Holy Office, on which were represented a gridiron, a pair of pincers, and a pile of wood, with these words—'JUSTICE, CHARITY, MERCY.' What an atrocious piece of irony! I was tempted more than once to singe, with my blazing taper, the hideous visage of one of these Jacobins, but my good genius prevented me. One of them advised me, with an air of mildness, to confess my sins. 'My great sin,' replied I, 'is to have entered a country where the priests trample humanity under foot, and assume the cloak of religion to persecute virtue and innocence.' 'Is that all you have to say?' 'Yes, my conscience is free from alarm, and from remorse. Tremble! if the regiment to which I belong should hear of my imprisonment, they would trample over ten regiments of Spaniards to rescue me from your barbarity.' 'God alone is master; our duty is to watch over his flock, as faithful shepherds; our hearts are afflicted at it, but you must return to your prison till you think proper to make a confession of your fault.' I then retired, casting upon my judges a look of contempt and indignation.

"As soon as I returned to my prison, I most anxiously considered what could be the cause of this severe treatment. I was far from suspecting that it could be owing to my answer to the mendi-

cant friar, concerning the Virgin and her lights."
[One of these having come to his chamber, presenting a purse, and begging a contribution for the
tapers to be lighted in honour of the Virgin; he
replied, "My good father, the Virgin has no need
of lights; she needs only to go to bed at an early
hour."]   "However, M. Aubert, being persuaded
that the Inquisition alone had been the cause of
my disappearance, placed spies upon all their steps.
One of these informed him that three monks of the
Dominican order were about to set out for Rome,
being deputed to the conventual assembly, which
was to be held there. He immediately wrote to
M. de Colet, commandant at Perpignan, to inform
him how I had disappeared, of his suspicions as to
the cause, and of the passage of the three Jacobins
through Perpignan, desiring him to arrest them,
and not set them at liberty, till I should be released.

"M. de Colet embraced with alacrity this opportunity of vengeance, and issued orders at the gates
of the town to seize the three reverend personages.
They arrived about noon, with high spirits and keen
appetites, and demanded of the sentinel which was
the best hotel. The officer of the guard presented
himself, and informed them that he was commissioned to conduct them to the commandant of the
place, who would provide for them lodging and
entertainment. The monks, rejoiced at this lucky
windfall, overflowed with acknowledgments, and
declared they could not think of incommoding the
commandant. 'Come, good fathers, M. de Colet is
determined to do you the honours of the city.' In

the meantime he provided them an escort of four
soldiers and a sergeant. The fathers marched
along with joy, congratulating one another, and
delighted with the politeness of the French. 'Good
fathers,' said M. de Colet, 'I am delighted to have
you in this city. I expected you impatiently, and
have provided you a lodging.' 'Ah, Monsieur
Commandant, you are too good; we are un-
deserving.' 'Pardon me; have you not, in your
prison at Barcelona, a French officer, the Chevalier
de St. Gervais?' 'No, M. Commandant, we have
never heard of any such person.' 'I am sorry for that,
for you are to be imprisoned, and to live upon bread
and water, until this officer be forthcoming.' The
reverend fathers, exceedingly irritated, exclaimed
against this violation of the law of nations, and
then said they resigned themselves to the will
of heaven, and that the commandant should answer,
before God and the Pope, for the persecution which
he was about to exercise against members of the
church. 'Yes,' said the commandant, 'I take the
responsibility upon myself; meanwhile, you will
repair to the citadel.'

"Now, behold the three hypocrites, in a narrow
prison, condemned to the regimen of the Pauls and
the Hilaries, uttering the loudest exclamations
against the system of fasting and the commandant.
Every day the purveyor, when he brought them
their pitcher of water and portion of bread, demanded
whether they had anything to declare relative to
the French officer. For three days they persisted
in replying in the negative; but, at length, the

cries, not of their consciences, but of their stomachs,
and their weariness of this mode of life, overcame
their obstinacy. They begged an interview with
M. de Colet, who instantly waited on them. They
confessed that a young French officer was confined
in the prisons of the Holy Office, on account of the
impious language he had held respecting the Virgin.
'Undoubtedly he has acted improperly,' said M. de
Colet; 'but allow the Virgin to avenge herself.
Write to Barcelona, to set this gentleman at liberty;
in the interim I will keep you as hostages, but I
will mitigate your sufferings, and your table shall
be less frugally supplied.' The monks immediately
wrote to give liberty to the accursed Frenchman.

"During this interval, vexations, impatience, and
weariness took possession of my soul, and made me
weary of life. At length, the Inquisition, reading
their brethren's letter, perceived themselves under
the necessity of releasing their prey. One of
them came to inform me that, in consideration of
my youth, and of my being a native of France, the
Holy Office had come to the determination to set
me free; but that they required me for the future
to have more respect for La Madonna, the mother
of Jesus Christ. 'Most reverend father,' replied
I, 'the French have always the highest respect for
the ladies.' Uttering these words, I rushed towards
the door, and when I got into the street, I felt as if
I were raised from the tomb once more to life!"

Charles IV. abdicated the throne of Spain, and
was succeeded by his son, Ferdinand VII., in 1808;
but Napoleon Buonaparte soon compelled him to

resign his throne, appointing his own brother Joseph to the throne, while he marched to the capital, and took Madrid on the 4th of December. Knowing the horrid character of the Holy Office, the same day he decreed the suppression of the Inquisition, that its revenues might be applied to the purposes of the government.

Pursuant to this decree, the palace of the Inquisition was demolished, some months after, in revenge for an outrage upon Colonel Lehmanowsky, an officer of the French army. His report of it confirms many of the foregoing details of that dreadful place. He states,—

"In the year 1809, I was attached to that part of Napoleon's army which was stationed at Madrid. Soult was commander-in-chief and governor of the city. My regiment was the 9th Polish Lancers.

"One night, about ten or eleven o'clock, as I was walking alone in one of the streets of Madrid, two armed men sprang upon me from a doorway; I instantly drew my sword, and defended myself as best I could from their furious attack. While struggling with them, I saw at a distance, crossing the top of the street, the lights of the mounted patrols. French soldiers on guard, with lanterns, rode through the streets of the city at all hours of the night to preserve order. I called to them in French, and as they hastened to my help, my assailants took to their heels; not, however, before I saw by their dress that they belonged to the guards of the Inquisition. Having been in the habit of speaking freely among the people what I thought of the priests and Jesuits, and the Inquisition, I have no doubt that these men were set to watch for me, and to assassinate me. It had been decreed by Napoleon that the Inquisition and the monasteries should be suppressed. Months, however, had passed away, without the decree being executed.

"I went that night directly to Marshal Soult, told him what had taken place, and reminded him of the emperor's decree. He said, I might go the next morning, and destroy the Inquisition; giving me charge, at the same time, to take care of the pictures, library, and other things of value. I replied, that my regiment was not sufficient for such a service, but if he would give me the 117th of the line, and another regiment, which I named, I would undertake the work. The colonel of the 117th, Colonel De Lile, was an intimate friend of my own, and is now the pastor of an evangelical church in France. Marshal Soult gave me the troops required. That night the expedition was arranged, and next morning we proceeded at break of day to the Inquisition, which was about five miles distant from the city.

"A wall of great strength surrounded the buildings. I went forward with a company of soldiers, and addressing one of the sentinels on the wall, summoned those within to surrender, and to open the gates to the imperial army. The man withdrew, and after conversation apparently with someone within, he re-appeared, presented his musket, and shot one of my men. This was a signal of attack, and returning to my troops, who had halted at a distance out of sight, I ordered them to advance, and to fire upon those who appeared on the walls.

"It was soon obvious that it was an unequal warfare. The garrison was numerous, and on the walls there was a strong breastwork, from behind which they kept up a destructive fire upon our men on the open plain. We had no cannon; our scaling ladders were insufficient, the walls being higher than we expected; and the gates resisted all attempts at forcing them. Wishing to get through the work as quietly, as well as quickly, as possible, I directed some trees to be cut down and trimmed, to be used as battering rams. Selecting a place where the ground sloped a little toward the wall, and so gave advantage to my men to cover with their fire those engaged in the assault, two of these battering rams were brought to bear upon the walls. Presently the walls began to tremble; a breach was made, and the imperial troops rushed into the Inquisition.

"Here we met with a scene, for which nothing but jesuitical effrontery is equal. The inquisitor-general, followed by the fathers in their robes, all presented themselves, as we were making our way into the interior of the place, with their arms crossed on their breasts, their fingers resting on their shoulders, as though they had been deaf to all the noise of the attack and defence, and had just learned what was going on. They addressed themselves in the language of rebuke to their own soldiers, saying, 'Why do you fight our friends the French?'

"Their intention, no doubt, was to make us think that the defence was wholly unauthorised by them, hoping, if they could make us believe that they were friendly, they should have a better opportunity of escaping. Their shallow artifice did not succeed. I ordered them to be placed under guard, and all the soldiers of the Inquisition, who had not escaped in the confusion, to be secured as prisoners.

"We then proceeded to explore the rooms of the stately edifice. We passed through hall after hall, richly furnished; we found splendid paintings; a rich and extensive library; and everywhere beauty, splendour, and order, such as I had never seen in any palace. The architecture, the furniture, the ornaments, were such as pleased the eye and gratified the taste. But where were the gloomy cells and horrid instruments of torture, which one had been taught to expect to find in an Inquisition? We looked for them in vain. The holy fathers seemed surprised at our expecting to find any such things; assured us that they had been belied; and that the holy Catholic church, in this as in other things, was grossly misrepresented.

"Although I saw through the cunning villany of the fathers in these remarks, and knew how the Romish church always affects to deny its crimes and cruelties when it carries them into execution, I was ready to believe, after our careful search, that this Inquisition was different from others of which I had heard. My friend, De Lile, was not, however, so easily convinced. 'Colonel,' said he to me, 'you are commander to-day, and as you say, so it must be; but if 'you will be advised by me, let us have another search; I do not believe we have seen everything yet. We accordingly again began to explore, especially in the parts under ground. By marking well what portion of the buildings we were beneath, we found that we had been under every part, except the great chapel of the Inquisition, and the buildings adjoining. The floor of this chapel was formed of vast slabs of rich marble. The floors of the other parts of the Inquisition were either of marble or of highly polished wood. We could find no entrance to vaults, or other indication of anything being below the chapel. Being now ready to give up the search, a thought struck Colonel De Lile, who was still sanguine of discovery. 'Let us get water,' he said, 'and pour it over this floor, and see if there is any place where it passes through more freely than others. Water was immediately brought, and a careful examination made of every seam, none of the slabs being cemented, to see if the water passed through. Presently one of the soldiers cried out that he had found it! By the side of 'one of the marble slabs the water was passing through fast, as though there were an opening beneath. All hands were now set at work for further discovery. The officers with their swords, and the men with their bayonets, were trying to clear out the seam and to raise the slab. Others began to strike the slab, with all their might, with the butts of their muskets, in

order to break it. The fathers, who had been looking on with the greatest dismay, now broke out in
loud remonstrance against our desecration of their
holy and beautiful house. As they were thus engaged, one of the soldiers, who was busy with the
butt of his musket, struck a part of the marble
under which was a spring, and the slab partly flew
up; then the faces of the inquisitors grew pale,
and they trembled, as Belshazzar, when the hand-
writing appeared on the wall. The marble slab
being raised, the top of a staircase appeared. I
stepped to the altar, and took one of the long
candles which was burning, some of my men doing
the same, that we might see to explore what was
below. One of the inquisitors here came up to me,
and laying his hand gently on my arm, said, with a
demure and holy look, 'My son, you must not take
those lights with your bloody hands; they are holy.'
'Well,' said I, pushing him back, 'I will take a
holy thing to shed light on iniquity; I will bear
the responsibility.' We proceeded down the staircase.

  " On reaching the floor, the first room we entered
was a large square hall, on one side of which was a
raised platform with seats, the centre one being
raised considerably, being the throne of the inquisitor-general. In the centre of the hall was a large
block, with a chain fastened to it, where the accused
were chained during their examinations.

  " On leaving the hall of judgment, we proceeded
along a passage with numerous doors. These were
the cells of solitary imprisonment, from which the

miserable victims were never brought out, except it were for torture. Within some of these cells we heard sounds as we advanced. On opening the doors we witnessed such sights as I wish never to see again, the details of which are too horrible to relate. *In some cells we found bodies apparently but a short time dead. Others were in various stages of decay; and we saw some, of which little but the bones remained, still fixed by chains to the floor of the dungeon.* To prevent this corruption being offensive to the occupants of the Inquisition, there were flues extending along the roofs of the cells and carrying the odour off to the open air. *Among the living prisoners we found aged men and women of threescore years and ten, youths and girls of fourteen or fifteen, and others in the prime of life.* Some had been there for many years, and had lost count of the time since they entered. The soldiers went to work to release them from their chains, and took from their knapsacks their over-coats and other clothing to cover their nakedness. They were eager to be taken to the light of day, but having heard of the danger of this, I caused food to be given to them, and then directed them gradually to be brought out to the light as they were able to bear it.

"We then proceeded to explore another room where there were instruments of torture. One of these was a machine, on which the victim was stretched, and every joint of the body, beginning with the fingers, was racked, until the sufferer swooned away or died. Another engine consisted of a box, in which the head and neck were immoveably confined by a screw, and over this box was a vessel, from which, drop by drop, water fell every second upon the head. This perpetual drop, falling on the same spot, caused most excruciating agony—agony, ending, ere long, in raving madness. Another infernal machine lay along horizontally, to which the sufferer was bound, and then was placed between two beams, on which scores of knives were fixed, so that by turning the machine with a crank, the flesh was torn from the limbs in small pieces. A fourth machine surpassed the others in fiendish ingenuity. Its exterior was a beautiful woman, richly dressed, with arms extended to embrace the victim; around her feet a semicircle was drawn. Whoever stepped over this line touched a spring, which caused the diabolical engine to open, and a thousand knives pierced him with deadly force.

"The sight of these engines of infernal cruelty kindled the fury of the soldiers, already enraged with the resistance they met with, and the death of their comrades in assaulting the walls. They declared that they would put their prisoners to the torture. I could not stem their fury. They began with the holy fathers. They put one on the machine for racking the joints. Another was put under the dropping water, and terrible was the agony he seemed to suffer. The inquisitor-general was brought before the machine called 'The Virgin,' and commanded to kiss it. ' You have caused others to kiss it,' said the soldiers, 'now you must do it.' They pointed their bayonets, and pushed him over the fatal circle. The beautiful image instantly prepared for the embrace, clasped him in its arms, and he was cut to pieces. My heart sickened at this awful scene, and I saw no more.

* * * * * * *

"In the meantime, the report had reached Madrid, that the prisons of the Inquisition were open! Multitudes already were hastening to the place. Fathers there were who found long-lost daughters; mothers their sons; wives were restored to their husbands; sisters and brothers met once more. Some were friendless and unrecognised. The scene of mingled joy, surprise, and anguish, no tongue could describe.

"While this was going on," said Colonel Lehmanowsky, "I gave orders for the library, paintings, and furniture to be carefully removed, and sent to the city for a large quantity of gunpowder. Placing this in the vaults and subterranean places of the buildings, and a slow match being set, we all withdrew to a distance, and awaited the result in silence. Presently, loud cheers rent the air; the walls and turrets of the massive structure rose majestically towards the heavens, impelled by the tremendous explosion, and fell back to the earth—a vast heap of ruins. The Inquisition was no more!"

Terrible as was this overthrow of the Inquisition at Madrid, it still existed in other cities of Spain; and Mr. Jacobs, travelling in that country, was permitted, in 1809, to view some of the buildings

of the Holy Office at Seville. But he was allowed
to see only the light, clean, and cheerful apartments,
being unable to obtain any reply to his inquiries,
whether there were any prisoners in dungeons, or
any instruments of torture!

Intelligence continued to advance in Spain, and
a reformation seemed determined on; so that, in
1813, the Cortes decreed the abolition of the Inquisition in every part of the country, as pernicious
to the interests of the community, and incom-
patible with the constitution. But Ferdinand
being restored to the throne, he entered Madrid,
May 14, 1814; and, influenced by the priesthood,
issued his proclamation, on the 21st of July, for
the re-establishment of the Holy Office. He
gave intimation of some alteration in its mode
of administration; and Don Francisco Xavier,
" the most excellent lord-inquisitor-general," published his first edict, April 5, 1815. Little im-
provement was effected in the court; yet it was
restrained by being partially under secular authority.
In 1820, however, the Cortes finally abolished the
Inquisition, and it has never since been restored in
Spain.

Blaquire, the historian of the Spanish Revolution,
states, in writing from Madrid, in October, 1820,—
" If reports which I have heard both here and at
Saragossa be true, the torture must have been
resorted to in several instances. Amongst the
memoranda found on the walls of the Inquisition
here, one, after declaring the innocence of the
writer, points out *his mother as his accuser*; another

seems to have been traced by a victim upon whom the torture of *la pendola* had been exercised. This was performed by placing the sufferer in a chair sunk into the earth, and letting water fall on the crown of his head, from a certain height, in single drops. Though far from appearing so, the *pendola* is supposed to have been the most painful operation practised by the defenders of the faith. In a third inscription, dated on the 11th of November, 1818, the writer complains of having been shut up for a political offence, and in consequence of a false denunciation."

When the Inquisition was thrown open, in 1820, by order of the Cortes, *twenty-one* prisoners were found in it, not one of whom knew the name of the city in which he was; some had been confined three years, some a longer period, and not one knew perfectly the nature of the crime of which he was accused. One of these prisoners had been condemned, and was to have suffered on the following day. His punishment was to be death by the *pendulum*. The method of thus destroying the victim was as follows:—The condemned was fastened in a groove upon a table, on his back; suspended above him was a pendulum, the edge of which was sharp; and it was so constructed as to become longer with every movement. The wretch saw this implement of destruction swinging to and fro above him, and every moment the keen edge approaching nearer and nearer; at length it cut the skin of his nose, and gradually cut on until life was extinct. This, it appears, was one of the substitutes for the

x

more barbarous exhibitions in public, when the
inquisitors did not dare to perform an *auto da fé*.
And this, let it be remembered, was one of the
modes of punishing those accused of heresy, by
the secret tribunal of the Romish Inquisition,
A.D. 1820!

Spain still groans under the dreadful domination of popery. Christian liberty is unknown to
her people. They are kept by the Romish priesthood in a state of the most debasing ignorance,
bound with the chains of a deplorable superstition.
They are still held by the gloomy spirit of the Inquisition, though its courts are not in operation;
but the more intelligent—and the number of this
class, even in Spain, is believed to be increasing—
enumerate, with horror, its past victims. The most
complete estimate of the wretched sufferers by the
"Holy Office" has been made by Jean Antoine
Llorente, Secretary of the Inquisition at Madrid,
in 1789—1790. In the "Preface" to his valuable
"History" of that court, he says, "My persever-
ance has been crowned with success far beyond
my hopes; for, in addition to an abundance of
materials, obtained with labour and expense, consisting of unpublished manuscripts and papers
mentioned in the inventories of deceased inquisitors
and other officers of the institution, in 1809,
1810, and 1811, when the Inquisition in Spain
was suppressed, *all the archives were placed at my
disposal;* and, from 1809 to 1812, I collected everything that appeared to me of consequence in the
registers of the council of the Inquisition, and in

the provincial tribunals, for the purpose of compiling this History."

Llorente gives the following as the total numbers of the victims, ascertained from the records of the Inquisition in Spain :—

Persons who were condemned and perished in the flames	31,912
Persons burnt in effigy	17,659
Persons condemned to severe penances	291,450
Total........	341,021

Besides these, however, it is presumed that very many died under torture by the inquisitors, and that large numbers perished in prison, without any record on earth being made of their sufferings or their names. The last person that was publicly burnt by the inquisitors in Spain, is said to have been a Beata; and she was charged with having entered into a compact with the devil : she suffered, November 7th, 1781.

Spain, at present, is proverbial for its degradation, under the blighting intolerance and bigotry of popery. This is testified by intelligent travellers, who represent the debasement of the nation as resulting from the past operations and the remaining spirit of the Romish Inquisition. The testimony of two of these discriminating observers of society may suffice for the present purpose.

Captain Widdrington, R.N., in his volumes on "Spain and the Spaniards," in 1843, cites from Gibbon, " What has Spain done with the *four hundred* cities she once possessed ? " and replies, " Spain might answer to the pithy question, ' Ask the *church*, they can, perhaps, inform you.' It is not owing to the *church*," he adds, "but to the ecclesiastical bodies under that name, whose will was the law for so many ages, that Spain has all but been erased from amongst the nations of the earth. The persecutions of the Jews; the expulsion of the Moriscoes; the locking-up of vast properties in mortmain; and the final establishment of the dreadful tyranny, to consolidate and keep these enormities together, have destroyed the resources of the country, and converted, probably, one-half of the finest part of it into *despoblados*. These causes, and not the discovery of America, have reduced this first of European kingdoms to the state in which we behold it. Where are the forty towns of Toledo, that have disappeared since the time of Philip II.? Ask the *priesthood*, for they are the real authors of such destruction. Where are the industrious people that teemed in Andalusia, the very names of whose locations are lost, although they once filled the country along the Guadalquivir, making it one vast garden and continued line of towns and villages? Ask the advisers and directors of the Catholic kings. Who have caused the reduction of Estremadura, nearly the most beautiful region in all Europe, to a vast *despoblado?* The same authorities. Let the traveller go from Burgos to Valladolid, and thence to Leon, returning by Benevente, or shape his course as he may in that region, he will see everywhere—amid the most fertile land, producing everything to gladden the heart of man—little more than the ruins of decayed villages and towns—the shadows and spectres of former wealth and prosperity; the same heads and hands have produced these fatal consequences—a state of things to which there is, happily, no parallel in Europe!"

Again, this intelligent author remarks :—"There is one very important historical fact to notice, which may help to explain some of the anomalies now daily being manifested. Until this generation, the ruling, consolidating, all-pervading, and all-managing principle of the government was the ecclesiastical power. This was the lever that raised the nation, and kept it up during the war of independence. Now this cause having been removed, as we have seen, rather abruptly—not lowered by gradual progress, but suddenly, and to many, unexpectedly—as yet no counterpoise has been applied to supply the place ; so that the people, in the time of public excitement, are like a vessel that has suddenly lost her rudder in an Atlantic gale."

Mr. Hughes, in his "Revelations in Spain, in 1845," states the hatred cherished by the Spaniards against the English—though so deeply indebted to our country for having effectually aided them against the French and Napoleon—on account of our being Protestants, of whose religious principles they are profoundly ignorant, through the misrepresentations of their Romish priests ; and he remarks, "If there is no Inquisition now-a-days invested with the ancient terrors, the dregs of its spirit survives in enforced religious observances. The regulation enforced by the council of Lateran,

which requires every member of the Catholic church
to approach the sacraments of confession and communion at Easter time, is sought to be made
universally stringent to this day, not by the ex-
ploded horrors of excommunication and deprivation
of Christian burial, but by minor pains and penalties.
A fine is levied from every person who does not
perform these religious functions at Easter. The
poorer classes throng the churches in crowds during
the latter weeks of Lent. The overworked clergy
perform their duties in a necessarily brief and
perfunctory manner; ten minutes dispose of each
loaded conscience, and absolution is pronounced.
Perhaps the worst feature of the system is the
coercion exercised upon the female population of
Spain. No young woman can manage to get
married, unless she produce a certain number of
tickets from her parish clergyman, attesting her
regular approach to the tribunal of penance at
stated intervals. There is need of much reformation in these respects; but there are few indica-
tions of an apostolical spirit in Spain; few tokens of
the energy of good ecclesiastics!"

Testimonies of this kind might be multiplied,
from most respectable authors, regarding the condition of Spain, not only declaring the desolation
of that beautiful country, but affirming that the
superstition and degradation of its people arise
from the blind policy, and the intolerant operations
of popery.

Spanish priests, educated and disciplined according to the established principles of the Romish

court, may well be presumed to be ignorant, in a great degree, that the evils afflicting their country result from their ecclesiastical system. But it can hardly be supposed that all of them are entirely ignorant of the Holy Scriptures, and the national benefits that flow from the acknowledgment of them as the Divine rule of Christianity. Many of them must have become acquainted with the sacred doctrines and holy maxims of the oracles of God; and, therefore, a fearful amount of guilt must attach to the superiors in the priesthood. They must be regarded as responsible to the Almighty for the evils prevailing in their country, and they must merit the severest denunciations uttered against the Scribes and Pharisees, who by their traditions made void the law of God. And while, by their priestcraft and disallowance of the Scriptures, they injure both the temporal and eternal interests of their people, the priests in Spain must incur the righteous displeasure of the Eternal Judge!

CHAPTER XXI.

THE INQUISITION AT ROME AND DR. ACHILLI.

The Inquisition continued at Rome—Its deeds and cruelties—
Pope Gregory—Pope Pius IX.—Memorial of the overthrow of the Inquisition in 1849—Letter to the Rev. E.
Bickersteth—Siege of Rome by the French—Imprisonment and Release of Dr. Achilli.

ROME, the seat and centre of papal intrigue, continued to maintain the Inquisition. Travellers

have remarked, however, that the abominations
and horrors of that tribunal have never appeared
in so shocking a point of view in that city, as in
Spain and Portugal. This, though matter of fact,
has not arisen from the superior clemency and
humanity of the Italians, or from the greater benevolence of their religion, but from peculiar circumstances. The avarice of the popes has dictated the
necessity of a less sanguinary policy at Rome,
while it has been enriched by multitudes of
foreigners of the higher ranks, who had been
attracted as visitors to Rome, to view the monu-
mental remains of its ancient greatness and glory.
But a feeling of dread would have prevented the
approach of many, if the tribunal in that city
had made a public exhibition of its victims. Persecution and punishments were, therefore, not permitted to the same extent in Italy as in Spain and
Portugal; though deeds of cruelty, at which humanity shudders, were perpetrated in the private
dungeons of the Inquisition.

Many serious persons were led to suppose that
the suppression of the Inquisition at Rome had
followed its abolition in Spain. This, however, was
far from being the case, as appears from the various
accounts given by recent writers, especially Dr.
Achilli, concerning the state of that institution in
Italy.

Pope Pius IX. knew that the regular staff of
ministers and officers of the Inquisition had been
maintained, with its confessors, familiars, and
guards, requisite for carrying out its sentences, by

his predecessor, Gregory XVI. And although there
had recently been no public executions, from what
was discovered in the palace of the Inquisition, when
it was taken, on the flight of Pius IX., it is clear that
only a very brief period had elapsed since its horrid
sentences were carried into execution on many a
miserable victim.

Pius IX., the present pope, although regarded by
many as far surpassing in benevolence almost every
former pontiff, has been a zealous supporter of that
tribunal. Hence, " A Narrative of the Iniquities
and Barbarities practised at Rome in the Nineteenth
Century, by Raffaelle Civeci, formerly a Cistercian
monk," published in 1847, declares, " in Rome the
Inquisition avowedly exists. In other parts of
Italy it has changed its name, but not its character ;
for a government, in a degree not less galling,
tyrannises over the consciences of men. Dominicans have given place to commissioners and
inspectors, without renouncing their right to search
out the secrets of all hearts, under the veil of a
supposed sacrament, satisfied to find victims on
whom to place their iron grasp. Whoever affirms
that the bloody persecutions of the Vatican have
ceased, asserts a falsehood."

Salvatore Ferretti, a native of Tuscany, but who
has been several years in London, editor of
L'Eco di Savonarola, appeals,—" Has Pius IX.
even abolished the infamous tribunal of the Inquisition at Rome ? the following will answer this in
the negative. 'Deceived by the display of be-
nignity and mercy upon the part of the new pon-

tiff,' says *L'Indicatore*, 'we spoke, in the seventeenth number of our journal, 1846, of the unfortunate Archbishop Cashiur, who for twenty-one years has been confined in the dungeons of the Inquisition at Rome, guilty of no other crime than having proved the infallibility of a pope to be fallible. We hoped, if not for his entire liberation, at least for some indulgence towards the unhappy man, from the high clemency of Pius IX.' Instead of this, our correspondent informs us that poor Cashiur is, by order of Pius IX., more severely treated than ever. The few concessions which had been made to him by Pope Gregory, have been taken from him by Pius IX. The pretext is, that the archbishop had had a dispute with brother Pius, a monk of the order of St. Dominick, and gaoler of the Inquisition; but the true motive, says our correspondent, is, 'that it is wished to conceal from the whole world the existence of the infamous tribunal; and the sight of Cashiur, although disguised, taking his walks accompanied by his keeper, would indicate the existence of the Inquisition.' O Rome, when wilt thou dare to raze from its foundations this infernal edifice? The sole remnant of the barbarism of the middle ages still exists within thy walls, and thou wilt call thyself civilised!

"What is consoling is the fact that Italy will not be slow to invoke the benefit of a religious reformation. There is only a Luther wanting to raise the first cry of alarm. It cannot be doubted that the papal religion in Italy is maintained only by the tortures of the Inquisition and the bayonets of Austria!"

Raffaelle Civeci gives the following statement regarding the way in which the inquisitor-general at Rome destroyed certain monks who, having found a Bible in the library, were desirous of introducing its study into their monastery. "The general, in order to crush the design, deemed it expedient to put in practice the celebrated maxim, *divide et impera*. The monk Stramucci was sent to the monastery of San Sevetinouelle Marche, where, owing to the insalubrity of the situation, or some other cause, he was, from a robust man, reduced to a skeleton. D. Andrea Gigli, curate in the monastery of Chiaravalle, was called to Rome. He was then in the enjoyment of excellent health, but in a short time his appearance was strangely altered, and after gradually sinking for two months, he was one morning found in bed a corpse. We were in the same college, and I was an eye-witness to the fact. D. Eugenio Gabrielli, who was in the flower of his youth, was, in the same manner, gradually declining for six months, and then, like the former one, died of what was called consumption. The Abbot Bucciarelli, a man of herculean stature, slept with his fathers after an illness of only three days. The Abbot Berti was, after two months, attacked by a slow fever, and expired after ten days' illness. D. A. Baldini, at the expiration of thirty-four days, was seized with violent spasms and inflammations, and went to rejoin, in heaven, those martyrs who had preceded him. The other six, through a special

interposition of Providence, escaped death; but all
had to sustain, for many months, a dangerous
struggle with this last enemy.   Only D. Alberico
and myself remained untouched by this *mysterious
agency*, but we lived in daily expectation of sharing
the same fate!"

Poison is known to have been administered, by
the agents of the papal court, to obnoxious individuals; and these unhappy monks appear to have
been carried off by that shocking means.   Various
forms of murder were practised also within the
dungeons of the Inquisition, as it was commonly
apprehended at Rome.

Dr. Achilli, for many years "Deputy Master of
the Sacred Palace," and himself a victim of that
court at Rome, in a recent work, entitled, "Dealings
with the Inquisition," testifies to the continued
enormities of that horrid tribunal.   He says, "This
disgrace to humanity, whose entire history is a
mass of atrocious crimes, committed by the priests of
the church of Rome, in the name of God and of His
Christ, whose vicar and representative the Pope,
the head of the Inquisition, declares himself to be
—this abominable institution is still in existence,
in Rome and the Roman states.   The Inquisition
existed in full vigour during the whole period of the
pontificate of Pope Gregory.   Pius IX. put on a
show of liberality; but this pope, believed so liberal
by many, was always secretly combined with the
Jesuits and the Inquisition."

Many were the victims of that atrocious court,
sacrificed with fiendish cruelty in the secret dun-

geons of the Holy Office. Appalling proofs of this
were discovered on the opening of the Inquisition,
on the flight of the pope, in February, 1848. The
celebrated Father Prout, a Roman Catholic priest,
present on the occasion, in a letter to the London
Daily News, therefore, describes the scenes that
were witnessed by the citizens, at the opening of
the dungeons of the Inquisition. "In one part,"
he states, "you see a quadrangular court, surrounded
by strongly barred dungeons; in another, a court-
yard, along which extends a triple row of cages,
resembling the port-holes of a three-decker; in
another, skeletons in recesses; in another, a vault
full of skulls, and piles of scattered human remains,
directly under a perpendicular shaft four feet
square, which ascended perpendicularly to the floor
of the building above, and was covered there with
a trap-door; and in another, two large subterranean
lime-kilns, if they may be so called, shaped like a
bee-hive, in masonry, filled with layers of calcined
bones, forming the substratum of two other chambers on the ground floor, in the immediate vicinity
of the very mysterious shaft above-mentioned.
These horrible sights may be seen by every one in
Rome. To-morrow," says Father Prout, "the
whole population of Rome is publicly invited by
the authorities to come and see, with their own
eyes, one of the results of entrusting power to
clerical hands."

Father Prout is believed also to have written
the following paper, which was published, as a
"Memorial regarding the tribunal of the Holy

Office, at the time of its suppression in February, 1849:"—

"In consequence of a decree of the Roman Constituent Assembly, by which the suppression of the tribunal of the 'Holy Office' was resolved, the government ordered that the fathers of the Dominican order, then inhabiting that vast locality, should remove to the convent called 'Della Minerva,' the chief seat of their order. They were in number eight, exercising the functions of commissary, chancellor, &c. The doors were then carefully sealed by the Roman notary Caggiotti, to prevent the abstraction of any object, and a keeper was appointed to the premises. These precautions taken, the inventory was commenced. The first place visited was the ground-floor of the edifice, where were the prisons, and the stables, coach-houses, kitchens, cellars, and other conveniences for the use of the assessor and the father inquisitors. This part of the building was to be immediately prepared for the reception of the civic artillery, with the train belonging to it.

"Some new doors were opened in the wall, and part of the pavement raised; in this operation, *human bones* were found, and a trap-door discovered, which induced a resolution to make excavations in certain spots pointed out by persons well acquainted with the locality. Digging very deep in a place, a great number of *human skeletons* were found, some of them *placed so close together, and so amalgamated with lime,* that no bone could be moved without being broken. In the roof of another subterranean chamber a large ring was found fixed. It is sup-

posed to have been used in administering the torture. It still remains there. Along the whole
length of this same room, stone steps, rather broad,
were attached to the wall—these, probably, served
for the prisoners to sit or recline on. In a third
under-ground room was found a quantity of *very
black and rich earth, intermingled with human hair,
of such a length that it seemed women's rather than
men's hair; here, also, human bones were found.*
In this dungeon a trap-door was formed in the
thickness of the wall, which opened into a passage
in the flat above, leading to the rooms where examinations were conducted. Among the inscriptions
made with charcoal on the wall, it was observed
that many appeared of a very recent date, expressing in most affecting terms the sufferings of every
kind endured in these chambers. The person of
most note found in the prison of the Inquisition was
a bishop named Kasher, who had been in confinement
for upwards of twenty years. He related that he
had arrived in Rome from the Holy Land, having in
his possession papers which had belonged to an eccle-
siastic there. Passing himself for that person, he
succeeded in surprising the court of Rome into
ordaining and consecrating him a bishop. The fraud
was afterwards discovered, and Kasher, being then
on his way to Palestine, was arrested and brought
to the prison of the Holy Office, where he expected
to have ended his days—less, as he expressed himself, to expiate his own fraud, than the gross blun-
der of the church of Rome, which had no other
means of concealing his character of bishop, its

own absolute laws preventing his being deprived
of it.

"The inventory of the contents of the ground
flat being finished in a few days, it was then thrown
open to the impatient curiosity of the public. The
crowd that resorted to the scene was very great,
and the public indignation rose so high, that there
was a loud and general cry for the destruction of an
edifice of such detestable memory. This feeling was
so strong, that on a Sunday afternoon, in March,
faggots were thrown into the cellars and other
under-ground rooms, with the intention of setting
fire to the building; and this would have been
accomplished, had not a battalion of civic guards
rushed to the spot from the Piazza di S. Pietro.
To the truth of all that is here related, thousands,
both Italians and foreigners, who visited the place
can testify; and there exists also a detailed account
of everything, written and solemnly attested with
legal forms.

"Passing to the upper flat, the attention of the
government was especially directed to the chancery
and the archives; the first containing all the current
affairs of the Inquisition; the second jealously
guarding its acts, from its institution until now.
Before commencing the catalogue of the contents
of the chancery, it was resolved to remove such
papers as might disturb or compromise the tran-
quillity of those persons who had relations with the
Holy Office.

"Attention was especially directed to the book
called 'Solecitazione,' (containing reports,) and to

the correspondence. This was done by order of the government, which thereby gave another proof of that moderation which its enemies deny to it. It appears, from a careful examination of these documents, which remain for the inspection of such as desire proofs, that the past government made use of this tribunal, strictly ecclesiastical in its institution, also for temporal and political objects, and that the most culpable abuse was made of sacramental confession, *especially that of women*, rendering it subservient both to political purposes and to the most abominable licentiousness. It can be shown, from documents, that the cardinals, secretaries of state, wrote to the commissary, to the assessor of the Holy Office, to procure information as to the conduct of the suspected individuals, both at home and abroad, and to obtain knowledge of state secrets by means of confession, especially those of foreign courts and cabinets. In fact, there exists long correspondences, and voluminous processes, and severe sentences, pronounced upon *La Giovine Italia*, *La Jeune Suisse*, the masonic societies of England and Scotland, and the anti-religious sects of America, &c. There is an innumerable quantity of information and processes on scandalous and obscene subjects, in which the members of regular religious societies are usually implicated.

"Passing from the chancery to the archives, which is in the second floor, it appeared, on first entering, as if everything was in its usual place; but on further inspection it was found, with much astonishment, that though the labels and cases were

Y

in their places, they were emptied of the packets of papers and documents indicated by the inscriptions without. Some conjecture that the missing packets have been conveyed to the convent 'Della Minerva,' or were hidden in the houses of private persons; while others suppose that they were burnt by the Dominican fathers. This last hypothesis receives weight from the circumstance that in November, 1848, shortly after the departure of the Pope from Rome, the civic guard came in much haste to the Holy Office, from having observed great clouds of smoke issuing from one of the chimneys, accompanied by a strong smell of burnt paper. But whatever were the means, the fact is certain, that, in the archives of the Inquisition, the most important trials were not to be found; such, for instance, as those of Galileo Galilei, and of Giordano Bruno, nor was there the correspondence regarding the reformation in England, in the 16th century, nor many other precious records. There remains, however, nearly complete, a collection of decrees, beginning with the year 1549, down to our own days. They were divided year by year, each volume containing the decrees of one year. Of these, of all that was contained in the chancery and archives of the Holy Office, a catalogue has been taken, with every legal formality of certification. It ought to be added that, after the above-mentioned threat of setting fire to the Holy Office, it was unanimously decreed by the Assembly that, instead of destroying that vast edifice, it should be portioned into dwellings for poor families of Rome. In consequence of this decision, the government was obliged to remove all the papers in the chancery and archives, along with three libraries existing in the Holy Office, to the Palazzo dell Apolinare, which was the residence assigned for the Minister of Finance.

" Of these three libraries one was private property, the other two belonged to the Inquisition. It must not be omitted to notice that the Holy Office had its independent revenue, arising from gifts of state property, chiefly bestowed by Sixtus V. and Pius IV., amounting clear to about 8,000 scudi. This sum was chiefly spent in paying the monks attached to the Inquisition, some of whom received considerable salaries. In the above income is not included the money exacted from prisoners as board; the account of what was paid, for example, by the famous Abbess of Monte Castrelli, was found to be 3,000 scudi. The authorised paid agents of the Holy Office, called ' Patentali,' were well remunerated; indeed, this was a system by which many persons were demoralised and corrupted, whose birth and education should have removed them far from such a base and guilty traffic, but who were tempted, perhaps, by necessity.

" To conclude, in a few brief categories we may sum up the results of this inquiry :—

" 1. That the court of Rome availed itself of the tribunal of the Holy Office for temporal and political ends.

" 2. That to succeed in its purposes, the Holy Office had especially recourse to confession, of which it made the most enormous and abominable abuse, not only violating secresy, but tampering with its integrity.

"3. By means of confession, the most odious licentiousness was insinuated in the confessionals. With this branch, the Holy Office occupied itself with extraordinary diligence, but without finding a remedy for the causes of such scandal.

"4. That the Holy Office corrupted all classes, buying information and secrets.

"5. That the ecclesiastical nuncios at foreign courts are in constant correspondence with the Holy Office, and from possessing means of procuring intelligence quite peculiar to themselves, keep the court of Rome informed of the most hidden political secrets."

Enormous as the abominations are which are thus testified concerning the Inquisition, they are only identical with what are recorded in the former part of this work; and this testimony is confirmed by the following paragraph in a letter from a friend at Rome, April 3, 1849, addressed to the Rev. E. Bickersteth :—

"The day before yesterday, the palace of the Inquisition was opened to the public. People crowded to see that horrible place, where so many good Christians have been tormented, under the pretext of being heretics. There were then seen the horrid dungeons where the victims of the papacy have been incarcerated.

"It seems that the inquisitors, in hopes of an intervention to bring back the Pope and cardinals to Rome, did not take sufficient care to remove certain objects which might betray their cruelty to the people. There were then to be seen in the lower dungeons, which are the worst, *the squalid remains of the dresses*, not only *of men, but of women and children.* On the walls are to be read expressions of grief written with charcoal, and *some with blood. A trap-door was to be seen, and a burial with human bones. But a subterranean cave occasioned special horror, covered with remains of bones and earth mixed, including human skulls and skeletons of different forms and sizes, indicating persons of different ages.* The only things which have not been found, with the exception of some things which might have been used for the purpose, are the instruments of torture, which were used to make the guilty confess. It seems that these they have been careful enough to destroy, if indeed they may not be found walled up in some corner; and for this end the government have determined to have the walls broken into, to discover what may be hid there. All who have seen those remains of clothing and bones, feel justly indignant at the inhumanity of *those assassins, who,* under the cloak of religious zeal, permitted every kind of cruelty. Would that those who wish to excuse that hellish tribunal, and who do not believe what others say to be truth, would come and see them with their own eyes. I wish that the friends and defenders of popery in England would come and touch these things with their own hands, and then tell me of what papal ministers are not capable, when they

have the heart to perpetrate such barbarities. I
shall urge the government to leave this place in
statu quo for some time, so that my friends among
the English may verify, with their own eyes, all
that they hear said concerning this 'Palace of the
Inquisition.'"

DR. ACHILLI AND THE INQUISITION AT ROME.—
Popish policy by the Inquisition, at the present
time, may be seen strikingly illustrated in the case
of Dr. Achilli. His instructive volume records,
according to its title, his "Dealings with the
Inquisition." He was born at Viterbo, in Italy, in
1803, and took the Dominican habit at the age of
sixteen. In the year 1821 he was ordained a priest,
and in 1826 appointed professor of various sciences
in the Seminary and Bishops' College at Viterbo.
He filled the chair of Theology in the college of the
Dominicans till 1833, when he was elected Regent of
Studies, and Primary Professor in the College of Minerva, at Rome. He was then appointed Visitor, in
the Roman States and in Tuscany, of the convents of
the Dominicans, among whom he continued till
1839, when, disgusted with his order of monks, he
left it by permission of Pope Gregory XVI., and
preached four years at Naples. He returned in
1841 to Rome, where he was imprisoned for a
hundred days in the Inquisition. From this he
was liberated, in July, 1842, on renouncing, for
perpetuity, all his honours and privileges; and the
Holy Office decreed his dismissal from all branches
of the ecclesiastical ministry. In October he left
Italy and became a British subject, being employed

as a professor of theology in the Malta Protestant
College, especially for the training of young men,
converts from Rome, for the evangelical ministry in
Italy. In 1848, he came to England; but the
revolution in Rome, and the flight of the Pope, led
him to return to that city, to advance the cause of
Christ, by preaching and circulating the Scriptures.
He left London, January 8th, 1849, and entered
Rome, February 2nd; on the 5th the Constituent
Assembly met, forming a republic. On the 24th
of June, Dr. Achilli married the daughter of Captain
Hely; and on the 3rd of July the French army took
possession of Rome, after a siege of three months,
restoring the government of the Pope, under a triumvirate of cardinals. The prisons of the Inquisition
were immediately crowded with their victims. No less
than sixty priests, who had ministered consolation to
the wounded and dying patriots, were seized and
imprisoned; and, by the authority of the cardinals,
aided by six French soldiers, three officials of the
Inquisition arrested Dr. Achilli at midnight, July
the 29th, and immured him in their dungeons. But
the great wall of the Holy Office having been
destroyed in the siege, he was removed next day to
the Castle of St. Angelo. His imprisonment was
soon known, and the religious community in England was roused at the outrage, so that the Council
of the Evangelical Alliance presented strong appeals
to the British and French governments on his
behalf, and sent two gentlemen as a deputation to
Rome. They were not allowed to see him; but, on
account of this excitement, he was treated with

comparative mildness: yet, it seemed, that he was designed to be sacrificed on the return of the Pope. The French government, perceiving their national honour tarnished by this imprisonment, contrived his liberation; and, notwithstanding the vigilant hostility of the cardinals, he was requested to give evidence before a military commission, and brought out, by two French soldiers, under this pretence, and furnished with all the means of escape in a military dress, January 19, 1850!

Dr. Achilli's imprisonment in the Inquisition, and his liberation by the contrivance of the French general, produced a powerful sensation throughout Europe. It led multitudes to contemplate, and even to execrate the Romish Inquisition, as ruinous to individuals, and hostile to the best interests of nations. And by the exhibition of the abominable character of that court, in the records of his book,—"DEALINGS WITH THE INQUISITION,"—Dr. Achilli has conferred a lasting obligation on the Christian public; while it cannot fail to excite the righteous indignation of all the followers of Christ against that tribunal, and against the whole system of popery!

Dr. Achilli's testimony, therefore, regarding his own imprisonment and the state of the Inquisition will be necessary in this place. He says, "I was imprisoned in the Inquisition from July 29th, 1849, to January 19th, 1850. Every precaution was taken to render my confinement severe, and every means of escape provided against. And, as it was imagined that the prisons of the Inquisition were

less secure than those of the Castle of St. Angelo,
I was speedily removed to that fortress. In fact,
every thing indicated a determination, on the part
of the church of Rome, to keep me in perpetual
incarceration.

  "The story of my imprisonment presents a new
feature in the annals of the Inquisition. Secure of
their privilege, satisfied with the possession of their
prey, which they were persuaded no earthly power
could force them to surrender, they delayed my
condemnation, partly because the tribunal was not
yet entirely re-organised, owing to the absence of
the Pope and the cardinals, and partly because—in
consequence of the fact of my imprisonment being
well known, and many persons of high consideration
having declared themselves interested in my favour
—they feared their designs might be frustrated,
were it made public that I had received my final
sentence. Their only course, therefore, was to
condemn me to suffer in secret. The fact was, that
I was detained captive, in order to grace the
triumphal car of Pio Nono, on his return to Rome.

  "The treatment experienced in this prison is
certainly not so bad, in most cases, as it is in every
other within the walls of Rome. The Castle of St.
Angelo is chiefly set apart for prisoners of distinction. Cardinals and prelates who fall into
disgrace with the Pope are confined in it. For this
purpose there are a variety of apartments; in one
of them are shown the iron rings that had the
honour of securing the cord with which the celebrated Cardinals Caraffa, Coscia, and others, were

hung. Pope Clement VII. was likewise a prisoner
in this fortress, at the time of its occupation by the
Imperial forces, which he himself had called into
Rome. The records of this edifice, which, as
everybody knows, was originally the mausoleum of
the Emperor Adrian, would throw considerable
light on the history of the papacy, and unfold
many of the evil deeds of the popes. It has been
the scene of the most unheard-of cruelties, as well
as of the most shameless and revolting obscenities.
The well-known orgies of Pope Alexander VI.,
which were celebrated partly in the gardens of the
Vatican, and partly in the Castle of St. Angelo,
have left a stain upon its walls which can never be
effaced. Like the Pope's bulls, it serves ' *ad per-
petuam rei memoriam.*' In one of the halls are the
notorious pictures by Julio Romano, of which it
would be difficult to decide whether the artistical
skill they display be more admirable, or the subjects
they represent more grossly indecent and detestable.
Colonel Calandrelli, one of the most valiant defenders of the republic, and a triumvirate after
Mazzini — a gentleman equally learned in the
history of his country, as he has shown himself
brave in her service—has assured me that he has a
work ready for publication, in which the whole
history of this celebrated Castle is unfolded from
authentic documents."—Pp. 4, 25, 26, 465.

Cardinal Wiseman having attempted a vindication
of the Inquisition, Dr. Achilli notices his jesuitical
effort; and he asks, " What, then, is the Inquisition
of the *nineteenth century?* The same system of

intolerance which prevailed in the barbarous ages.
That which raised the Crusade, and roused all
Europe to arms at the voice of a monk [Bernard]
and of a hermit [Peter]. That which—in the name
of a God of peace, manifested on earth by Christ,
who, through love for sinners, gave himself to be
crucified—brought slaughter on the Albigenses;
filled France with desolation, under Domenico di
Gusman; raised in 'Spain the funeral pile and the
scaffold, devastating the fair kingdoms of Granada
and Castile, through the assistance of those detestable monks, Raimond de Pennefort, Peter Arbues,
and Cardinal Torquemada. That which, to its eternal infamy, registers in the annals of France the
fatal 24th of August, and the 5th of November in
those of England. That same system which at
this moment flourishes in Rome, which has never
yet been either worn out or modified, and which,
at this present time, in the jargon of the priests, is
called, 'The Holy, Roman, Universal, Apostolic
Inquisition!' Holy, as the place where Christ was
crucified is holy; Apostolic, because Judas Iscariot
was the first inquisitor; Roman and Universal,
because from Rome it extends over all the world.

"But what is the Inquisition of the present day
in Rome? It is the very same that was instituted,
at the council of Verona, to burn Arnold of Brescia;
the same that was establised at the third council
of the Lateran, to sanction the slaughter of the
Albigenses and the Waldenses, the massacre of
the people, the destruction of the city; the same
that was confirmed at the council of Coustance, to

burn alive two holy men, John Huss, and Jerome
of Prague; that which, at Florence, subjected
Savonarola to the torture; and at Rome condemned
Aonio Paleario, and Pietro Carnesecchi. It is the
self-same Inquisition with that of Pope Caraffa,
and of Fr. Michele Ghistieri, who built the palace
called *The Holy Office*, where so many victims fell
a sacrifice to their barbarity, and where at the present moment the Roman Inquisition still exists.
Its laws are always the same. *The Black Book, or
Praxis Sacræ Romanæ Inquisitionis*, is always the
model for that which is to succeed it. This book is
a large manuscript volume, in folio, and is carefully
preserved by the head of the Inquisition. It is
called *Libro Nero, The Black Book*, because it has
a cover of that colour; or, as an inquisitor explained
to me, *Libro Necro*, which, in the Greek language,
signifies, *The Book of the Dead*."—Pp. 106, 109.

Dr. Achilli mentions some cases illustrative of the
atrocious wickedness of the inquisitors: one of
these will strikingly exhibit "the mystery of iniquity" in their system. He says, "During my
residence at Viterbo, my native town, where I was
public professor and teacher in the church *di Gradi*,
I was one day applied to by a lady of prepossessing
appearance, whom I then saw for the first time.
She requested, with much eagerness, to see me in
the sacristy; and as I entered the apartment, where
she was waiting for me, she begged the sacristan to
leave us alone, and suddenly closing the door, presented a moving spectacle to my eyes. Throwing
off her bonnet, and letting loose in a moment her

long and beautiful tresses, the lady fell upon her knees before me, and gave vent to her grief, in abundance of sighs and tears. On my endeavouring to encourage her, and to persuade her to rise and unfold her mind to me, she at length, in a voice broken by sobs, thus addressed me:—

" ' No, father, I will never rise from this posture, unless you first promise to pardon me my heavy transgression.' (Although much younger than herself, she addressed me as her father.)

" ' Signora,' replied I, ' it belongs to God to pardon our transgressions. If you have in any way injured me, so far I can forgive you; but I confess I have no cause of complaint against you, with whom, indeed, I have not even the pleasure of being acquainted.'

" ' I have been guilty of a great sin, for which no priest will give me absolution, unless you will beforehand remit it to me.'

" ' You must explain yourself more fully; as yet I have no idea of what you allude to.'

" ' It is now about a year since I last received absolution from my confessor; and the last few days he has entirely forbid me his presence, telling me that I am damned. I have tried others, and all tell me the same thing. One, however, has lately informed me, that if I wished to be saved and pardoned, I must apply to you, who, after the Pope, are the only one who can grant me absolution.'

" ' Signora, there is some mistake here, explain yourself: of what description is your sin?'

" ' It is a sin against the Holy Office.'

"'Well, but I have nothing to do with the Holy Office.'

"'How? are you not Father Achilli, the vicar of the Holy Office?'

"'You have been misinformed, Signora; I am Achilli, the deputy-master of the Holy Palace, not Office: you may see my name with this title prefixed to all works that are printed here, in lieu of that of the master himself. I assure you that neither my principal nor myself have any authority in cases that regard the Inquisition.'

"The good lady hereupon rose from her knees, arranged her hair, wiped the tears from her eyes, and asked leave to relate her case to me; and having sat down, began as follows:—

"'It is not quite a year since, that I was going, about the time of Easter, according to my usual custom, to confess my sins to my parish priest. He being well acquainted with myself and all my family, began to interrogate me respecting my son, the only one I have, a young man *twenty-four* years of age, full of patriotic ardour, but with little respect for the priests. It happened that I observed to the curate that, notwithstanding my remonstrances, my son was in the habit of saying that the business of a priest was a complete deception, and that the head of all the impostors was the Pope himself. Would I had never told him! The curate would hear no further. 'It is your duty,' said he, 'to denounce your son to the Inquisition.' Imagine what I felt at this intimation! To be the accuser of my own son! 'Such is

the case,' observed he, 'there is no help for it—I
cannot absolve you, neither can any one else, until
the thing is done.' And, indeed, from every one else
I have had the same refusal. It is now twelve
months since I have received absolution; and in
this present year many misfortunes have befallen
me. Ten days ago I tried again, and promised, in
order that I might receive absolution, that I would
denounce my son; but it was all in vain, until I
had actually done so. I inquired then to whom
I ought to go, to prefer the accusation; and I
was told, to the bishop, or the vicar of the Holy
Office, and they named yourself to me. Twice,
already, have I been here, with the intention of
doing what was required of me, and as often have I
recollected that I was a mother, and was overwhelmed with horror at the idea. On Sunday last
I came to your church, to pray to the Virgin, the
mother of Christ, to aid me through this difficulty; and I remember that when I had recited
the rosary in her honour, I turned to pray also to
the Son, saying:—'O Lord Jesus, thou wert also
accused, before the chief priests, by a traitorous
disciple: but thou didst not permit that thy mother
should take part in that accusation. Behold, then,
I also am a mother; and, although my son is a
sinner, whilst thou wert most just, do not, I implore
thee, require that his own mother should be his
accuser.' Whilst I was making this prayer the
preaching began. I inquired the preacher's name,
and they told me yours. I feigned to pay attention
to the discourse, but I was wholly occupied in

looking at you, and reflecting, with many sighs, that I was under the obligation to accuse to you my own child. In the midst of my agitation a thought suddenly relieved me, I did not see the Inquisition in your countenance. Young, animated, and with marks of sensibility, it seemed that you would not be too harsh with my son; I thought I would entreat you first to convert him yourself, to reprimand, and to threaten him, without inflicting actual punishment upon him.'

"I shall not recapitulate my injunctions to this poor woman, to tranquillise her mind with respect to having to denounce her son. I advised her to change her confessor. But, had I really been vicar of the Holy Office, what was my duty in this matter? To receive the accusation of this mother against her own son. An unheard-of enormity! She naturally would have made it with grief and tears, and I should have had to offer her consolation. And since this horrible act of treason has the pretence of religion about it, I should have employed the aid of religion to persuade her that the sacrifice she made was most acceptable to God. Perhaps, to act my part better, I might have alluded to the sacrifice demanded of Abraham, or Jephtha; or cited some apposite texts from Scripture, to calm and silence the remorse of conscience she must have experienced, on account of the iniquity of bringing her child before the Inquisition." — Pp. 115-119.

CHAPTER XXII.

FEMALE INQUISITIONS IN ROME.

Policy of the Inquisition in the Romish Church—In Nunneries
—They are Prisons—Testimony of Rev. B. White—Case
of Abduction at Turin—Testimony of Rev. M. H. Sey-
mour—Society in Rome—Italian estimate of Woman—
Reasons for Nunneries—Their walls and iron gratings—
Their secrecy—Testimony of an Officer—Religious temp-
tations—Impurity in Nunneries—Instances of wickedness
—Suicide of an Abbess—Popery as regarded by the
Romans.

ROMISH policy in the Inquisition, as we have
seen, is not limited to the Holy Office. Its influence and its morals are felt throughout the whole
circle of society in popish countries; and its operations extend to all classes, even to the educational
and public institutions. It is seen in the religious
houses. We have, in Chapter XIX., some affecting examples and illustrations of the enormities
and immoral practices of the *celibate* priests, among
all ranks. And such evils are known to have been
common in convents and nunneries. These have
been considered as so many "Female Inquisitions."
Many of them are, in a proper sense of the term,
prisons, whose unhappy inmates are altogether in the
power of the priests. They are governed and regu-
lated by rules framed or sanctioned by the "Holy
Office;" and in what manner soever the recluses

z

are treated, they have no means of redress, being entirely removed from the jurisdiction of the civil magistrate, *secluded in secret apartments, to which priests only have access.*

What is the general character of both priests and nuns, in Roman Catholic countries, is testified by many; and the testimony of the Rev. Blanco White, formerly chaplain to the king of Spain,—as he had the best means of information,—will be satisfactory regarding his own country. He says,— "Men of the first eminence in the church were the old friends of my family—my parents' and my own spiritual directors. Thus I grew up, thus I continued in manhood, till at the age of five-and-thirty, religious oppression, and that alone, forced me away from kindred and country. The intimacy of friendship and undisguised converse of sacramental confessions opened to me the hearts of many whose exterior conduct might have deceived a common observer. The coarse frankness of associated dissoluteness left, indeed, no secrets among the spiritual slaves, who, unable to separate the laws of God from those of their tyrannical church, trampled both under foot in riotous despair. Such are the sources of the knowledge I possess : God, sorrow, and remorse, are my witnesses.

"What need I say of the vulgar crowd of priests, who, coming, as the Spanish phrase has it, from *coarse swaddling clothes*, and raised by ordination to a rank of life for which they have not been prepared, mingle vice and superstition, grossness of feeling and pride of office, in their character ? I have known the best among them; I have heard the confessions of young persons of both sexes, who fell under the influence of their suggestion and example; and I do declare that *nothing can be more dangerous to youthful virtue than their company.* How many souls would be saved from crime but for the vain display of superior virtue which Rome demands from her clergy!

"The picture of *female convents* requires a more delicate pencil, yet *I cannot find tints sufficiently dark and gloomy* to portray the miseries which I have witnessed in their inmates. Crime, indeed, makes its way into those recesses, in spite of the spiked walls and prison gates which protect the inhabitants. *This I know,* with all the certainty which the self-accusation of the guilty can give. It is, besides, a notorious fact, that *the nunneries in Estremadura and Portugal are frequently infected with vice of the grossest kind.* But I will not dwell on this revolting part of the picture!"

"Auricular confession," with its authorised rules and *questions,* seems, above everything in human intercourse, adapted to corrupt the heart of the priest, and prepare him for the most vicious practices. And the dangers to unprotected nuns cannot but be inexpressible. How can a virtuous mind contemplate this practice, in the nature of things, without revolting from it with indignation? The MIND surrendered to the keeping of a fellow-being, who probes every feeling and knows every thought!—the MIND forced into a mould, as of iron, and there held by an unholy priest!—*maidens*

unbosoming themselves in secret to unmarried men,
—to men who are trained up from childhood for
the priesthood, as the sure means of a respectable
livelihood! *Married women* exhibiting the inmost
recesses of their hearts to strange men! Is there
not iniquity unspeakable in this practice? It
seems necessary, therefore, to complete the present
work, to offer some exhibition of the state of those
prisons of females, kept under the government of
priests,—and especially as they exist in the metropolis of the Roman pontiff. This appears essential
to the "INQUISITION REVEALED."

Popish policy regarding convents, and the fact
of their being secret prisons, similar to those of the
Inquisition, will appear more fully from an atrocious
case of priestly intrigue, in violation of the law of
God, the particulars of which are given in *The
Times* newspaper of Friday, November 15, 1844:—

"A popular French writer has recently asserted,
in a work of fiction, in which he virulently, though
not always unjustly, assails the policy of the Romish
clergy, that the pretensions of the more unscrupu-
lous agents of that church openly defy all the most
sacred relations of mankind; that they dare to set at
nought even the ties of filial duty; and that no
artifices are too base for them to resort to, in further-
ance of their ends. But we have met with nothing
in the pages of fiction which illustrates these
serious and almost incredible charges more forcibly,
than an occurrence which has actually taken place
in the course of the present year, in one of the
capitals of the south of Europe. We feel impelled

to give to these painful events, and most sinister
machinations, a greater publicity than they have
hitherto received; not only because it is well that
the actors in such transactions should learn, that
they cannot escape the animadversions of Europe,
but because the case we are about to relate affords a
warning not to be overlooked by our Protestant
fellow-countrymen, whose families may chance to fall
within the reach of the same dangerous influences.

"The post of Dutch minister at the court of
Turin had been reputably filled, for some years, by
a Protestant gentleman of the name of Heldivier,
who resided with his family in that city, until, in
consequence of some new diplomatic arrangements
on the part of the Dutch government, he received,
in May last, his letters of recall. Some domestic
anxiety had been occasioned to this family by one
of the daughters, a young lady of ardent and independent temperament, who was supposed to have
formed an attachment to a young lawyer of the
town, whose character and position did not make
him a suitable match for her. Their departure was,
therefore, hastened; but after M. Heldivier had
presented his letters to the king of Sardinia, he
was accidentally detained, by the illness of another of his children, for a few days, in an hotel
at Turin. On the 8th of June, a display of fire-
works took place, in honour of the birth of an heir
to the duke of Savoy. The ex-minister and his
wife were induced to attend this fête, and very
reluctantly to leave their daughter, who excused
herself on some pretext, at home. They were

absent but a short time; yet, in the interval, the vague apprehensions they seem to have entertained were fatally verified. Their daughter had disappeared—and for ever. At that hour of the night she had quitted the hotel, alone, and without even a change of dress. The police were immediately sent in search of the fugitive. The young advocate, who was at first suspected to have had a hand in the elopement, was examined, but he proved himself to be totally ignorant of the occurrence; not a vestige of her was to be found within the jurisdiction of the authorities of the city; but this absence of all evidence raised a strong presumption that she would be found in the precincts of some convent, more inaccessible than a prison or a tomb.

"Application was made to the archbishop of Turin, as the supreme ecclesiastical power of the kingdom, for leave to pursue these inquiries, or for information, if he possessed it, on the subject; for, meanwhile, the anxiety and anguish of this unfortunate family had been raised to a pitch which we shall not attempt to describe; and even the public, startled by the actual disappearance of a young lady, *still a minor*, the daughter of a gentleman who came amongst them as the representative of a foreign sovereign, took the liveliest interest in their extreme distress.

"The archbishop thought fit to reply to this application, that he had reason to believe that Mademoiselle Heldivier had indeed sought refuge in a convent, but that he was unable to state where she was at present. A few days more, however, brought the whole transaction to light. When the archbishop of Turin asserted that he was unable to state where the young lady was, *he might have stated, and he did afterwards acknowledge*, that *no person living had had so great a hand in the affair as himself*. For two years he had been carrying on *a system of secret communication with Mademoiselle Heldivier!* Thwarted by her parents in her attachment for the young advocate, she had sought to avenge herself upon them by transferring her confidence from her father to this priest—from her natural protectors, to the jealous arms of the church of Rome. The archbishop, *unwilling to commit himself by a written order, had furnished his convert with one-half of a sheet of paper, cut in a particular manner;* the other half was given to the abbess of the convent of Santa Croce, in Turin, with orders to receive the bearer of the corresponding fragment at any hour of the day or night. Provided with these credentials, the fugitive found shelter in the convent walls; but, *by the advice of the archbishop,* her flight was deferred until her father, by the delivery of his letters of recall, had, as these clerical conspirators contend, surrendered those diplomatic rights and privileges which would have been fatal to their scheme.

"The fact being thus ascertained, a strong effort was made to bring the authors of this plot to account for their action, and to yield up the young person whom they had gotten into their possession. Setting aside the odious secret arts by which this alleged conversion had been effected, and the

irreparable injury done to an honourable family,
the case was one which demanded the strongest
remonstrances, as an unparalleled invasion of the
law of nations, and of the rights of diplomatic
persons. A Dutch subject—a minor—the child of
a Dutch minister—is encouraged to quit her father's
abode, received into a convent, and there detained,
not only by moral but by actual force, since every
attempt even to search these convents was success-
fully resisted by the clergy. His Majesty granted
him an audience; but, in answer to the prayers
and demands of M. Heldivier, that his daughter
might be restored to him, the only reply which the
absolute monarch dared to make was, that *whatever
might be his own opinion on the subject, if he presumed to interfere with the ecclesiastical jurisdiction
of the convents, he should be excommunicated!* Such
an answer, on such an occasion, might have been
expected from a Philip II. of Spain; and such
powers as are thus recognised and established fall
little short of those of the Inquisition! The principle contended for, on behalf of the church of
Rome, is this—that *any child, having completed the
age of twelve years, may, for any cause, motive, or
pretext, throw off the parental authority, and fling
itself under the protection of the church.* If the
child be a Protestant, so much the better, since,
while it abjures its filial duties, it abandons its
religious faith; but, whether Catholic or Protestant,
the protection of the church, thus sought and thus
given, is absolute and inviolable!

"There are few countries now, in Europe or the

world, where such a doctrine as this would not be demolished by the ordinary notions of civil rights and justice. But the dominions of the king of Sardinia are not one of those countries. In vain did Mr. Abercromby, our own intelligent minister at the court of Turin, and Baron Mortier, the representative of France, represent that M. Heldivier, as a diplomatic person, had an incontestable right to quit the country in peace, taking with him all his family. The inexorable grasp of the infallible church prevailed. The king of Holland appears to have taken this outrage upon the family of his minister with a most unbecoming indifference and pusillanimity; and Mademoiselle Heldivier remains in the convent of Santa Croce, where she has formally abjured the Protestant heresy, and will, probably, take the veil on the completion of her noviciate.

"We have no wish to draw any excessive or unjust inferences from this strange occurrence, which seems to belong, not only to another country, but to another age; but *it exhibits an awful picture of what the uncontrolled power of the Romish clergy may still dare to effect, and a humiliating example of a government, which has allowed the ties of private right and public law to be broken asunder*, because it is itself a victim to the worst form of bigotry, and the most servile subjection to spiritual oppression!"

Rome must be regarded as the fountain of the papal Catholicism. In that metropolis is concentrated the wisdom, the authority, and the perfection of that system, which has been established by the pretended "Vicar of Christ." We are bound, therefore, to examine the institutions of him who is entitled "His Holiness," and worshipped under the designation of "Most Holy Father!"

Nunneries abound in Rome; but they are, in reality, so many prisons, and most of them appear to be governed by the most intolerant rules, framed under the authority of the Inquisition, and administered in its spirit, as testified by the most respectable writers. Perhaps no one will be esteemed more worthy of credit than the Rev. M. Hobart Seymour, M.A., a clergyman of the highest reputation in the church of England. In his "Pilgrimage to Rome," written after his visit to that city, at the close of 1844, and in the early part of 1845, he testifies concerning the condition and character of society among the Romans, as shall be quoted from his instructive volume.

Regarding the city of Rome itself, he declares, "Although the hotels are admirable, the best of them being under the management of foreigners, every species of filth and every kind of odour greet the visitant on his entrance among the streets of this city of the church. For filth, for odours, for indecency, for all that is offensive to the eye, to the feelings, to the habits of a cleanly and orderly people, the city of Rome surpasses almost any city in the world!"—Pp. 139.

In testifying concerning the Roman convents, he says, "The subject of monasteries, as nunneries are called in Italy, is beset with considerable difficulties.

The conclusion at which we have arrived, after all the information we could obtain, is this:—that however unmixed the evils of such a system may seem—however inexcusable and unredeemable in France or England, in Germany or Switzerland,—the establishment of monasteries in Italy bears a different complexion; not, indeed, from anything in the nature or conduct of such establishments themselves, but from the state of society in Italy.

"The social state of that beautiful land is as sad and melancholy, as its skies are bright and joyous. In the addresses of the preachers at the several receptions of novices and nuns, at which we were present, there was one pervading idea—one, too, not lightly put forth or incidentally alluded to, but running through the whole discourse, and forming the main substratum of everything else. I allude to the idea, that it was very difficult for a young female to preserve herself pure and holy from the sin and vice of the world, except within the walls of a monastery. These preachers had never witnessed the social system of England, or other lands; they had seen only that which pervaded Italy, and especially that of Rome. They were *unmarried men, who knew nothing of the purity, the modesty, the virtue, that belongs to a high-toned state of female society.* They had seen only the remains of the loose, wanton, and licentious spirit that breathed through every part of Italy during the last century; and every one who has the means of observation or information, seems to feel that the judgment of these men, though overstrained, as applied

universally, is too correct in the main, as applied
to the tone of society in Italy, and especially in
Rome.

"I was much struck with this idea, when put
forth so strongly, as expressing the conviction of
those men ; and it soon appeared to be a very general
feeling among the laity as well as among the clergy.
And I was surprised at finding that, even among
the women, who had themselves borne the most respectable and irreproachable characters, there was a
strong conviction, that however objectionable the
life of the cloister, it yet was the safest life for a
female. My wife had much communicated to her
by ladies, who were mothers of families, and were
conversant with the difficulties that surrounded
them. And the general impression was, that the
state of society was so ill-arranged—that the tone of
feeling was so loose—that moral principle was so
lightly valued—that regard for female purity was so
little cherished — and the whole frame-work of
the social system so loosened and disjointed, that
there was neither a due respect for female character, nor sufficient protection for female purity.
Living under governments essentially despotic—
living under laws that are framed only to screen the
authorities—living in lands where justice can be
bought and sold, like any other marketable commo-
dity—living among a people ever ripe for any and
every revolution—living in this state, they live sus-
picious of each other ; and being without commerce,
without education, without employment, they too
often make vice and intrigue, and at all events plea-

sure—the business, and education, and employment of life. In such a state of things among the men, women become regarded by them merely as a means to an end, merely as a means to minister to the pleasures of the hour; till too often she sinks into that state in which character is an incumbrance, and modesty is unknown.

" This is a dark picture, though a faithful one, of Italian society. It was drawn for us by Italian hands, in the freedom and frankness of private intercourse; and strongly illustrates the ground of their great predilection for monasteries. A young Italian lady, before her marriage, is not permitted to stir out of the sight of her mother; and no acquaintance with men, and no intimacy even with her own brothers, in the sense in which we regard acquaintance or intimacy, is permitted. The mothers seem to act as if they thought it was morally impossible their daughters should not fall, if only they had a moment's opportunity; as if they thought their daughters were seeking the opportunity, and were restrained only by the strict superintendence of parental presence. This is a state of society unknown in England, and almost as unintelligible as unknown. And, strange to say, all the warm and affectionate intercourse of brothers and sisters, and all the frankness and confidence of respect and protection that characterises the intercourse of unmarried persons in society in England, are things utterly unknown and unintelligible in Italy."—Pp. 168–171.

Nunneries, therefore, in the present state of

society, in the opinion of Mr. Seymour, are
necessary in Italy. He says of them, "There are
two very cogent motives towards the maintenance
of nunneries in Italy; one, as a means of safe and
secure seclusion from the hideous forms of vice and
immorality that characterises Italian society:—the
other, as an easy and convenient means for settling
and providing for the unmarried daughters of the
land.

"The feeling, that the life of the cloister is the
only safe and secure protection for an unmarried
female, is warmly cherished and most deeply seated;
and it is carefully fostered by the parents, in order
to induce their daughters to remain in the cloister.
It is no less carefully cherished and fostered by the
priesthood, to conceal the *penetralia* of conventual
life; and so far is this carried, that if a novice,
having taken the white veil, should, at the conclusion
of her noviciate, refuse to take the black veil, she
would be regarded as a reckless, wilful girl, who
preferred a life of exposure to the worst temptations
of the world, to a life of holiness and peace in a
nunnery. Her parents and relations would refuse
to receive her; or, if they did receive her, it would
be as a fallen and unhappy one. And as, in England, a family would weep and mourn over one of
their number who had fallen into sin, and shame,
and sorrow, bringing ruin upon herself and disgrace
upon her family; just so, in Italy, would a family
regard the girl who had finished her noviciate, and
refused to proceed further. She would be kept
from contact with her other sisters; she would be

removed out of sight, that no stranger should see
her; her name would never be heard in conversation; and, even in her own family, it would never
be breathed, save in those low and whispering
tones in which we speak of those that have fallen.
With such a prospect before her, as a matter of
certainty, it ceases to be any cause for astonishment that the young novice should persevere, and
lay aside the white veil, and assume the black,
becoming a recluse for life."—Pp. 173, 174.

Mr. Seymour's representation of the condition of
nuns is most affecting; but only in accordance
with what is declared by others who are competent
to form a correct opinion. He says, of the wretched
victim of this system, "At the last day of her
noviciate she is nominally free, and then, on
assuming the black veil, *she becomes a prisoner for
life.* If she escapes from the monastery, or
attempts to fly, the law proclaims her an outcast,
and all the ministers of justice *pursue her as a
felon,* and *she is seized and punished as a criminal,*
and confined, if possible, still more closely than
before. I cannot say precisely what are the provisions of the law respecting such runaways, but the
notion that it is a sin *deserving* death is carefully
propagated, and the belief generally prevails that
imprisonment in a dungeon for life is the destined
penalty within the walls of a convent. The terrors
of the law are thus one great security against any
attempt at escape from a nunnery. And, besides
this, escape is next to impossible; for the monasteries are so constructed, that the inmates are as

much prisoners within them, as criminals are prisoners in the public gaols. The windows are barred; the gates are chained; the walls are lofty. Exteriorly they always present this sad appearance, and interiorly it is necessary to pass through one, two, and sometimes three massive gates or doors, made as strong as wood and iron can make them, and locked and chained as securely as art can effect. It has always appeared to me, when examining these monasteries, that it was physically impossible for a young female to make an effectual attempt to escape. She cannot escape; and if she could, she would immediately be seized by the police, and remanded to some worse punishment in her prison.

"I have examined the exterior of many monasteries, and have been admitted into the interior of some, so as to be allowed to converse with the nuns at the grating: my wife has been admitted into the *intima penetralia* of others. The impression left on her mind, as on my own, has been the same— that there is no possibility of escape; and that the nuns must remain, in general, not because their home is happy, but because they have no means of leaving it. It is often indeed said, and great care is taken to propagate the idea, that their home is happy—that their occupations are innocent—that their hearts are peaceful; while all within is a paradise of holiness and happiness, the very type and shadow of our home in the heavens. It is carefully reported, that this fulness of happiness, this repletion of peace, this secret and holy com-

munion of sister with sister, and total separation
from all the ties of a family, and all the cares of
life, is the real magic that binds, as by a spell, the
hearts of novices, and the minds of nuns; so that
they would not exchange their nunneries for the
noblest palace—their simple repast for the most
joyous, festive scenes—their life of dull monotony
for the most brilliant society; or the companionship
of the sisters for the society of the most affectionate
of husbands. All this is so often said, that in Italy
it is as familiar as a household word; but all
appeared otherwise to us. We felt, that if, indeed,
they were so happy, there was no necessity for
such lofty walls to keep them there; that if, indeed,
all within was such a perfect paradise, there was no
need of such pains to prevent their deserting it;
that if all was a type of heaven, it seemed strange
to have such bars of iron, and such gratings of iron,
to compel these spirits of holiness to remain in the
enjoyment of it. In England, these lofty walls and
iron bars bespeak a prison, to confine the criminal
and prevent his escape; and, certainly, in Italy they
look as if designed for the same purpose. And it
is nothing else than rank hypocrisy, to say that
these lofty walls and iron bars are designed for any
other purpose than the enforced constraint and
imprisonment of the inmates of the monastery.
To so cruel and tyrannical an extent is this imprisonment carried, that no nun is permitted to speak
with any one, even through the grating, unless in
the presence of a second nun as a spy, to prevent
any plan of escape, or aught else concerted with

the stranger, or any conversation passing to the prejudice of the monastic life, or to the unveiling of the secrets of the nunnery. It is all a part of the system to surround the inmates with every imaginable check and restraint, to preclude the hope and prevent the possibility of escape, and so secure the nuns as prisoners for life, and recluses for ever. At one nunnery, where we were conversing with two nuns at the grating, having visited them in company with the relations of one of them, I observed that the iron was double, the two gratings being some inches apart, so that even hand could not touch hand through them. I asked the reason of such double defence, begging to know whether, as all was such a paradise, it was designed to keep the ladies in, or to keep the gentlemen out. I was merrily answered on the instant, ' O, Signor, one grating will keep the ladies within, and the other will keep the gentlemen without!' "—Pp. 177–180.

Mr. Seymour obtained information of the most appalling character, from persons who possessed intimate acquaintance with these " Female Inquisitions" at Rome. Their testimony, therefore, could not be invalidated. He states on this point,—" A gentleman, who holds an official station in the papal court, and who, from the nature of his office, has been obliged to accompany the cardinal-vicar in his visitation of some of the nunneries, communicated to us, in private, the impressions created on his own mind. He was a man of years and experience—was the father of a large family, was a very domestic, amiable and religious man, for a Romanist

—and certainly was the most respectable character, as an Italian gentleman, it was our good fortune to meet in Italy. He and his wife communicated many things which we could not otherwise have learned, and frequently, by introductions, put us in the way of ascertaining matters in which they themselves could not prudently appear. He used to say, that when the novices became nuns at an early age, as eighteen or twenty, they seemed to be sufficiently happy for two or three years; at least, that for that time there seemed to be nothing remarkable; but that when they became old enough to see and understand well what were the consequences of the step they had taken, and that now there was no hope before them, they soon gave way to sorrow and despair. He spoke with deep feeling of the effect of this on the spirits and appearance of the young ladies. He stated that the broken-hearted look—the shades of indelible sorrow—the lines of settled and unalterable sadness—the expression of resentment or despair—that characterised many of these young creatures, used to affect his heart, sadden all his best feelings, and trouble his very dreams. He could not think or speak of the subject without such feelings that tears would come into his eyes; saying, that it was inconceivable the number of nuns that went to an early grave under this system. Those who awoke to the reality of their state, and thought of all the ties of home and affection, and their exchange of all freedom for the dull monotony and useless employments of the cloister, soon pined and saddened, and sinking into despair, died of madness; while some others, like gathered flowers, plucked from their native gardens, where they might long have bloomed and gladdened the scene, soon faded and withered and died. He always said that this was the melancholy destiny of the greater portion; and that nothing on earth could induce him, with the knowledge he possessed, to allow one of his daughters to take the veil; for that *the majority of nuns at Rome died of madness before they were five-and-twenty* years of age!"— Pp. 181–183.

Surely no one can read this testimony concerning the condition of *nuns at Rome*, without the deepest emotion and horror. The system that requires it must be inhuman and execrable; and those who administer it, though titled dignitaries in a priesthood, must be fearfully guilty. It may be said that the ladies are carefully taught in their seclusion the duties of religion, and directed to its divine consolations. But Mr. Seymour further remarks on the morals and religion of the Roman nuns. Referring to the testimony of his friend in the "papal court," he says, "Now all this, though very different from our notions on the subject, seems very natural. There are some monasteries where the inmates have many privileges and many comforts, and can enjoy the world in a measure. There are some, too, where the nuns occupy themselves in the education of the young, and this gives an object of interest to their hearts and to their minds. But all these are the higher order of nunneries. The great majority of the nunneries of

Italy are very different. There are no occupations
for mind or body—there is no object before the
mind; so that, with thousands, the heart is left to
prey upon itself. For the greater part of the day,
the sisters are left to themselves, to brood over the remembrance of the past, or to talk to each other about
nothing. There they live, with far less enjoyment
for the present, and infinitely less hope for the
future, than those ladies of an eastern harem, on
whom we think with so much compassion. They
have no objects in which they can take an interest;
they have no persons on whom their affections may
be placed; and they have no means of being practi-
cally useful to others.

"Such a state of existence is not conducive to
the growth of a true and healthful religion in the
soul. Accordingly it is found, that wherever there
is religion in a nunnery, it runs into that wild and
prurient thing that we rightly call ' *monomania*,' and
results in the most extravagant claims to visions and
revelations. It is the religion of madness; or perhaps, more correctly speaking, it is madness taking
the direction of religion.

"Once, my wife and myself, in company with a
married couple of Italians, were in consultation
with two nuns related to our friends, one of whom
was stating that no man except the Pope himself
was ever permitted to enter that monastery. This
she spoke of as a privilege of which they had some
right to be proud. But while she was speaking,
the confessor made his appearance! He was a good-
natured, merry-looking man, of about thirty-five

years of age. I have often been struck with the fact, that in almost every instance the confessors of these nunneries were younger men than myself, even when I was married. On his withdrawal, I asked the nun, of what use was the confessor? She replied that it was necessary for the nuns to confess their sins. I said, that I understood they had entered the nunnery to escape the sins of the world; and I asked, as all temptation to sin was thus supposed to be excluded, what kind of sins had they to confess. The question perplexed them not a little, and they could answer me only by laughing. I persevered, however, and at length they told me, that the nuns had so many quarrels and differences among themselves, that it led to much that required confession and absolution! I thanked them for the information, and only remarked that this showed that, after all, the lofty walls and iron bars of a nunnery were no protection against sin.

"It is a curious fact, that in all the lives of holy and sainted nuns that have been given to the world, the arch-tempter is always described as tempting them through the passions. He invariably is made to appear *in the form of a very handsome young man!* It is equally observable, that in the lives of holy monks and sainted friars, the arch-enemy is usually said to have appeared *in the form of a very lovely young female!* All this is very natural; and it shows, that even within the walls of both the monastery and the convent, the monks and the nuns are sometimes thinking of other subjects than those of heaven!"—Pp. 183–186.

Although the internal economy of nunneries is generally concealed with the utmost vigilance from the public, yet many things transpire at Rome, from time to time, that indicate the state of morals among their occupants, and to demonstrate the wickedness that is practised by them in secret. Mr. Seymour states some fearful facts. He remarks,—"Every one who knows anything of Italy, and especially of Rome, is aware that the most debauched and profligate characters in the land are among these inmates of the cloister. At present, the question concerns the moral character of the nunneries. So many things have of late years been stated—so many narratives of vice have been published—so many personal histories of victims to the system have been given—and so much has been said and written as to the dangers of the confessional, that I feel justified in saying a few words as to the moral state of the nunneries in Italy.

"I entertain a favourable opinion of many of these nunneries; believing that they realise that for which they are designed, namely, a safe retreat for unprotected females, and are conducted in a manner that bespeaks a moral and religious sisterhood. But I entertain a less favourable opinion of others. It should ever be remembered, however, that from the very nature of some of these establishments, *there is no possibility of knowing what passes within them. Immured within those lofty walls and iron bars, none can go forth to reveal what may have passed within:* so that, though possibly *the most hideous forms of vice may reign throughout—though*

*every chamber may be a polluted place—though
violence and murder may stain every gallery;* yet
there is no voice to tell it to the world. I have
already stated that an official gentleman, who, at
times, was obliged to attend the cardinal-vicar at
the formal visitation of monasteries, gave us some
information on the subject. His wife informed my
wife, that on one occasion, shortly before our visit to
Rome, they found in a nunnery, which they named,
and which was not ten minutes' walk from our
residence, that no less than *four* of the nuns were
enceinte! They were immediately removed to
another establishment; the reverend confessor was
removed elsewhere, and the whole affair was kept
as secret as possible. *It would never have been
known,* were it not that this nunnery was one of
those whose inmates are occupied in teaching the
young ladies of Rome, and young ladies *will* talk.
And matters became more canvassed, owing to the
impression that the poor confessor was only a
scape-goat for a higher personage, whose guilt was
to be concealed by the dismissal of a subaltern.

"But there are some establishments from which
even this suspicion could never go forth. They are
so closely kept, that mortal eye can never see the
intima penetralia. The *'sepulte vive,'* for example,
that is, the *'buried alive,'* are establishments of this
kind. The young creature, as a part of the ceremonial of admission, is laid alive in her coffin; and,
when once admitted, she is, in fact, as if dead and
buried to her friends; for she is never allowed to
see again father or mother, brother or sister!

Once a year, on an appointed day, the parents of
the 'buried alive,' may attend at the nunnery, and
the young creature within may hear their loved and
familiar voices, but she must never see them; and,
as no kind of intercourse is ever permitted, she can
never know whether they are living or dead, except
as she hears or does not hear their voices on that
day. If a parent has died during the year, the
abbess assembles the nuns, she tells them that the
parent of one of them is dead, and desires all to
pray for the soul of the departed; but she never
reveals the name of the dead; so that all the nuns
are left in a state of agonising suspense, till the
one day comes round, and all listen to catch the
tone of their parents' voices; and the absence of
the longed-for voice tells the tale of the bereaved
recluse! Such, at least, is the account the Romans
give of these establishments, which thus seem the
very climax of cruelty, rending and agonising the
hearts of the inmates, under the pretence of a desire to wean them from the world!"—Pp. 186–188.

Language fails to characterise this system of
manifold iniquity and refined barbarity. But deeds
even worse than these may well be imagined. Mr.
Seymour observes, therefore, "But that which
concerns our present subject is the veil of secresy
that covers all within such establishments as these.
There may be—I must not say there is—there may
possibly be the most frightful vice—there may be
the most ruffian violence—there may possibly be
the veriest climax of profligacy—there may possibly
be all this, and the public never know it. History

has recorded the fact, that in the apartments of the inquisitors of Spain there were found *sixty-two* young women, who had been corrupted and ruined by the inquisitors, and kept there where the public can never know it. The French soldiery flung open the Inquisition, and revealed the secret." [See Chapter XIX.] *"There is no security against the same evil in a very large proportion of the nunneries; for every crime of earth and hell may possibly be rife throughout their cloisters, and the cry of innocence and outraged virtue, stifled within the walls, may remain unheard by the world without.* While we were at Rome, an abbess of one of the nunneries rushed forth frantically from the opened gates, plunged into the Tiber, and there sought, in its deep waters, to drown the memory and remorse of the past! We were surprised at the pains taken to deny and conceal this fact, though known and witnessed by hundreds. The ecclesiastics could not bear to hear it mentioned!"—Pp. 188, 189.

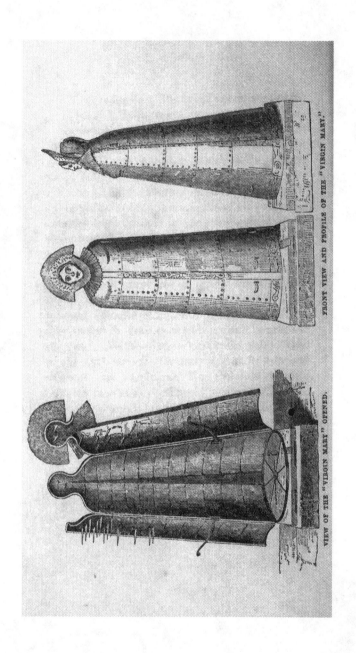

FRONT VIEW AND PROFILE OF THE "VIRGIN MARY."

VIEW OF THE "VIRGIN MARY" OPENED.

CHAPTER XXIII.

"THE KISS OF THE VIRGIN MARY."

Reality of the Iron Virgin—Researches of Mr. Pearsall in Germany—His discoveries in Austria—Description of the Machine—Its origin in Spain—Victims of the Virgin.

CRUELTY, as we have seen, is the distinguishing characteristic of the Romish Inquisition. And torture, as employed by that hated court upon its unhappy, helpless victims, was inflicted in various modes. These are described, generally, in Chapter XIII. But there is one particular machine for punishment, referred to in Chapter XIX., as employed by the inquisitors in Spain, of the most horrible kind; and which Colonel Lehmanowsky, who witnessed it in the Inquisition at Madrid, correctly declares, that it "surpassed all others in fiendish ingenuity." This machine was denominated "THE VIRGIN," or "THE VIRGIN MARY."

Many persons have denied its existence, as too horrible to be credible; but, besides the evidence already adduced, from the testimony of that military officer, and of Madame Faulcaut, who had seen it in the Inquisition of Saragossa, it appears to have been common in Germany. The following testimony is from a work called "THE KISS OF THE

VIRGIN; a Narrative of Researches made in Germany, during the years 1832 and 1834, for the purpose of ascertaining the mode of inflicting that ancient punishment, and of proving the often denied and generally disputed fact of its existence: by R. L. PEARSALL, of Willsbridge, Esq., in a Letter to the Rev. H. T. Ellacombe, F.S.A., Vicar of Bitton in Gloucestershire."

This narrative was read, January 12th, 1837, before the Society of Antiquaries, and published in their "Transactions," vol. xxvii., pp. 227-256.

Mr. Pearsall remarks, "In England, thanks to the publicity of our judicial proceedings, those who fell under the hands of the executioner perished before the eyes of the world, in a mode prescribed by the law. This was not the case in other countries. Wherever there was a despotic monarch, or an irresponsible corporation endowed with an unlimited criminal jurisdiction, men were accused, imprisoned, and never more heard of. Their probable fate could be guessed only from circumstances, or from some unguarded expression from the lips of such as were likely to be aware of it.

" 'PASSER PAR LES OUBLIETTES,' was a well-known phrase in France; and yet few were able to define its meaning accurately. Every one, however, understood that when a man was considered by the tribunals to be guilty of certain crimes, he was doomed to pass, as it were, into oblivion, by descending through trap-doors, called *oubliettes*, into the nether regions of the prison, from which he never returned.

" 'THE KISS OF THE VIRGIN,' (or *Jungfern-Kuss*), was an equally well-known phrase in Germany, and its import was almost as little understood. A general impression, however, reigned among the multitude, that, in certain towers and prisons, there was a terrible engine, which not only destroyed life, but also annihilated the body of the person sacrificed; and this, from being constructed in the form of a young girl, was called '*The Virgin.*'

"During a residence in Germany, some years ago, chance threw me in the way of hearing much of this engine, without being able clearly to understand what it was, excepting that it exercised the functions of executioner in the form of the Virgin Mary, and exterminated its victims by hugging them in arms furnished with iron blades. Thus they were soon deprived of life. It was said to have existed in many towns and castles, and even *convents*. Some represented it to be an image of the Virgin Mary, which the culprit was told to kiss, and which, on being touched by him, was set in motion by inward machinery, which caused the figure to fall down and crush him. Others said, that its arms expanded and clasped him to a breast, out of which poniards protruded. Others, again, represented it merely as an emblem of *Justice*, placed above a trap-door, on which the culprit trod, as he advanced to pay her his homage, and which, being left unbolted, sank underneath his weight, and precipitated him into an abyss.

"The difficulty of obtaining evidence respecting

it, and the contradictory and, consequently, unsatis-
factory nature of the little that I did for some time
obtain, made me begin to treat the stories which I
had heard as the result of popular error. Added
to this, I found almost all the members of the
modern school of philosophy prepared to treat the
thing as an old woman's tale; and one of them told
me that the whole affair was a mere monkish lie.

"Discouraged as I was by the result of my
inquiries, I could not altogether hold the thing as
utterly without basis. And being loath to treat as
mere idle rumour that which had been heard of by
every German, and was believed by the great
majority of the people, I was tempted to take a
middle course between belief and unbelief, and to
conclude that the *Virgin* must have been the *plank*,
or German *guillotine*. The conclusion which I
arrived at was, however, disturbed by a passage
which I accidentally met in a book, entitled,
'Materialen zur Nürnber-gerischen Geschichte
herausge geben von D. T. C. Siebenkees, Nürnberg,
1792.'

"The passage in question is represented to have
been extracted from a Chronicle (which the author
has not indicated), and may be thus rendered in
English :—' In the year of our Lord 1533, the
Iron Virgin was constructed, for the punishment of
evil-doers, within the walls of the Frogs-Tower,
opposite the place called *Die Sieben Zeiler*—that is
to say, the Seven Ropes; so, at least, it was publicly
given out, to justify the thing. Therein was an
iron statue, *seven feet high*, which stretched abroad

both its arms in the face of the criminal, and death by this machine was said to send the poor sinner to the fishes. For, so soon as the executioner moved the step on which it stood, it hewed, with broad hand-swords, the criminal into little pieces, which were swallowed by fishes in hidden waters. Such secret tribunals existed formerly in many countries."

Mr. Pearsall pursued his inquiries with indefatigable industry in the German cities, and made many discoveries in secret "torture chambers." "Many persons of the better class," he remarks, "to whom I spoke on the subject, denied that the Virgin had ever existed in Austria; but my *laquais de place*, and others of the lower class, told me, that when they were young, it was said to be standing in a tower which hangs over the canal that runs through Vienna into the Danube, and that whenever the water there looked a little red (as was usually the case after a storm), nothing was more common than to hear people say, 'So, the Virgin has been at her work again.'"

Mr. Pearsall made important discoveries at Nuremberg. There he was aided by Dr. Mayer, keeper of the archives of the city. "Dr. Mayer told me," says he, "that the passage from the Chronicle, quoted by Siebenkees, was no fable; that the machine had formerly stood in a vault near to the *Sieben Zeiler*, and that he himself had seen part of the machinery which belonged to it, although the figure itself had disappeared. 'The figure,' said he, 'stood at the brink of a trap-door; and when

B B

the individual who had suffered by its embraces was released from them, he fell downwards through it on a sort of cradle of swords, placed in a vault underneath, and which were arranged so as to cut his body in pieces, which dropped into running water, over which the machine stood.'

" Desirous of seeing the spot where the Virgin stood, I procured permission to visit it from the city architect, who sent me the keys by a man named Kiefer. This man has been a long time in the employment of the magistrates, and he accompanied Dr. Mayer and myself to the spot in question. He was a stranger to Dr. Mayer; but he had himself, many years back, been in the vault. He found no stream of water there, although the place was extremely wet and damp; and on one side of the vault, which was drier than the other, *there was a sort of grave, in which were many human skulls and bones.* He told me that in his youth he had known an old man, named Kaiferlin, who had seen the machine in a perfect state. He stated, also, that Kaiferlin told him, that two or three days before the entry of the French into Nuremberg, the Virgin and all the instruments of torture formerly kept in the place where she was, were taken away by night in a cart, and that neither she nor they had ever been heard of since."

Mr. Pearsall at length found this Virgin in the Castle of Feistritz. Baron Diedrich informed him, "I bought it of a person who obtained it, *with the left hand,* during the French revolution, and had with it a great part of the contents of the arsenal of Nuremberg. From him I received it *in a cart*, with several things which had formerly belonged to that arsenal. It came to me rusted and in bad condition, deprived of its machinery, but accompanied by the pedestal on which it now stands, and which seems to have been made for it."

"The construction of the figure," says Mr. Pearsall, "was simple enough. A skeleton, formed of bars and hoops, was coated over with sheet iron, which was laid on and painted, so as to represent a Nuremberg citizen's wife of the sixteenth century. The front of the machine opened like folding doors, the two halves of the front part of it being connected by hinges with the back part. On the inside of its right breast are *thirteen* quadrangular poniards. There are *eight* of these on the inside of the left, and *two* on the inside of the face. These last were clearly intended for the eyes of the victim, who must have, therefore, gone backwards into it, and have received, in an upright position, in his breast and head, the blades to which he was exposed. That this machine had been formerly used cannot be doubted; because there are evident blood-stains yet visible on its breast, and on the upper part of its pedestal. How it was worked is not known, for the mechanism which caused it to open and shut is no longer attached to it; but that there was some such mechanism, is clear from the holes and sockets which have been cut out on the surface of the pedestal, showing the points where parts of the apparatus intended to work it must have been inserted. It stands, at present, on castors, and there

are two iron springs, which its present proprietor has
caused to be placed in it, for the purpose of making
its sides to open whenever it is moved forward;
but this is done to startle, by way of pleasantry,
those who see it for the first time."

Mr. Pearsall traces the origin of this machine
to Spain, and in connexion with the Inquisition.
He says, " In the year 1835, I met at Liege with a
very well educated and accomplished man of letters;
he was a Frenchman by birth, and had been attached
to the court of Joseph Buonaparte, when he was
promoted by his brother Napoleon to be king of
Spain. There, my informant told me, that he had
an opportunity of inspecting the chamber of the
Inquisition at Madrid, and that, among other
instruments with which it was provided, he found
an image of the Virgin Mary, composed partly of
wood and partly of iron. This engine was called
' *Mater Dolorosa*,' and with it was administered the
last and severest degree of torture. Its ordinary
position was that of a woman standing erect, with
her arms crossed on her bosom; but there was a contrivance by which she was made to expand her arms,
and then the inside surfaces of them were seen to be
garnished with a number of small points or stilettoes.
The person to be tortured was placed opposite to
her, breast to breast, and then her arms were
brought round his back, and by means of a powerful screwing implement made to grasp him tightly,
so as to inflict great pain, and to render it impossible that he could fall from her gripe. Whilst she
held him thus firmly, a trap-door was opened under

his feet, so as to cause him to hang in agony over an abyss. In this position he was importuned to confess his guilt, while the arms of the machine were slowly and gradually screwed tighter and tighter, till life was squeezed out of his body. The corpse was then released, and fell through the trap-door into a sort of *oubliette.* Now, I am much inclined to think that the machine in the possession of Baron Diedrich was made to do its inhuman duty somewhat in the same manner as the machine in the Spanish Inquisition."

Priestly cruelty in Spain appears to have derived this instrument from the invention of this kind by Nabis, tyrant of Sparta. See Hampton's Polybius, vol. ii., p. 291. Mr. Pearsall remarks, " Perhaps, also, the merit of having invented the Virgin is due to the genius of Spain; and it is by no means impossible that it was thence transplanted into Germany during the reign of Charles V., who was monarch of both countries. According to M. de Pfeffel, *(Abrégé de l'Histoire d'Allemagne,* p. 414) there were great tumults in Germany during the years 1531 and 1532, and continual quarrels at Nuremberg, between the Protestants and Catholics. 'In 1532 was published,' says he, 'the famous Criminal Code of the Empire, which was the most severe and the least observed in Europe.' In 1533 the Iron Virgin was, according to the Chronicle cited by Siebenkees, constructed at Nuremberg.

" I cannot fix the time when this machine was first employed in Spain; but I was told by Mr. Gévay, a learned Hungarian in the Imperial

Library at Vienna, that he had read of this machine in Spanish romance of the early part of the *sixteenth* century, which proves that it was known in Spain at the period in question. The author, also, of a French romance, published at Paris in 1828, and entitled 'Cornelia Borogina,' makes mention of it as Spanish, and this attributes it to the same epoch. Add to this, that it is an instrument much more congenial with the genius of the Spanish nation than with that of the Germans.

"Probably one might find in Spain other specimens of this machine; perhaps some may exist in Italy; for I have heard that at the close of 1814, there was something like it at Florence. But after having seen the engine in the possession of Baron Diedrich, one can no longer doubt that others of its species were employed as appendages to the ancient tribunals; and one is, therefore, obliged to regard the story of '*The Kiss of the Virgin,*' not as a popular legend, but as history."

Reflecting on popery, existing thus in Rome and other countries called Catholic, degrading all classes of the community in every nation, we cannot but consider it deserving the execration of mankind. It is a system of priestcraft grafted on the Gospel, a "mystery of iniquity," utterly at variance with the first principles of humanity, as well as the letter and spirit of Christianity, as taught in the Scriptures. Its dreaded Inquisition, in all its various agencies, is regarded with the utmost abhorrence by the more intelligent people of Rome and of the other States of Italy. The Catholic priests, too, are hated generally, as the crafty oppressors of the laity; and, though this might be denied by the adherents of the Pope, the fact is notorious, from the late revolutions in Europe, and especially from the present condition of the Italian States, whose governments require to be severally supported by the military power of Austria, while Rome itself is occupied by a French army, as indispensable to the support of "*the Most Holy Father*," against his *beloved children*, in *his own city!*

Intelligent persons, in all popish countries, regard the Romish priesthood with mingled contempt and dread. This is testified by every well-informed writer. As an evidence of this, it may be stated, that a merchant from Portugal, recently in London, being asked by an English merchant, freely, in his counting-house, whether he allowed his own parish priest familiarly to visit his family,—consisting chiefly of daughters,—replied, "No, indeed! on no account whatever would I suffer him to enter my house!" and, laying his hand upon the desk, he declared, with peculiar emphasis, "I would rather suffer this hand to be chopped off, than allow the priest to associate with my family!"

Priestly influence is reluctantly endured by the Catholics, though ignorant of pure Christianity, while sensible men groan under its oppressive intolerance. Hence, the intelligent author of "Rome in the Nineteenth Century," referring to the jealousy and domination of the priests, remarks, concerning a Catholic friend, who had travelled in other countries, that he cherished the utmost

Printed in the USA
CPSIA information can be obtained
at www.ICGtesting.com
LVHW041252151023
761121LV00001BB/80